A ROSIE LIFE IN ITALY 5

ROMULUS AND SEAMUS

ROSIE MELEADY

ENVY PUBLISHING

For

James, Jamsie, Jim, Seamus, Jimmy, Jim Bob

Love you to all the planets

Star Trek visited and back

PROLOGUE

I have a confession to make.

In book four I wrote about my cousin Rob who found out he had incurable liver and bowel cancer a couple of weeks after my dad died. I don't have a cousin called Rob with incurable cancer. I made him up.

I'm sorry for the deceit. I have three older brothers, I really could have done without inventing a brotherly cousin to complicate the story, but there was a reason for me having to create him as a character.

You may recall from previous books in this series, the brother I am closest to–Jim. Family and friends know him by several varieties of his birth name, James. As a child I called him James or Jamsie. And then, because of the influence of 'The Waltons' TV show on the eight of us living in our little childhood family home, I used to say, 'Good night Jim Bob' and he'd respond, 'Good night Mary Ellen'. So from time to time, I still call him Jim Bob.

His wife calls him Jimmy, his friends call him Jim and my other two brothers call him the Irish version of James; Seamus. He can carry so many names as he is a man whose personality and love of the world is enough to fill ten bodies.

It was Jim who asked "How much would a house like that cost?" when we were driving past the derelict 'Sighing House' in Umbria with the ageing 'Vendesi' sign. His question spurred me on to call the estate agent and arrange a nosey visit the following day.

When sitting on the terrace of our rented house the evening after the viewing, discussing the potential of 'The Sighing House', it was Jim who took out of his pocket the small iron figurine of the she-wolf with her two human cubs, Romulus and Remus.

"I borrowed it from the house."

"You nicked it?" I said, shocked by his Christian light-fingers which literally would not harm a fly. I really do mean that. Saint Francis of Assisi, patron saint of animals was Jim's idol growing up and through his adult life.

Jim can catch a fly buzzing around his house with chopsticks and put it outside–he watched the Karate Kid too many times in the Eighties.

"Just borrowed it," he said, rubbing the ten years of derelict-house dust from the crevices of the wolf. "I mean if you don't buy the house whoever does is just going to go in and gut the place and throw everything out, so I saved the wolf from doom. But I have a feeling I just borrowed it."

I didn't know what he meant until we were back in Ireland the following Christmas and Jim gave me a small tightly wrapped gift. We had just signed the 'compromesso' or sale agreement for The Sighing House.

As I opened it and the small iron figurine revealed itself, Jim said, "I told you I just borrowed it. It's time for her to return to the house."

"Romulus and Seamus," I laughed, renaming the founders of Rome after one of Jim's many names.

So I brought the wolf back to The Sighing House and carefully placed her on the stone mantel, where she kept a watchful eye as we renovated our loving lair over the next three years into something we could call home.

It was Jim who planned the surprise going away party when we had packed up our camper van during Ireland's only hurricane to move to Italy. While I was feeling sick with anxiety; boxes still only half filled for storage, Jim issued me an order to go shower while he organised the remaining chaos into the boxes.

"Now come and eat."

As soon as we arrived at his house for dinner, I heard the soundtrack of 'The Godfather' playing. A giant 'Arrivederci' sign hung over the dining table. My parents and nieces and nephew all waiting for an Italian feast made by Jim.

The next time we were together was in Italy for my parents' surprise sixtieth wedding anniversary party. The perfect night I had always dreamed of; dancing under the stars with my dad, Jim and his wife, while my Mam and two other brothers watched and sang at a long candlelit table surrounded by family and friends.

It was Jim, not my fictional cousin Rob, who came over to Italy the previous spring and toured the city founded by Romulus and 'Seamus' as detailed in book four of this series; visited the Colosseum, ate double fried artichokes in the Jewish quarter and soaked up all the beauty and history Rome could offer, before coming to Umbria to stay with us at The Sighing House for the first time since he'd seen it derelict.

The progress we had made with the house blew him away and by the time he left, we were already planning to conquer Pompeii on his next visit.

It was Jim who called to tell me our dad had passed away suddenly that November.

And it was Jim, not Rob, who was diagnosed, the week after our dad died, with liver and bowel cancer.

Jim didn't let his diagnosis take over his life. He didn't tell people he had cancer, there was no need. He did his treatment and got on with work and life as he always did.

His diagnosis profoundly affected how I dealt with the grief of our dad and why our mother couldn't stay living in Ireland, so I couldn't leave it out of book four. But I wanted to respect Jim's privacy, and so I invented Rob.

Jim never mentioned the word incurable, but Ronan did the research and we knew there was a time limit.

1

—————

When a doctor starts a conversation with, "I don't want to alarm you. There is nothing to worry about but..." during a scan, you know it's time to worry.

I didn't even need a bloody scan. It was just because our young Italian GP–whose surname translated to 'chicken' and whose first name was Fabrizio, so he of course became to us Doctor Fab Chicken–had bought a new ultra-sound machine.

"It is a smaller version of the powerful scanning machines they have in Milan," he said, completely chuffed with himself.

It serves me right for being envious of the rest of my family having had a go of it; Ronan following his scorpion attack, Izzy a sore shoulder scanned, Luca's wrist after he sliced his artery. They had all come out of the doctor's office telling me fascinating details about the view they'd had of their insides.

The last straw was when I took my mother for her follow-up

appointment after her allergic reaction to a mosquito bite and she got a scan of her knee. I think I was actually jealous.

"The appointment wasn't even about your knee and you got a go of his machine?"

So, when Mam couldn't find her prescription two weeks later, I saw it as the perfect opportunity to get in on the action.

The pharmacist in Ireland sent over a list of the medication Mam was on and I texted Doctor Fab Chicken and asked if he could write a prescription for them.

"Come to the hospital tonight at 8pm," were the only words he texted back. It made me feel I was on a secret mission.

I arrive but even though Covid restrictions are a thing of the past, I forget I still need to wear a mask to enter a hospital in Italy.

This is the area of the hospital day-patients come to for appointments, so at 8pm it is empty, except for one man sitting in the waiting area looking at his phone with his satchel on the chair beside him. A sign blocks his head from view.

I text the doctor; 'I am outside but I have forgotten my mask.'

It is only when he gets up from his chair, I realise the man in the waiting area is Doctor Chicken, waiting after his shift in the hospital for me so he can write a prescription for my mother.

He jogs off to a reception area to get me a mask and by the time he returns another client has arrived to discuss a prescription with him. Once he's finished a long-winded conversation with the man, Doctor Chicken leads me to a consulting room.

This is the same hospital I'd taken Ronan to with his pancre-atitis during Covid. In fact, the area I am in is the same place I thought I was going to run into zombies as the situation felt so dystopian. That was over a year ago.

I take a seat in the consultation room. The posters on the wall suggest it is usually used by an ear consultant.

"I will complete the prescription on the EU form so you do not have to pay for the medication," Doctor Chicken smiles.

This takes time as he needs to fill out a separate form for each medicine.

"So you have just finished your shift in the hospital and you are now running your GP practice?" I ask, making casual conversation as he writes.

"Yes, I now have more patients for my GP practice as there is a doctor retiring."

"Gosh, you are busy, you don't take a break at all."

"Well, on Friday I go to a conference in Milan. I like conferences, they are relaxing. They are in the cities of Italy tourists pay a lot of money to come and see. So I get to go to visit the cities and there is always good food. I enjoy them." Doctor Chicken is in his late twenties and has no ambition to leave his beautiful Italy.

"I am sorry for my hands," he says, pausing between prescriptions and tilting his hands up. They look red and shiny. Not raw, just shiny. "I bought a coffee machine, and I cleaned it myself today, so my hands are..."

"You bought a coffee machine for the office and you had to clean it?" I ask, confused at how a busy doctor was expected to do a menial task while on his shift.

"No, not a machine. Here, I will show you."

He scrolls through the photos on his phone and shows me an image of a silver coffee pot, sugar bowl, cream jug and some other pieces on a silver tray.

"Oh, you collect antiques?" I say, trying to understand what I am looking at.

"No, it is from 2005 and a famous Italian brand. But it was all black, and the seller did not know what they had." He does an evil little laugh. "So I spent a lot of time cleaning it myself with a special cloth today."

Before I had left for the appointment with Doctor Chicken, my mother was listening to the Irish news. Ireland's health care crisis was the dominant story. It's not new news, it's been in crisis mode for years. Over four thousand people on waiting lists.

The government has thrown a red herring at the media. 'We are going to give free GP visits to everyone in the future,' says someone official. The report switched to an interview with a GP who explained that there is a massive shortage of GPs in Ireland, and no GPs in the country can take on any new patients. They can't take holidays as there is no one to replace them. If you move to another county in Ireland, you need to keep your old GP as you won't be able to transfer to a new one. Making GP visits free is only going to increase the frequency of people's GP visits. The GP looks frazzled.

Meanwhile, in Italy, my young, new, enthusiastic GP is available to me on WhatsApp any time of day and will wait after his shift in the empty hospital to see me. He has time to polish silver and spends his days off staying up to date at medical conferences.

Doctor Chicken is asking about my family and talking about their insides which he has seen with his magic scanning machine. He is still in love with it. He particularly asks about Izzy as he knows she works in the movie industry and he is a big movie fan.

"Can I have a go of it?" I ask, nodding at the scanning machine carry case he had left on the bed. I had planned to be more subtle but my curiosity has become too much.

"Sure we can do it this moment if you wish. There is no harm being reassured everything is okay."

But everything was not completely okay. He had found something.

"You have a cyst on your liver, it is liquid, it has probably been there since you were born but has grown in size. It is 11cm by 10cm."

"Bloody hell!" My shock was spiked with the fact my brother Jim had been diagnosed with liver cancer only months before. Was I facing the same prognosis? How was I going to manage this? How was I going to get back to be with him and deal with my own at the same time while looking after our mother? The thoughts flit through my head faster than light but are called to a halt as Doctor Fab Chicken quickly elaborates:

"It is okay, I can see it is full of liquid. Many people have these cysts on their livers and never know, but they are usually smaller. Yours is quite large, in fact it is so big I cannot see your gall bladder. But it is absolutely nothing to worry about, it is completely liquid."

He has eased my worries enough for me to breathe again.

"Gin or wine?" I ask.

"What?" He says, still pressing the ultrasound machine scanner on my tummy while looking at the screen, fascinated.

"What type of liquid is it full of? Gin or wine? It's obviously my body being clever and keeping a reserve."

He doesn't laugh.

"The good news is that when you get the cyst drained, it will reduce at least ten centimetres from your waistline. It will be like you have had a baby."

"Oh, bring it on!"

He does a quick scan of everything else in my stomach cavity and confirms my separated torn muscles since pregnancy will mean I will never have a flat stomach even with the 10cm reduction. "I'm sorry," he says as if telling me of a death, followed by a moment of silence for my once flat stomach.

"With the separated muscles you need to be careful of the stomach exercises when you are at the gym."

"I always am. I am so careful I just avoid the place altogether."

"Who is in the movie Izzy is working on?" He asks, changing the subject.

I mention the headline actor's name not expecting him to know him.

"Oh, he is one of my favourite actors!"

"Ah nice to hear, but can we get back to the water balloon inside my belly? So I should get the cyst drained?" I say, sitting back up.

"Yes, I think so. They usually can be left, but yours is so enormous I think it would be good to get an MRI scan and for me to book you an appointment with a liver specialist so he can tell you the best course of action." This sounds serious again. "Can you get me his autograph?"

"The liver specialist's?"

"No, the actor's!" His face looks animated with excitement.

Before I moved to Italy my doctor in Ireland had put me on a waiting list for a non-urgent MRI scan for something, and the appointment in Ireland came through eighteen months later. It was for the week after I returned to Italy with my Mam following dad's funeral so I had to cancel the appointment and a year later I am still waiting on a new one. As I am now resident in Italy, I am no longer relying on the Irish health system, thankfully.

I just need to get into the Italian national health system which requires getting a Tessera Sanitaria (TS) - the national health card. In most regions, as a European, I would get the TS as soon as I became a resident in Italy, but not in Umbria, the region where we live. Italy is festooned with different shades and quantities of red tape depending on the region and even the local comune where you live.

To get the TS, I need to be employed by a company here, be a pensioner, be married to a pensioner or be resident for five years. And without the Tessera Sanitaria, life can be complicated when it comes to issues such as health checks.

"How long should I expect to wait for the appointments?" I ask.

As this was another non urgent MRI, I brace myself for his answer in years.

"It would be quicker if you get the Tessera Sanitaria card," he says, packing up his machine. "Without it, you could be waiting a month," he adds apologetically. "But you should try to get the Tessera Sanitaria otherwise you will have to pay for the appointments."

Ronan has been entitled to apply for the Tessera Sanitaria since he got his pension eight months ago. And as the wife of a pensioner, I heard I would be eligible for one too.

"Right, when are you going to apply for the Tessera Sanitaria?" I ask Ronan as I flop back into the car beside him. "I might need to get a procedure. There is nothing to be worried about but he has advised I get it dealt with sooner rather than leaving it on the long finger."

Ronan is reluctant. "Can't you get the TS card some other way?"

"What the hell? Why are you so bloody reluctant to do this?"

"Because if I become resident I won't be able to drive the the Irish car here when it's fixed, as it's right-hand drive and registered in Ireland," Ronan says.

"Bloody hell first I am coming second to the dog and now I am coming second place to the twenty-year-old car? Fine! I'll sort it myself."

"No, Rosie I'll do it, of course your health is more important. And you never came second place to a dog."

"You moved out of our marital bed because I didn't want Paddy in the bedroom and you chose to move to a bedroom with the dog. That is coming second to the dog."

"Marital bed? When did we step back into the 1940s? And don't be ridiculous, Paddy was traumatised when we adopted him, I was just helping him settle in. I can move back in if you like?"

I don't answer.

"See! You love having your own room, writing as late or early as you want and me not snoring beside you."

He was trying to make it light, but I was grumpy as hell. The cracks that started with him moving rooms had got wider and were being filled with my regular floods of annoyance at everything Ronan did or didn't do, such as delay getting his TS card which I now need to have.

"I just need to research how I can keep the Irish car on the road, it might be old but it's a great car," he said, getting back to the subject.

But I wasn't letting him off that easy. "Just register it here if you are so in love with it, it's not like you hadn't had three years to think about this and find an alternative solution, if there is one."

"It's also because I want to stay under the radar until they've finished the whole mafia gun thing."

Like Jim's cancer, Ronan's mafia charges have not been something I could talk about... until now.

2

The mafia thing happened to us while we were renting from Giovanni, before Covid and before we had found The Sighing House. It was really the cat's fault.

Moonface was the more courageous hunter of our twin cats. While Spooky focused on chasing uncatchable butterflies and jumping on lizards, Moonface focused on bigger fry, regularly leaving us 'gifts' in the corner on the front terrace. Usually they were cute dead mice but sometimes a rat. And sometimes her 'gifts' were not quite dead.

As The Sighing House is further away from crop fields than our rental was and Moonface now resides in our pet graveyard, we no longer get rat gifts. Spooky prefers to catch lizards and brings the odd snake home to play with.

Countryside rats here are stereotypically Italian; they look well-groomed with beautiful coats, and clean, fluffy fur underneath their well-fed plump bodies.

One morning there was, what looked like, an expensive toupee in the corner of the terrace. Ronan prodded it with a stick and turned over a really big rat. It was massive and I couldn't help but think it must have had a great hair care routine. It had the silkiest hair I'd ever seen.

It was the toupee rat that led to one of our most eventful episodes of living in Italy. Something that has now gone on for four of our years here.

"Oh no, I think it's still breathing," said Ronan, horrified while I let out a suppressed scream only bats could have heard, jogged on the spot and ran into the house.

"Deal with it Ronan. Put it out of its misery."

"How?"

"I don't know, maybe bring it to the vet?"

"Oh, I think it's stop breathing... Yep he's dead. That's it, I'm going to get a BB gun to deal with any future half dead gifts from Moonface."

He found a BB gun in some market shop and stuck it on top of the wardrobe for future rat emergencies.

I had forgotten about it until 10am one weekday morning and the gate buzzer buzzed. Ronan was just getting up while I was having a lazy morning having got back late from working on a wedding the night before. My discarded clothes, including underwear, were artistically strewn on the floor, adding to the already messy room thanks to the unusable coffin wardrobe and a busy few weeks of work.

Ronan buzzed the gate open and went down expecting to do the usual; take a delivery of something we forgot we had ordered. The dogs were barking but over the din I heard voices and Ronan talking excitedly to someone coming up the outside steps.

Was he bringing someone into the house? I was trying to think what I could have ordered that would require the person to come all the way down the drive with Ronan.

I sat listening to see if I could identify the male voice in the sitting room Ronan was still talking to, and then I heard Ronan's footsteps coming down the hall.

"Aw it's just the (muffled word I couldn't understand, but it sounded like 'bees'), they're just looking for the (another muffled word I couldn't understand, but it sounded like 'bun')," Ronan said coming quickly into the room, smiling like a madman as he took giant steps towards the coffin wardrobe.

I was already out of bed, pulling on jeans and a sweatshirt.

"It's who?" I said. "Bees looking for a bun?"

But I didn't wait for an answer. I was out the bedroom door and down the hall to the sitting room to see what Ronan was talking about.

Four men in their forties and early fifties stood in our tiny square sitting room, facing the door to the short hallway to our bedroom, sandwiched in a half-moon shape between the sofa and dining table forming a perfect barrier to the front door.

All so distinctively different, they looked like they were fresh off the set of an Italian undercover cops TV series. There was the tanned bald, muscular guy who looked like he would mangle you in a second with his bare hands, not in a thuggish way but in a Ninja way but with a thuggish look. Well, as far as an Italian could carry a thuggish look while remaining handsome.

The tall lanky guy with shoulder-length thick wavy greying hair and matching goatee. His aged leather jacket, Chelsea boots, designer jeans and suede waistcoat over a t-shirt finished the look perfectly of a sophisticated art hippy type who could infiltrate a drug ring.

And then there was the duo; the bigger guy, not fat, just bigger with see-into-your-soul eyes that could sum you up perfectly in a minute. He'd be the one at the whiteboard drawing connecting lines frantically as he solved five twenty-year-old cold cases at once during a press briefing.

The see-into-your-soul eyes good cop was the perfect yin to the last guy's yang. The bad cop. He was the smallest of the bunch, not much taller than me. His face was heavily lined, black hair greased back, large brown eyes with long thick lashes, but he was not someone you could ever describe as cute without the risk of getting your brains blown out.

The warning signs were in the scars on his face and neck. He was ready to pounce like a vicious little terrier the others had to control. But he was the one giving the orders. The boss. The Don. I called him Donatello with the other half of his duo being Angelo. The tall guy Leonardo, and the baldy ball of muscle Raphael. These were not their names, just what I called them instantly in my head and, yes, I realised afterwards I had named them after the Ninja Turtles without actually knowing the names of all four turtles.

I never found out their real names as there were no introductions. They just stood there, and I found myself saying... "Well hello Boys," like bloody Marilyn Monroe. 'What the hell Rosie??' My inner voice screamed. 'Did you really just say that in a seductive voice to four policemen?'

They didn't look like policemen, because they were undercover cops. But these were no ordinary undercover cops, these were the frigging anti-mafia flying squad. Unlike the Ninja Turtles they weren't carrying swords, their very visible holsters were carrying pistols. Except for Donatello. I guessed his was tucked into the back of his jeans like in all good cop movies.

"Parla Italiano?" asked Angelo, the good cop.

"Un piccolo," I answered, smirking.

'Please wipe the smirk off your face,' screamed my inner voice.

"It's okay I speak some English... You are his wife?"

"Yes."

"We need to see the gun your husband bought."

"Gun? Oh that thing. It's only for dealing with rats."

He looked at me with smiling eyes.

"Rats like the mouse?" he asked.

"Yes, of course. Mickey Mouse style rats... not rats as in people who tell secrets on us."

'Shut the hell up,' screamed my inner voice again.

Ronan walked up behind me, chattering away in English as if talking to a group of friends.

In the following split seconds, I froze without them needing to say 'freeze'.

Their hands all went to their holsters except Donatello who reached around to the back of his waistband. I was right.

I was trying to think of the word for 'freeze' in-case they did shout it. It's something to do with gelato, I think. If they shouted 'gelato' should I shout back 'Pistacchio' just to cool off the situation?

It was then I saw why they were on high alert. Ronan was holding a gun—holding it out for Leonardo to take, still talking away as if telling a story over a pint, unaware he had just raised the adrenaline levels in the room by a thousand percent.

Donatello's non-existing patience snapped, he said something in Italian and stepped towards me. Angelo translated, "It's nothing to worry about but we need to search the house."

Donatello went to brush past me.

"NO! Not in there. I need to tidy up first," I said, running past him into the bedroom and picking my knickers up off the floor. He was behind me shouting something. I think it was 'gelato'.

"I'm sorry the place is a mess, the wardrobe is like a coffin and yesterday I was working," I said.

I heard Angelo use the words for embarrassment and the verb conjugation for 'to clean' and the word for 'bedroom' as they overtook me.

"Why are they are looking for my camera?" Ronan said, following them in confused.

"Camera means bedroom Ronan, you need to learn bloody Italian."

I backed out to the sitting room. Donatello was back in the sitting room with Angelo, following me in case I was hiding the arms stash, leaving the hippy and Muscle Man with Ronan in the bedroom. The cupboard under the sink was flung open, the chimney checked, and the attic–Ronan's smoke-filled office–which led to further embarrassment by me, as it was even more untidy than our bedroom.

By the time they came back down the stairs, the other two Ninjas were out of the bedroom. Muscle Man had stepped onto the terrace outside the front door. I'm not sure if he was on guard, scoping the outside for possible accomplices escaping across the fields, or just having a cigarette.

From the bedroom, Leonardo carried a rectangular breadbasket; the one Ronan kept his BB gun in on top of the wardrobe.

But there were two guns in the basket.

"You have two?" I asked Ronan.

"Yeah, the one I got in the market didn't work, so I ordered a similar one online," he said hesitantly.

"You bought a gun online?" I spat out the words in disbelief.

"Yeah, from Germany."

I knew this tone; he was trying to be matter-of-fact when he knew he had messed up big time.

"Why the hell did you do that?"

"It was after the toupee rat thing. You know I can't watch an animal suffer." His effort to appeal to my soft side was not working. "I asked the company if it can deliver them in Italy and they said 'yes'. I have the email to prove it... they said something about registering it, but I thought they were just trying to get my details to spam me with newsletters so I paid little attention to it."

Later, when I read the email, I could see it was clear they said the gun needed to be registered with the authorities, but Ronan never reads any instructions, whether it is how to cook a frozen meal, put furniture together or when buying lethal weapons online.

"But it's only a BB gun, isn't it? There's no license needed for them," I said, giving him a defence. I'd seen them for sale in the tourist shops that also sold medieval crossbow replicas and wooden slingshots.

"Well, actually... it's a 2.2. It looks similar to a BB gun but its bullets are... well they are bullets." Ronan sounded guilty.

"You bought a proper gun?" I am back to hissing in sheer disbelief. "... ONLINE?"

Ronan pulled his mouth wide like in a cartoon when a person slams something into another person's face by accident and is waiting for their reaction.

"And what's that?" I said, pointing at a round orange cylinder about twice the size of a can of beans. It was in the basket on the table the hippy cop was guarding while the others were still roaming swiftly around the house in perfectly choreographed moves.

"It's for launching fireworks on New Year's Eve. I was going to surprise you."

"Really? Oh... thanks?" I said as one cop opened the door to Luca's room. It all happened so fast I hadn't time to wake Luca or tell the cops there was someone in the darkened room.

To make it worse, this was when Luca was going through a phase following some weird-ass minimalist life health program involving ice cold showers and sleeping on the floor.

When Luca does something, he goes all out. So to him, being minimalist meant he had cleared his room including the bed mattress and every piece of furniture except for his desk and built-in wardrobe.

I had ordered him a futon as I couldn't stand seeing him sleep in a sleeping bag on the floor on my yoga mat with some cardboard underneath it.

But the futon had not arrived yet, so when the cops opened the door to the darkened room and opened the shutters, they just saw a teenage boy in a sleeping bag against the wall on some cardboard in an otherwise empty room.

After a quick 'ciao' to a half-woken Luca and a look in his wardrobe, they left his room without batting an eyelid, or taking us in for child abuse or questioning for kidnapping. Perhaps they just thought we couldn't afford furniture.

"You'll need to come to the station with us, it is nothing to worry about, it is just procedure," said the good cop.

"The station down the road?" I asked.

"No, the police station in Perugia. Not you, just your husband."

"Do I have time for a quick coffee?" asked Ronan who is neanderthalic before his morning coffee.

"No, I'm afraid not. You can drive your car to the station so you can drive home when we are finished with you."

I watched as they led Ronan away to the car, sandwiched between all four cops with the hippy cop carrying my breadbasket. The good cop sat in the passenger seat beside Ronan–in case he made a run for the Mexican border, I thought, even though we were in Italy.

I was not nervous about this, actually I felt somewhat amused.

I wasn't nervous until Ronan called from the police station.

"Rosie this is really serious."

3

"I got up to go to the toilet, and a cop came in with me," Ronan said sounding panicked on the phone. "There are 'Wanted' posters some with an X through them on the walls like you see in the movies."

"Is your face on any of them?"

"Rosie this is serious. I asked what are we waiting for, and they said an official translator. I think I'm being charged."

An official translator did raise the seriousness by several levels as it meant they were ensuring he understood what was being told to him. His rights.

It was about three hours before he got home with a five-page summons signed by him.

"The translator was crap, I understood more in Italian than her English. I was signing papers she was translating. They were mostly just declarations saying they showed me and my family respect when they came to the house... But Rosie, there will be a court case and they have assigned a solicitor... I'm thinking I should go back to Ireland?"

"Let's not panic. Hold on... do you mean go on the run?"

"No! I could just forget this happened and go back to Ireland."

"If they are criminal charges I think leaving the country would be considered going on the run if you don't have permission to do so?"

"Bloody hell, you are right. And they weren't normal police, they were the mafia squad. They think I'm working with the mafia all because of Moonface and her rat collection."

"The rat pack and the mob... It takes on a whole new meaning," I said, trying to keep things light. It couldn't be that serious, surely? It was just an Irish man doing something stupid. Wasn't it?

I took the document and tried to read it. It looked very official and seeing a set court date sped up my heart.

"Let's call Lucia and ask her to help us translate and understand what you are being charged with," I said, taking a deep breath.

"I already did from the car on the way home. She will be here in about ten minutes. I told her the name of the solicitor who is in charge of the case—some guy called Fabrizio Rana—and she said that was 'terribile', because he is very good. He is famous in Perugia for winning a case against a big American company, apparently."

"Fabrizio Rana?" I asked.

"Yes, do you know him?"

"No.. but... never mind." What I had to say could wait.

I put on the kettle and as I waited for it to boil. I consoled Ronan the best I could. "I believe prison food in Italy is very good. A prison in Volterra runs a restaurant, it has great views too, we could try to get you in there if you have a choice."

"Are you joking Rosie?"

"Of course I am!" I finally snapped. "Because I am trying desperately not to scream at you. How can you have been so bloody stupid? Jeopardising our lives here all because you can't follow the instructions on something so serious? The small print, which I've checked, and it isn't small at all, but quite prominent saying you needed to register a firearm?"

"I thought it was a BB gun."

"No, you did not. You can't fool me."

"Well, a BB gun wouldn't kill a rat, I needed something a little more powerful."

"Yes, a bloody proper gun that could kill someone!"

"Ah, no it wouldn't."

"Don't tempt me. If we get it back, I might just test my theory on you."

There I had done it. I had vented my anger at him just before the doorbell chimed.

"That will be Lucia," Ronan said jumping to his feet, happy not have to answer me as he knew there was nothing he could say.

Once Lucia and I had our usual warm up chat about how good it was to see each other again and admiring each other's hair, she sat down to business.

"Ah, Fabrizio Rana. It is not good that he is defending you. He is very aggressive and good," tutted Lucia grimly.

"Fuck, fuck, fuck," said Ronan grabbing the crown of his head with both hands.

"Hang on," I said. "Did you say he is defending Ronan? If he is defending Ronan then he is on Ronan's side?"

Instantly Lucia's face brightened, and her voice animated. "Ah sì sì! My English is like iron at the moment, you know when it goes sour?"

"Rusty is the word you are looking for."

"Yes, yes, and you are right. He is defending Ronan, so he is the lawyer they have assigned for the case. Ah then it is okay. He is on your side and he is excellent. He is my cousin!"

"Oh, bloody hell." Ronan inhaled a sharp breath and sat back down, relief running through both our bodies.

"But don't worry," said Lucia. "These things go on forever in Italy. My family have been in the same trials over a house for twenty-six years. You will probably be dead before this is completed. But it is good he is on your side.

"The letter says you need to call him, he speaks very good English so it will be okay. I have many chickens today so I cannot stay."

We knew she was talking about check-ins at her agriturismo, not her egg layers. Before she left, I need to say what I wanted to say earlier. I can't wait, I might burst.

"Rana means... frog... right?" I asked Lucia.

"Yes, that is correct."

"So we now not only have a fab chicken in our lives but a fab frog too?"

"Yes, I suppose you do! To us they are just surnames," she laughed. "Congratulations, you are not Italian without a trial of some kind," she said to Ronan as she got up to go. "Everyone has them, so you are one step closer to being a proper Italian. And don't worry it will all blow over, lots of people have guns in Italy, they just are not stupid and ordering them online."

Just then our son Luca with disheveled hair, rubbing his sleepy eyes came out of his room.

"Morning," he said, greeting us with a yawn, even though it was afternoon. "I had this really weird dream that an Italian guy came into my room and rooted around in my wardrobe, and he had a gun in a holster on his belt."

The following day Giovanni sent Ronan a message with an attachment.

"Oh fuck," Ronan said, holding out his phone to me with the attached file open. Ronan's two guns and his firework thing were the front-page picture of the region's newspaper.

I couldn't copy and paste the text to Google Translate, so I sent it to Karen. Karen is like my English sister from another mother, who has lived up a mountain in Tuscany with her family for about fifteen years now. She and Lucia are my saviours when anything needs to be translated in a hurry; "Please help. What does this say?"

She responded:

"Irish man taken in for questioning by anti-mafia squad regarding illegal firearms and missile launcher possession...

Have you got dodgy Irish neighbours?" asked Karen with a line of laughing face emojis.

"No, but our neighbours do... This is about Ronan."

"OH SHIT! what the hell has he done, joined the Mafia? Missile launcher?"

"I know, it sounds like we are in the Taliban. They advertised it for setting off fireworks safely. Bloody hell! One of our neighbours must have seen Ronan target shooting in the garden and reported us."

As our car was the only Irish car we ever saw in the region, it would be quite apparent to anyone who had read the article that it was about Ronan... which meant us. The article had failed to mention one gun was a BB gun. Instead, we are two Irish bad asses with a pistol each—Bonny and Clyde as far as our neighbours are concerned.

"I'm not going out in that car ever again, oh my God this is disastrous," I said, pacing the floor.

After reading the not so small print on the email from the seller for a third time, it clearly stated something else Ronan had failed to take notice of; the seller must inform the appropriate authorities in Italy of anyone buying firearms from them. So that is how the police found out, not a scared neighbour, thankfully.

Giovanni arrived and started pacing the sitting room of the house we were renting from him. He was not happy. He was talking in Italian and I was picking up some of it but we called Luca out of his empty room to translate.

"This is not good for him. He wants us to leave."

———

The following day Lucia arrived in a rage. "I am so angry. I was just at Mick Kelly's about something I need to get done at the restaurant and as I walked into the office, Giovanni was there with his back to me telling him about your guns and talking shit about you."

I've never seen Lucia so furious. "I shouted at him, 'Giovanni stop. Stop talking shit about them, they are good people, they would do anything to help anyone, better than a lot of Italians around here and you are talking shit about them? If I ever hear you talking like this about them again, I will chop off your balls and shove them down your throat'."

Giovanni was back being his friendly self to us that evening and told us we didn't have to leave.

The following week, the hippy policeman was back again. Ronan looked nervous as he drove up the driveway and went down to meet him.

I watched from the bedroom window as he got out of the car and opened the back door. I thought he was ushering Ronan in, but instead he took something out of the back seat and got Ronan to sign a piece of paper. A receipt for the goods he was returning–our breadbasket and the BB gun–as they were not illegal to own. Anyone can have them... especially the breadbasket.

This all happened back in 2019. Then Covid hit and court dates were postponed. Now, four years later, Ronan's court date is looming. Will it be thrown out? Will it be postponed again? Or will he be enjoying prison food with a beautiful view of Volterra before I have finished writing this book?

4

Mam went back to Ireland just as the hot summer of 2022 started. She had spent every day of the previous eight months with me as we both adjusted to life without Dad.

I thought it would be easier, but I surprised myself by evolving into a woman with a very short fuse. Before my mother left, she threw a couple of 'jobs' my way. Don't get me wrong, I like doing things for my Mam, but sometimes the way she wants them done, makes something easy ten times more difficult and time consuming for me.

"I was talking to Maura back home in Ireland and I want you to contact the health service and get the forms to fill in for the home aides I have here. Like the hand bars in the bathroom and the walking frame."

This was one of the last hot topics we went head-to-head on before she left.

"It's okay, Ma, I'll just order them for you, no need to go through the Irish health service."

"Don't be ridiculous. I don't want you spending your money on things I am entitled to get for free or at least discounted from the government," she scoffed.

"Ma the things will cost about €100 to buy. If I call the health service they will probably have me on hold for five hours, then we'd have to wait for the forms to arrive, and then fill them out with every detail of our lives including what we had for breakfast that day, before they get lost in the Italian postal system and then having to repeat it all again. The money saved just wouldn't be worth the time I'd have to invest."

"I'm not worth your time? Just do it."

I knew she was joking, playing on my words, but my short fuse had been lit. "Will you stop trying to fill my days with unnecessary jobs? I've enough to be thinking about. I'll buy them online, it will take me ten minutes rather than weeks of stress. And they will be there and put up by Jim before you get back," I said, over reacting and storming out of the room.

It wasn't the first or last time I raised my voice at her about 'jobs' she'd constantly give me. Whereas with Ronan, I was the one constantly giving him jobs to do and then losing any sense of reason when he didn't do them or didn't do them the way I wanted them done.

I put my anger issues down to perimenopausal hormones, but I was beginning to hate the person who was emerging from beneath the surface of my skin.

Luca, our nineteen-year-old son, moved back to Ireland the

same day my Mam left, leaving two huge voids in the house, and my life. I had no one to care for except myself.

Over the following days, I wandered the rooms rearranging furniture and keeping myself busy but the heat was restrictive and when I stopped hauling stuff around the 'lost' feeling crept in.

Every time I sat, Spooky hopped onto my lap, her neck arched up and her eyes seductively squinted 'pet me, pet me how can you resist.' Her soft slick hair and the motion of petting relaxed my tense throat.

Maybe I had it wrong, maybe she was saying 'pet me, I'm here to help.' Allowing me time to take deep breaths.

I needed to get out and explore and remember why I was in Italy.

―――――

We are still waiting on the €40k we are due back from the 50/50 government bonus renovation repayment. All the paperwork was submitted to the bank over six months ago by Mick Kelly our renovation project manager, so it should be completed soon and then we can use that money to finish the bits left to do in the house, such as replacing the small roof, refurbishing more doors and starting work on the garden.

"Let's go to Spello," I announce to Ronan the following day. "Now that we are free, and while we wait to continue the renovations, we can tick a few things off the bucket list to remind us why we love Italy."

I had never been to Spello, the tiny Umbrian hilltop town encased by medieval walls, but it has on my long 'Italy To

Go' list a long time. We enter Spello, walking through one of the three entrances. Porta Consolare, Porta di Venere and the Arch of Augustus date back to when it was a Roman colony from the first century BC. Along with the old Roman aqueduct, the entrances are just some of the two-thousand-year-old things still standing, absorbing everyday history.

Women like me have walked through these portals going about their daily business for over two millennia. Each woman carrying her own history in her body. Troubles and joys some shared, some kept deep within. I wonder if the town was always this beautiful, dripping in geraniums, petunias and succulents from every window box and railing.

Spello is getting ready for its most famous annual event–La Infiorata–where the town's narrow pavements and roads are carpeted overnight by artists and locals with detailed mosaics made from dried rose petals.

Boxes of petals lie on the steps of a church in the sun waiting for their big moment to arrive when they will be part of a masterpiece; pinks, blues, saffron yellow, deep orange.

We stop by a trattoria.

"What's the difference between a ristorante, a trattoria and an osteria?" Ronan asks me as we dig into a wonderful lunch of egg and truffle, artichoke and cinghiale ragu.

This is something I know from my wedding planning. "Well, a ristorante is the most formal with printed menus and linen tablecloths. They'd have the higher prices."

I take a slurp of my crisp cold wine and unmuddle in my head how to differentiate between a trattoria and an osteria.

"A trattoria is usually hosted by a family who are the owners. It's simpler than a restaurant and usually cheaper. And an Osteria was originally like an inn with rooms to stay in with pub grub. They don't offer accommodation anymore but usually do simple, low-priced homemade food."

Over the next few days, the heat ramps up to the point of making me feel my blood has thickened and a weighted body suit made of unbreathable fabric lined with plastic has encased my body. I find it difficult to do anything other than sit on my bed. Now I understand why so many Italians take August off and head to the mountains or the beach. Although this year is hotter than ever. In fact, it is the hottest summer on record.

The river Po has dried up and I've never seen the lake behind our house this low—no one has in living memory. I remember Mick Kelly telling me we needed the earthquake band around the house to protect it or hold it together should the lake dry up too much as the land underneath the surrounds of the lake may then move ever so slightly. "But the lake never dries up so this will never happen," he reassured me.

Well, guess what? We've arrived and the lake is drying up, so it's just as well we got our fortified band installed.

For some crazy reason, July is the month when a lot of towns in Italy have festivals and medieval days. Our town, Passignano sul Trasimeno, is no exception.

There are four districts in the town and they compete in several events to win the annual Palio delle Barche.

The palio re-enacts the events from an attempted invasion in 1495 when the noble Baglioni and Oddi families fought a fierce battle here. Some exiles from Siena and Perugia invaded the castle at Passignano, but were so intimidated by the locals' violent reaction, they fled the town carrying their boats on their shoulders.

The race involves all four districts of the town and around one hundred and sixty competitors. They complete it in three stages.

Firstly, the boats row across the lakefront and around a buoy then back to the pier. Here the flag bearing girl gets out of the boat and runs to the street where she hands over the district flag.

Once the flag has been passed, a team of about fifty men run, balancing an upturned boat, around a circuit through the steep hills and passageways of the old town, echoing how the Oddi family had to flee from the castle, swapping places as needed while still running at high speed, until they return to the starting point. The flag is passed back to the girl who runs back to the boat. Finally, the boat and the girl with the flag are then rowed to the finish line.

The boat race starts at 6.30pm. It's 10.30am and I've already heard drumming in the distance for over an hour. Today, there will be locals in full medieval costume parading through the street in thirty-six degrees.

Medieval costume parades are another common sight in old towns of Italy during the spring and summer. These events are not just some old people playing dress up. Dozens of people come out in their finery of all age groups, children to grannies get decked out in heavy velvet costumes. The most prevalent age group is fifteen to forty-year-olds. Strong teenage boys and girls proudly dressed in costume march along the roads to the beat of drums.

Of course, there is food involved. A sagra where the community comes together to eat all evening.

In town we bump into Mick Kelly. "You have come to see the race?" he asks, smiling.

"No, I thought the race is on tomorrow?"

"Tomorrow is the boat race, today there is the Race of the Jugs. The women of the town with big jugs need to run in their hysterical costumes. With no wobbling. My sister is in it."

Luckily I have heard of this before. But Ronan has not and is looking bewildered at Mick Kelly's description of his own sister.

I quickly explain to Ronan before he says something inappropriate, "They run at high speed, carrying pitchers of water on their heads in their 'historical' costumes. It pays homage to the women who protected the castle's water supply by carrying jugs of water with speed from the public fountain to the castle gates. Don't you dare to make a comment about the size of their jugs."

Italians like carrying heavy things up hills in the summer heat and creating a festival around it, such as boats in Passignano, wine barrels in Montepulciano, giant wooden pillars known as the candlesticks in Gubbio and a large variety of bigger than life ancient religious statues in other towns. Maybe it explains why Italian men tend to be shorter... it's all the weight of these heavy things which honor for their town obliges them to run around with, pressing them into the ground.

Even though Montepulciano's Bravio delle Botti Festival is held at the hottest time of the year, it is still on my 'Italy To Go List'; the Bravio delle Botti, involves men racing uphill pushing heavy barrels of wine. It goes hand in hand with lots of wine tastings, what is there not to like?

But I can't go to Montepulciano this year as I feel like crap. My memory foam mattress has kept in its memory all the heat that has passed through the room in the last few weeks, making sleeping only an occasional possibility. I feel like a slab of turkey in a roasting tin basted in sweat.

I am shivery and then sweating again.

It's too hot to move, to do anything in the house or garden. Any exertion feels like I am doing it with a heavy blanket thrown over me. My head feels like it's bursting and my whole body is in pain. My energy goes from low to medium. I take a Covid test and it's positive. How the hell did I get Covid? I haven't been near anyone in over a week.

We had walked down by the lake and got an Aperol Spritz from the bar. A kid stopped to pet Juno but only for a second. Maybe it was the bartender.

So I isolate in my bedroom–my lovely room with the free-standing bath I've hardly used, double aspect windows and a perfectly plastered, mould-free ceiling I still rejoice in seeing every morning. Considering Ronan is the only other person in the house, and has his own bedroom and study across the hall-way, it is easy to stay isolated.

The first few Covid days are energy draining and I am sweating. Covid, perimenopausal hot flashes and the heat of the Italian summer cause a perfect heat storm through my body. As I drift in and out of consciousness, I have flashbacks of self-combustion reports on 'Ripley's Believe it or Not' in the Eighties. People's boots being found with ash of their bodies around them but the boots remained not even singed. Self-combustion and quicksand were two things pre-teen me found terrifying. They turned out not to be that important in adult life–but an epic pandemic was–which I vaguely remember being mentioned as a 'what if' on Ripley's Show.

Lying in bed, while Ronan dutifully keeps me supplied with ice packs to ease my fear of self-combusting, I'm counting down to my new life by weddings left to plan. Only four weddings to go before my new life starts as a full-time author. Burnout and a tough year had me pushing myself out of bed some days and just putting one foot in front of the other through the day. I had people's weddings to plan; the best day of their lives couldn't be affected by the worst time of my life.

As my Covid-fuelled days go on, I feel somewhat better with my energy creeping back up to the level where I can sit up in bed and stay conscious for a few hours at a time. Mundane tasks, like cleaning up the thousands of dealt-with emails and wedding plans stored on my computer system dating back ten years, keep me busy and feel therapeutic.

It's like I'm having an elective hysterectomy after just giving birth to make sure there will be no resurrecting of my wedding business in the future. There will be no going back–no matter what shade of financial hardship the rose-tinted glasses turn up in.

I spend the best part of the following day unsubscribing to things I have never read, deleting photos from my phone and going through contacts to see who I haven't caught up with in a while.

Mick Kelly is one of them. I write to him for an update about the €40k refund we are waiting on to finish the renovation work.

His reply adds another layer of sweat to my clammy skin; "The banks have paused the offer. We have to wait and see."

5

"Pasta Palace. Mamma Mia Manor. Pizza Piazza. Gelato Getaway. Tiramisu Terrace."

"Are you hungry?" I ask Ronan, who is rhyming off potential house names as we clean the kitchen together. "Or are you planning to open a restaurant here?"

"You said the house name needs to be Italian and most of the Italian words I know are food related... Paddy's Palazzo, Craic Casa, Dolce Dubs, The House of Missing Doors."

"Okay, you can stop now," I snap. "This is more difficult than naming our kids."

It's thirty-six degrees and rising. It is so hot, even the solid stone steps in the centre of our house that no direct sunlight reaches are very warm under bare feet. Italians don't recognise the need for air conditioning but the opening and closing of shutters is not doing it for me. The dogs just lie panting rapidly in front of the electric fans.

Ronan's crazy house name roll calls over the last few weeks normally drive me nuts after five minutes. However, the anger monster inside me is surprisingly quiet this week. It could be because Shelly has persuaded me to go to the Tom Jones concert in Perugia. She had bought tickets for her and Sherwin but he has had to return to the UK for the weekend.

We drive to the mini metro. I'd heard of it but never quite understood where it went from or where it went to. "It's the best way to get into Perugia," Shelly says. "It takes all the hassle out of driving into the city."

About ten driverless aluminium pods, each with a capacity of twenty-five people standing, go on a constant circuit from the massive car park up into Perugia's centre. It's like something a kid would have drawn in the Fifties, imagining how we would be travelling in 2020.

The bubble metro car takes us up to the road to the old town before we walk through what looks like a medieval underground village–the basement of Rocca Paolina–a fortress built by the Pope in the 1500s. But this was not a fortress to protect the people, it was a fortress to control the people of Perugia after the Pope had defeated the Lordship of Baglioni in a battle over salt.

Perugia was a free comune until 1370 before being 'incorporated' into a Papal State. But Perugia kept some of its autonomy, giving its citizens certain freedoms including freedom from paying taxes on salt. Salt was used to preserve food, so it was an important and critical commodity.

Successive Popes tried to quash Perugia's autonomy, but they resisted. However, in 1539 there was a disastrous harvest. So what did the then Pope do? He upped the taxes on salt. The people rebelled but on the fourth of June 1540, Papal troops led by the Pope's son (!), forced the Perugians to surrender. The Pope's gang then built an enormous fortress, Rocca Paolina, to stop the Perugians rebelling against the Holy See ever again.

For this reason, Rocca Paolina was hated by the citizens of Perugia for centuries and systematically demolished in the decades after the Unification of Italy. However, the basement remained.

"Bloody hell, were we just in some sort of time travel machine?" I ask Shelly as a series of escalators near the bus and train station, take us deeper into the medieval underground.

Any other country would have it as a museum but here in Perugia anyone coming into the city by the bus or train, gets to experience the feeling of entering the deepest Middle Ages.

Walking through history daily is the way of life no matter where people grow up or decide to live in Italy. Each building has a rich episodic story to tell.

"This is really beautiful during Christmas time with the market stalls standing along the path leading to the top and during Perugia's Chocolate Festival in October," says Shelly.

The Umbria Jazz Festival is on and the city is alive with live bands. Families and groups of every age fill the streets with chatter and laughter. As I hadn't been to Perugia since before Covid started, I forgot how the boho boutique shops are much more to my liking than the big name stores of Florence. They are all closed for the evening, but the lit-up displays are calling me to come back another time.

Mr Tom Jones plays a blinder of a concert, we sing and chair dance to all the hits he bellows out. This eighty-two-year-old gives me hope about getting old, something I've recently added to my fear list of heights, escalators, quicksand and self-combustion.

It's close to midnight when we leave the arena. We trace our route back along the full streets still vibrating to the sound of trumpets, double basses and jazz singers hitting notes so deep they sink into the city's Etruscan foundations.

Kids and adults are enjoying their midnight snacks outside a gelateria and people are just finishing meals and having a last drink.

No one is drunk, well no one is obviously drunk. As an Irish person, this feels like some sort of crazy anomaly of Italy. While I don't like stereo-typing Ireland with a drink culture, festivals in my home country do involve a lot of drinking without the accompaniment of long leisurely meals. Walking through a street festival in Ireland at twelve at night without seeing a lot of drunk people just wouldn't happen.

We walk back through the medieval underground maze of brick-built streets with arched windows and secret passages.

There's no way would I walk through somewhere like this in Dublin or any city in Ireland or the UK without feeling on my guard with the possibility of robbery or attack during the day, never mind at midnight.

I have a glancing thought of how amazing this place is, as if I'm a tourist–but this is the capital city of the region where I am a resident. This is now my capital, this is where I live, my brain gives myself a little squeeze. I need to visit more often and stop feeling like an alien.

6

——————

It's late summer, I open half of the windows and doors on the ground and first floor and let the warm strong breeze filter through the magnolia trees into The Sighing House. I stand and bask in it. Not only does it have a drying effect on my sweat patches, but it comforts me to think the worst of the intense summer heat is over.

I took advantage of it being too hot to leave the house and embraced becoming a hot sluggish mess, sitting on my bed most of the day writing furiously.

Apart from the intense heat, this was my idea of heaven. Sitting quietly and writing. Many words. Two novels in two months in fact.

We go to Ben's house for dinner. This is the first Italian family dinner we have been to other than Lucia's. Ben and his wife have a wedding business and I am edging the management of all my weddings towards them.

They bought a renovation house project the same time as us but further up a mountain with an amazing view.

"Bella Vista," says Ronan driving up to Ben's gate and rolling the name of the house off his tongue. "How about that for ours?"

We are still trying to find the perfect name. I'd only named it 'The Sighing House' when it was waiting for the right owners to buy it, and now that it had found us, I didn't feel it needed to be sighing anymore.

It was temporarily called The Work House when it was roofless and ripped to shreds, but the connotations of the name in Irish history were not pleasant or fitting for an Italian villa.

"Because we don't have a Bella Vista, unless you are an avid train spotter?" I say, referring to the train track running between the end of our garden and the lake. Usually, I would have said this with humour but even I recognise my tone as being sarcastic.

Ronan verbalises an endless mind dump of house name ideas whenever there is a lull between us. "Villa Magnolia, Rosie's Hole, The Wreck, The Money Pit, Villa Vino, Casa WTF, The Mouldy Forest, Unstable Gables". At first it was funny but I am sick to my teeth of endless stupid suggestions and it really isn't helping the anger management issues I am having.

Under the dense undergrowth at the back of their house, Ben uncovered a stepped garden with two beautiful stone statues and a stone table with stone benches under a tree. He has a profusion of stringed lights hung around the garden, traversing from one tree to the next.

Under the strings of light is the table set for dinner; homemade bread and peppery olive oil made from the early season batch of olives from their grove of forty trees. The table overlooks the grove where fireflies blink in the darkness.

Ben and Ellie have two are very cute and polite girls, "Can I have some prosciutto?" asks the five-year-old, helping herself to the aperitif food. "Can I have some cheese? Can I take a fig?"

No coke or fizzy drinks. Water and maybe an orange juice for the kids and wine, of course, for the adults. In Italy there are no kids' meals at restaurants. The parents might request some simple pasta with tomato sauce for the youngest 'bambini' but otherwise kids help themselves to what the adults are eating.

"Your kids are so good," I say, remembering how happy I used to be when someone would comment on my kids' behaviour. It makes parents feel less desperate.

"Oh, don't let their sweetness deceive you, they fight like cats which is just the way with Italian sisters but at the same time they would also die for each other."

Looking at them you would never think they were sisters. The youngest has typical Italian dark hair while the eldest has thick blond hair. "She gets it from my side," says Ellie. "There is a thread of this hair running through my mother's family. But they look so different, people comment all the time, but sometimes not in a nice way."

She explains, "This woman came up to me at the supermarket and looks at Ben and says to me 'Ah she's corno.' And I say 'no' and the woman is saying 'ah yes you have a cornuto'."

"What's cornuto?" I ask.

"It means the child is from a different father than your husband. In Tuscany they have no restrictions on their mouths, they can say anything and it is okay."

"Say a child is cornuto in Sicily and your throat would be slit," laughs Ben, laying a platter of salami slices on the table. The tray reminds me of the time we rushed Luca to ER and I arrived shouting I had a platter of salami cuts–'tagliere'–instead of using the verb 'to cut'–'tagliare'–to tell them my son was bleeding to death.

I'm not a salami fan but as Ben insists, "You must try it! It's salami with fennel," I take some out of politeness. It blows my tastebuds into a whole new taste universe.

"Oh my God, that's amazing, I'll have to get some for Jim the next time I am going back to Ireland."

On every phone call I have with Jim, he asks me what I have eaten recently. I know my food-passionate brother thinks Italy is wasted on me as I am not trying every piece of offal and oddly named meat available.

"I have a question for you Rosie," says Ben. "The groom's first name we recently did a wedding for was 'Ryan'. But that is a surname yes?"

"Yes, it is a common surname in Ireland."

"That is what I thought. It is unusual for me, as a surname would not be permitted as a first name in Italy. Ryan would be allowed of course, but an Italian surname as a first name is not allowed. The law in Italy is strict about names," Ben continues while topping up my wine and Ellie places a second platter of meats on the table. "For instance, a boy baby cannot be named after his father if the father is alive. If you want to name your child after a living family member, it can only be as a second name, you must have a different name in front of it."

Ellie adds, "Traditionally a child was given the surname of the father but only this year the courts have ruled babies should be given both parents' surnames unless the parents decide to opt for one or the other."

Through my wedding planning days and dealing with legal documents for foreign weddings, I know all the issues with surnames and birth names in Italy.

In Italy a woman keeps her birth name for life, they don't take their husband's name at marriage. All children born in Italy are assigned a sixteen-digit code fiscale as is anyone living in Italy or doing business in Italy. The first letters and numbers in the code comprise of your initials, year and month of birth. This cannot be changed, so women, like men, sign everything using their full birth name.

Registering a child's birth needs to be done carefully in Italy. One of my brothers is Anthony, Francis, Luke (Mam wanted to give all the names she liked to the last child she thought she was going to have, then I came along).

Except there are no commas on his registered birth cert. If that happened in Italy, the combination of names would all be considered his first name and he would have to sign documents with all of them. Commas between first and second names are important in Italy.

Ben has added cheeses to the table from their holiday to the Dolomite mountains close to where Italy borders Switzerland.

The first was delicious, served with jam made from their own apricots. Next was the creamy coloured cheese with an orange tint through it. I munched, and it tasted wrong. It was mould central, strong mould.

'No, no, no,' my brain said 'do not swallow!' I slyly spit the gross tasting cheese into my napkin.

In the meantime, Ellie and the kids were showing their disgust for the cheese less discreetly, by spitting it on the ground. Whereas Ben, thought it was the most delicious thing he had ever tasted.

"What's the name of that cheese?" I ask gulping wine trying to get rid of the taste. "I need to know so I never buy it."

"Puzzone di Moena," Ben says, laughing at our reactions," in Italian it means 'Stink from Moena'."

7

S ince Mam went back to Ireland, I am adapting to the Italian way of life with a power nap in the afternoon.

Like the way brunch is between breakfast and lunch, rather than having lunch and dinner we have 'lunner'–one main meal between lunch and dinner. Since Ronan still considers spaghetti bolognese as one of his essential daily food groups, we usually eat separately and have different meals. I can no longer stand the sight of it and I am leaning more towards vegetarian food.

With my wedding business slowly migrating to Ben and the house empty, I fill any space in my workaholic schedule with writing. Some days I spend ten hours working on my rom-com series. It's not a genre I usually read but I enjoy writing it.

I'm trying to think of romantic ways to describe kissing other than using the words mouth or lips. A thesaurus can usually help in these cases, but for 'mouth' my choices are gob, cake hole, trap and mush. "She stared longingly at his cake hole on his handsome mush and her gob became dry." While it has a certain ring to it, it is not quite the style of phrasing I was looking for.

Mam reads romances so I call her up for some brainstorming.

"Well, funny you should ask, I am just reading a book where the hero is kissing the heroine and the description is 'His tongue darted between her lips like a bird out of a cuckoo clock'."

We're both laughing hysterically, something we didn't do much of together when she lived with me and I have missed it.

Asking my eighty-six-year-old mother's help with sex scenes was probably not the best idea, so I start at the beginning and look into the history of kissing. Of course, most records are about the Romans.

Apparently, a kiss on the lips was not always sexual for the Romans. It was largely in the family circle, between relatives or people closely related. While they usually used kisses on the cheek in social life, they kissed their wives on the lips to see if they were drinking wine–a banned substance for wives to indulge in.

The ancient Romans had different names for the types of kisses they gave. Osculum on hand or cheek was for greetings. Baccio alla Romana or barium, was the more intimate one to see if herself indoors had been at the wine. Then there was savium, which is described as 'a passionate kiss men only used with prostitutes'. I can't find a description but I am guessing savium is what I am after for my books.

But kissing will have to wait. We're working on clearing out the room we have been using for storage on the first floor. Ronan's method is to take a box and move it across the hall to sort out later. So basically transferring the storage from one room to another, turning the other non-storage room into a storage room. I get it, there is method in his madness as he sees big objects like bed frames or major items that need chucking, whereas I am a detail person, wanting to go through every box and find a place for each thing or dump it.

These are the last two rooms of twenty-two we need to sort out, so it is getting more difficult as the things that have been moved in here are the items moved from elsewhere under the title; 'What-will-we-do-with-this?-I-don't-know...keep-it-and-we'll-sort-it-at-another-time.'

So while Ronan flings things to be dumped out the window like a rockstar in a hotel in the Eighties, I go through the boxes in the new storage room. I proceed with caution as the dusty, mostly paper-filled boxes are the perfect nesting ground for scorpions.

First up are the pile of medical magazines from the early Fifties found in the attic. I'm not interested in reading about the latest medical discoveries from seventy years ago, but I am interested in the eight-page glossy central pull-out feature in each of the five magazines, about diverse topics such as sea urchins, the zodiac, the history of bathing and medieval herbal medicine.

Each have fantastic illustrations. The herbs article in particular has beautiful, colourful, medieval paintings. So I go on a hunt for picture frames in the household department of our local DIY store. The price of picture frames with Perspex, not even glass, is exorbitant. So I go online and source a box of mixed sized frames for €30.

I am excited to get to work cutting out the black and white

detailed line drawings of the anatomy of sea urchins to form a series of four framed pieces; perfect for the main bathroom.

I've calculated that with twenty-two rooms, we have eighty-eight walls to decorate. Not all will require art but some, such as the hallways, will require more than others.

The small medieval colourful illustrations are next. I create a gallery of nine and arrange them on a leftover piece of jungle wallpaper to figure out a template for the nails to go in the wall to hang them the way I want.

The wooden head of Buddha that Ronan bought me about fifteen years ago, which never really found a place in any of our previous houses because it was too big, fits perfectly on my bedroom wall, adding to the serenity of the fern plant and large Aladdin-style brass bed.

The oil painting of a donkey my mother painted for my previous birthday, nicknamed 'Rosie's Ass', hangs in the guest kitchen on the first red brick wall we discovered. The red brick still needs to be re-mortared like the dining room, as does the one in the big kitchen but it will be done with time.

During the room clear out, Ronan finds a USB in a padded envelop and we can't remember what it is. So he sticks it into the back of the TV and discover it's our wedding video his brother made. We have not watched it in twenty years.

There, in front of me, is my Dad and Eileen moving and talking and dancing with me. Tears flow.

"Hang on what date is it?... Today is our wedding anniversary, how did we forget?" Ronan says.

"We've been just taking one day at a time and losing track of dates... Let's go out for dinner," I suggest, not so much to celebrate but more to get away from having to go back to clearing the rooms.

We leave the rooms as they are, get ready and go to the local fish restaurant, where red and white gingham covered tables sit under an alley way shaded by a bamboo mat roof.

"We should do this on the walkway to the vines," Ronan says, pointing at the roof. It gets us started on talking about plans for the garden and on the back of a napkin we sketch out a design over dinner. Of course, after a while, it turns ridiculous with us drawing a Trevi Fountain type structure, phallic statues and massive pools.

"Okay so it's agreed; when we get the €40k credit back from the bank we do the small roof and the garden."

"But in the meantime, we should book a holiday," I say because I am always the instigator. "To celebrate us retiring from weddings and bringing up two kids."

"What about the dogs?"

"I love our dogs but I wouldn't put rearing them in the same category as bringing up our kids!"

"No, I mean who will look after the dogs while we are away?"

"I'll find someone to look after them, but I really would like to experience a holiday where I just lie on a beach and read and swim and eat nice food with no work involved. I can't remember the last time I had a non-work-related holiday. In fact, I don't think we have ever booked a holiday together just to have a holiday."

"Where do you want to go?"

"I've always wanted to go to the Greek islands, it niggles in the back of my mind that we should have checked out Greece before buying in Italy. I love it here, but perhaps Greece has something else we don't know we are missing... Like the sea."

We bump into Shelly and Sherwin on our way home and end up going for a drink with them down by the lake.

"We want to go on a holiday to Greece," I tell them. "An island with a warm, blue sea and a sandy beach is all we require, where would you recommend?"

They have travelled a lot more than us, all around the world.

"We really liked Corfu."

"Cyprus it is then," I say feeling lightheaded from the wine at dinner, the fresh air and follow up drink at the bar. So I go home, get online and book a holiday in Crete.

I initially chose a hotel on the west coast but after a frustrating two hours of trying to choose the right place to stay, I book somewhere random close to beaches and a town and go to bed feeling very accomplished.

"How did you get it so wrong?" asks Ronan the following morning when I tell him what I have done. They all begin with C and are in the same sea, a carafe of wine and a warm night, is the only explanation I can give him.

I am looking forward to finishing the last wedding, when I will have head space. Time to think. Time to adjust to everything that has gone on. Time to get my house and my new life organised.

I read a quote once that said; You have two lives: One life and then the second life starts when you truly realise you only have one life.

I feel my second life will start when the final wedding is done.

8

It's near to the end of summer and the suffocating Italian heat wave we have been wrapped in for weeks is loosening its grip, but it's still bloody hot. Izzy is moving to a new apartment so helping her to move is a good excuse for me to fly to cooler London for the weekend.

I've flown over the Alps many times and I have never seen them so snowless. The green valleys between the soaring heights, houses dot the snaking rivers like feet of a centipede. Parts of the riverbeds are a pale tan where aquamarine blue would normally be. It seems no part of Italy was spared from the heat of this summer.

While in London, I book a haircut as I still don't trust being able to explain what I don't know what I want done to my hair in Italian. The hairdresser assigned to cutting my hair in the salon in London is Matteo. He is from Milan and when he hears I live in Italy, he babbles away in Italian explaining what he's going to do to my head. I nod as I am too embarrassed to admit my Italian is still crap after four years. Matteo does a good job on my hair, it should get me through another three years or at least long enough for me to learn Italian.

I also get my eyes tested while in London. I know I need reading glasses but going for an eye test in Italy would be too confusing as 'I' is pronounced EE and they have weird names for 'H' and 'Y', so my mispronunciation could lead me to having a very incorrect test leading to much stronger glasses than I need. Not only that, but glasses are very expensive in Italy. Ben paid €900 for his. But then again, they all go for designer frames. Cheap and cheerful does the trick for me.

It's so lovely being able to book a last-minute flight over to see Izzy. I still hesitate and hold back thinking it's difficult to do since all the Covid travel drama and trauma. But here I am walking in a park chatting with my lovely girl, groups of people sitting on the grass, gathered in bars and restaurants enjoying the sun and not a face mask in sight. It's so good to see this as normal again.

"Dave and I are talking about buying a house together," Izzy says.

"Oh wow, that's amazing when and where?"

"Well, it will be in the UK, near London. And the when is, when we can afford it. He has savings but I want to be equal in it from the start. So hopefully in a year or two when I have work again."

Mad guilt washes over me. If she hadn't invested in The Sighing House, she would have money to invest in her own dreams. None of us imagined the knock-on effects of the worldwide pandemic would included her losing her job, after the TV series she was part of got cancelled.

I need to think of a way of getting her back her investment.

When alone, I call Ronan. "We need to talk. Izzy and Dave want to buy a house."

"Great!"

"Yes, but she is putting her dreams on hold because she doesn't have an income and she invested all her hard-earned cash in The Sighing House. So I'm thinking we should give her the €40k when we get the 50/50 back and just save up for the work that needs to be done."

"Good idea."

Even though I have texted Mick Kelly a few times since I had Covid, he hasn't responded with any further updates about the government reimbursement. So I text him again. "Hey Mick, is the bank processing the 50/50 or have you any news?"

"Some weeks ago the bank answer me to say they stopped to taking the credits, but they were waiting some news from the government. Next week I try to speak with them again."

Ronan picks me up from the airport and, while driving back, we see dark clumps of black smoke rising and puffing on the olive hill with the castle topper that sat behind our rental house at Giovani's.

Fire helicopters scoop water from the receding lake and drop it on the billowing smoke. There is one fire truck ahead with just one fireman. His truck has run out of water and he tries to beat flames licking up one of many ancient olive trees on fire, before giving up. It's doomed like at least one thousand other olive trees that scatter the hill we used to look out at from the kitchen of our rental. We need rain. The land is parched crisp, a vast tinderbox. The fire is not near our house but we have a better understanding of why there are fines when the grass of a property is not cut, and why the neighbour reported the overgrown garden of The Sighing House the week before we bought it.

I wait until the next morning to discuss what's on my mind with Ronan. "I have a bad feeling we are not going to get the €40k reimbursement from the 50/50, but we need to give Izzy a chunk back."

"So what do you want to do, sell it?" he says, slurping up his breakfast cereal with his eyes on his phone screen.

"Sell it?" I couldn't understand how he could say it so casually and quickly. "Can you put your phone down for a moment and talk to me?"

"Sorry."

"Sell it?" I repeat, still in twisted shock.

"It's the obvious thing to do. Sell this place and give Izzy back her investment and buy a smaller place. It's too big for just the two of us. Sorted and less work."

"Sell The Sighing House?" I am in disbelief. I also can't believe out of all the names we have gone through we are still calling it The Sighing House.

"For God's sake, Rosie are you hard of hearing. What's the alternative?"

"Well, I was thinking perhaps starting a BnB and then getting a mortgage."

"A mortgage? You wouldn't get one at your age."

"My age?" Now I am getting annoyed. Not that I want a mortgage, I've had enough of them and all the stress that goes with having one. But implying I was too old at fifty to qualify... was I too old?

"Could you imagine trying to apply for a mortgage in Italy?" he says. "The paperwork involved would be a nightmare. And besides we don't have fixed regular income other than my pension."

"I don't think we can sell it," I say, giving his idea some space once the initial shock had subsided. "There was a clause in the purchase that we cannot sell it for five years otherwise we had to pay a much higher tax rate."

"Well, no harm in getting the house valued and have a discussion with the notary to see what the situation would be in regards tax." His eyes went back to his phone. "It could be on the market for years before we find a buyer. We should run it as a BnB in the meantime, it would give a regular income if you wanted to go the mortgage route."

"But what if we find a buyer within months?"

"Then we sell it," he says matter-of-factly.

"Sell it?" I am back to my shocked state.

"For goodness' sake Rosie are we back to this again? Sell it, give Izzy back her investment and buy a small place for us with the remainder. Simple."

I'm sweating. Sell The Sighing House? Small place? Sharing the same room again? I had got fond of my own space, more than fond, I loved waking up early and writing in blissful quietness after a good night's sleep with no snoring or anyone else to think of.

And then there was of course Mam. I needed a place for her to come during the winter and spring. How would that work?

Later, I overhear Ronan chatting with Izzy on a video call, she is showing him around the flat she and Dave have moved into.

"Rosie was telling me you are saving up for a house together. We were talking about a way we could get you back the money you put into this place, so we're going to look into selling it and buying a smaller place."

Her answer is muffled but I can hear the delight and excitement.

He shouldn't have said anything yet. But the seed has been planted and I can't tear it out of the ground now that it has taken root.

9

The idea of running a BnB has put a tight band of stress around my stomach. It is not a dream I ever had. Cleaning toilets and washing bed linen after strangers does not fill me with a sense of joy.

And I know the breakfasts will fall on my shoulders as Ronan is not a morning person. And mornings are my precious writing time. I'm going to be back doing two jobs before I've even had a chance to experience just doing one for the first time in my adult life. Ronan, on the other hand, has finished his last wedding and is officially retired. I'm jealous.

There's no point in suggesting he runs the BnB as he'd never do the cleaning to the level I would want it done and since his lack of reading emails properly could already land him in prison by the end of the year, I wouldn't trust him with bookings. And I am not ashamed to admit, I am a control freak.

However, the good thing is, he now has the time and head space to apply for his residency. As he is an EU citizen and has a regular pension, this is or should be straightforward.

We still have the list of requirements needed for residency from the time I applied. One requirement is health insurance. So we go to our house insurance broker and take out two months health insurance to cover the application period, like we did for mine.

"I have put you down as a professional," says Barbara our insurance broker, who is the mother of the guy who fixed our internet, that's how we found her.

"No, I am a pensioner," says Ronan, proud of his newfound status.

"But you are the same age as my husband, and he is not a pensioner? He can still work and you look so much younger than him," says Barbara sitting back aghast.

"Maybe I look younger than him but it doesn't change my age or my status as pensioner, I need it correct so my application for residency and Tessera Sanitaria goes through automatically."

She reluctantly changes it. But on presenting all his documents to the comune there's a glitch with his insurance document. "You need health insurance for one year, this is just for two months."

"But two months of insurance was all my wife needed?"

"It has changed."

"But it only takes a maximum of two months for residency to be approved and, as I am a pensioner, I will automatically get the Tessera Sanitaria and be entitled to free public health care and won't need private health care."

Well, that is what Ronan would like to say but he can't because he doesn't speak Italian so we make an effort through Google Translate and just get told again he needs private health insurance for a year.

"Six hundred and fifty euro!" exclaims Ronan back in Barbara's office.

"It is the cost," Barbara says, filling out the application to extend the insurance on her computer and giving us the printout of it.

So we go back to the comune with just the application. And it works. Ronan's residency application is accepted and Barbara tears up our application of insurance extension without us needing to pay the extra.

A few weeks later there is a policeman standing at our gate. I recognise him as the same one who came to verify I was living here for my residency. I stick my head out the window and wave at him. "Uno momento," I say as Ronan makes his way down the four flights of stairs.

The policeman stays outside and asks Ronan a few questions in English from his application, verifying his name and that this is the house where he lives. He gets to profession, and Ronan says "Pensionato".

The policeman looks at him and hesitates about writing it in.

"But you are too young to be a pensionato."

"I am sixty-six."

He still hesitates, "Yes but you look too young."

"So I look too young for residency as a pensioner?" I hear Ronan ask as I reach the gate to see what the delay is.

Just then Patricia, our postwoman, arrives with our mail and she and the policeman have a full serious discussion about how Ronan is too young to be sixty-six. They nod and look sad for him but then are laughing and the policeman gets Ronan to sign the document and is on his way.

"I am sorry, I hate to give you these," says Patricia.

The utility bills have been coming in fast and are mounting. Weddings were still taking up my time, but the backlog of unpaid bills is really because I procrastinate about having to suffer the hostility of the clerks at either the bank or the post office.

And because I procrastinated the gas, electric and water companies have all sent reminders which I have to sign for on the same day the new bills have arrived including the TARI bill, which is for the refuse collection.

Also, in a kitchen drawer, there's a letter from the water company I just haven't had time to translate yet.

"I can return them and say you were not here to receive them if you wish?" says Patricia giving me the option to postpone paying the overdue bills even longer.

"No, it is okay, I just hate going to the bank or post office and having to queue to pay them."

"You know you can pay utility bills and fines in the supermarket?" she says, pointing to the supermarket across the road from the house.

"Really?" This is an amazing discovery. I take the bills with the payment slips attached and practically skip into the supermarket.

I hand my pile of bills to Fred–the good-looking guy who acts like he owns the place but doesn't–and he scans the QR codes.

The four months of three different utility bills add up to a lot, nearly €1400 to be exact. The water bill had additional payments to be made since I translated the letter from them asking me to email the meter reading as they could not get into the house to do a reading themselves. So, the bill had been estimated until now, including the time they were doing a lot of work in the house and needed water for cement, grout and coffee, lots of coffee.

"No! This is too high! Mamma mia. It is too much," says Fred.

"Tell that to the utility companies," I say.

"No, I mean it is too much. We can only take payment for bills up to one thousand in one day." And without pause he continues, "Do you have a loyalty card for here?"

"No."

"You should get one. You can get points for the bills you pay here."

"Always a silver lining. Okay can I have one?"

"Well..." he hesitates. "They are €25."

"I have to pay for a loyalty card?"

"I am afraid so." He is cringing asking for the fee, but we shop here a lot and if we are going to pay our bills here...

"Okay go on then, I'll get one anyway it will be worth it."

"But it is €25?"

"Yes, I know, can you give me one?"

"No," he says, looking like he is turning down a proposal of marriage.

"What?" I say as if I was the one who proposed after fifteen years of being together.

"Oh, hmm I don't have the forms here. Come back on Thursday."

"I don't want to wait until Thursday to pay these bills so let me pay half of them and the other half on Thursday."

"Okay," he says looking relieved.

Thursday comes and I go to pay the rest of the bills and get the loyalty card.

"Is Fred here?" I ask the cashier who doesn't speak any English.

"No, he does not work on Thursdays."

"Can I get a loyalty card?"

"No, I cannot fill out the forms. You need to talk to the manager on Tuesday."

I just pay the bills anyway.

On the way home I bump into Sherwin coming into the supermarket. "Sherwin, do you have a loyalty card for here?"

"No. They told us we should get one, but no one seemed to know how to sign us up for it."

I give up on trying to get a loyalty card, I'm just glad I don't have to face the bank or post office to pay bills any longer. Amongst the post there is also a reminder from Doctor Fab Chicken to get in touch with him regards booking a specialist appointment about my water baby–the name I fondly call my cyst.

Now that my worst fear of living in Italy–having to deal with hospitals–has manifested itself, I pledge to make a new effort in learning Italian. It will also be necessary if we are running a BnB.

I am back home from the supermarket just in time to take my online group Italian class. We are going over the verb 'To Understand'.

Io capisco

Tu capisci

Lui/Lei capisce

I get to the 'we plural' form of the verb, 'Noi capisciamo', and in my pronunciation I include the ish sound in the middle of the conjunction. My teacher corrects me.

"You need to be careful with this one. The correct form is 'Noi capiamo'. The way you said it is a vulgar word for urinating."

"Oh my God, I used that lots while we were building the house, when the builders were explaining what or why they were doing something. So instead of saying we understand I was saying... 'we are pissing'?"

I think back and maybe my verb usage wasn't too off, as sometimes we were pissed off with them. It did feel at times, we were pissing money against a wall or pissing against the wind trying to get things done and sometimes, we were pissing ourselves laughing at their estimated quotes. And, to get through it all, sometimes I felt the need to get pissed.

Lucia calls me with a question about my next and final wedding at her agriturismo. In passing, I mention the idea of us starting a BnB at the house and she responds; "Oh great, I have four additional guests arriving for a wedding next week and I have no rooms for them. Can you take them, it will be good practice for you?"

"Oh, em, I'm not ready."

"What you need to do to be ready?"

"I don't have linens."

"I will give you them."

"I need a cleaner to help prep."

"I will send you one."

I have no more excuses so I say okay.

What have I agreed to? We are starting a BnB?

10

It's all a bit of a rush getting the house ready. It is in good shape but I've discovered as soon as you know a stranger is going to come into your home and pay to be there; you look at it with completely fresh eyes.

"We will need to get air-con installed next year and mosquito screens for the windows if we are going to do BnB next summer," says Ronan collecting the rusting paint tins which have sat on the balcony for months.

"Even if we don't do a BnB, I can't do another summer of this heat without air con in my bedroom," I say to Ronan before I leave.

"Why don't you just move to a different room?"

He has a point. My room is in the southeast corner of the house so it is sun-baked all day.

"We'll also need a friggin' name for the house. I can't believe we can't think of one... and before you start," I quickly add, "rhyming off a load of stupid suggestions is not funny anymore, let's seriously try to think of a fitting Italian name for the house–"

"I've got the perfect one, how about–"

"Think before you speak," I interrupt. "If it is comical or not Italian, do not say it, as it might cause a divorce."

"Oh, okay. That's my suggestion of Villa la Spaghetti gone then," he says, scooting past me with the tins. He just about gets away with it as I'm not my usual flaming enraged self today.

Besides the cleaning and the breakfast commitment of a BnB, the constant changeover of people coming and going through our house on a rotating basis really does not appeal to me either. I like to get to know people, hear their stories, bond, make a connection. However, I am hoping having Lucia's over-flow guests will help change my mind.

There are two women from Sweden coming and a couple from Florida. Both just for two nights; the night before their friend's wedding and the night of the wedding. We can do this.

Ronan happily volunteers to collect the Swedish women from the train station at lunchtime and I will collect the Florida couple who are arriving from Naples later the same day.

I have the rooms perfect; the window is open with a warm breeze blowing through, there's a vase of lilies on the bedside table and fresh new linens and towels on the bed. I'm quite proud of it... until Spooky runs in with Juno in hot pursuit, she jumps up on the bedside table between the two twin beds and topples the large jug perfectly onto one of the beds. It's not just water, the pollen from the lilies makes it look like skid marks were left on the bedsheet.

I, of course, have bed sheets but I don't have spare crisp, professionally-laundered sheets Lucia gave me and I don't want to let her down by lowering her standards. Panic sets in. I pull the sheets off to find a bigger problem; the mattress is soaking, and it's not the type you can flip.

"Ronan where are you?" I say, without saying hello while I pace the floor.

"I'm just at the station. I think I spot them. Two tall blondes, definitely not Italians."

"Wedding?" I hear him call out.

"Yes, it's them," he says back down the phone to me.

"Okay, listen, you need to stall bringing them back, take them for a drive, show them the sights or something. I have a bit of an emergency here and it will take me an hour or two to fix."

"An hour or two?" He sounds horrified.

"Maybe less than an hour. Look I will be as fast as I can, I'll call you."

And I hang up. I need to think fast, so I flip the mattress onto its side and stick the fan on high speed in front of it before grabbing the sheet and putting it on a fast wash. It's a double size sheet, so I figure I can take the sheet off the bed for the couple arriving later.

Luckily the water had only done surface damage to the mattress, it had not the time to soak deep and together with a fan and a hair dryer I have it as dry as Luca's sense of humour within twenty minutes.

I call Ronan, "Okay you can bring them to the house."

"We're just having some lunch. I brought them for a drive but they hadn't eaten since early this morning. They don't speak a word of English but we are having a good laugh."

"Seriously, how do you do it?" I'm still envious of Ronan's ability to make friends without being able to speak the language.

I have the bed made and the welcome pack supplied by the wedding couple in the room just as Ronan pulls in through the gate.

We bump their large suitcases up the two flights of stairs.

"You are very welcome," I say smiling as we get into their room. They are delighted to see the welcome basket.

"I just need your passports to take a picture of..."

They don't understand English nor Italian. "Passporto? Passports?"

"Ah yes," one translates for the other and she unzips her handbag and pulls out a travel wallet with both their passports in it.

"'Welcome from Patrick and Clare?'" The tallest girl reads aloud, just as I look confused at the front of their passports from Latvia.

"Wedding of Hanns and Johanna?" she states to me.

"Oh Ronan you didn't?" I say, knowing by his face he has not copped on as to what has happened. Neither has one of the girls, she is already starting to unpack and about to sit on the bed I have perfectly made for the second time.

"You have brought back the wrong people," I say just as my phone is buzzing. It's Lucia.

"Rosie where is Ronan? The Swedish guests are waiting at the train station for him."

"Emm, there has been a mix-up. He collected them but they are not them, so we are just trying to sort it out. Tell the Swedes to have a coffee, he'll be back there in twenty minutes."

Enraged self is back. Why do I always have to fix his mess ups? Lucia had texted him yesterday telling him to send a photo of their passports as soon as they meet, so she could start on the check-in paperwork for me. Of course he didn't read the text because it included instructions which Ronan has a strong aversion to. If he had read it and followed the one line of instructions, then this mess would not have happened which I now have to fix.

Both Ronan and I go to the station and I find the two Swedes sitting enjoying a gelato opposite the entrance while Ronan goes to explain to the driver standing with a Johanna & Hanns sign scribbled on the back of an A4 envelop looking very fed up. The Latvians have been on their phones continuously since we left, talking rapidly and excitedly with their friends who are waiting for them at a different villa.

"You basically kidnapped two Latvian models," I say trying not to lose my cool with him.

"Kidnapped? If someone kidnapped me and brought me sightseeing then to lunch, I would be delighted."

The Swedes speak perfect English and find our explanation of being late amusing and 'unique'. I'm guessing they think we just made it up.

"It is okay to deliver us to the party, we will come to your accommodation later," one of them says. So we drop them and their small bags off at La Dogana and continue on home.

I volunteer, or should I say insist on, going to meet the Americans. They are older and this is the first time one of them has been outside of Florida, never mind the US.

"So how has your trip been so far?"

"Awful" says the man, exasperated. "There's no Starbucks anywhere, and I can't live without my daily java chip frapacino. I thought frapacinos were Italian, why don't they have them here?"

I don't know how to answer this, I should have let Ronan collect them.

But Bill doesn't wait for an answer and just continues. "And Cheryl got robbed in Naples train station. They took her entire bag of jewellery out of her hand luggage while she was carrying it. We only realised it was gone when we got to the place we were staying in a small town outside Rome last night. We went to report it to the police station today, and they were closed for the afternoon. Can you believe it? They were closed for riposa whatever that is. That's why we had to get the late train." Bill is loud and exasperated by Italy already.

"The police were helpful, but they didn't have a list of pawn-shops in Naples to contact. That's what they would do in the States; contact the pawn shops and offer a reward if any of the valuables came in. Cheryl is devastated, aren't you Cheryl?" Bill doesn't wait for a response.

"A string of pearls her mother gave her and pearl earrings I gave her were in the bag." I look back at Cheryl in the rear-view mirror, she is dressed from head to toe in branded Versace, which basically has 'rob me' written all over it when walking through Naples train station dragging a load of designer suitcases.

"Never again, I'm staying in Florida," says Bill, holding on to the door for dear life as I follow the snaking road with olive groves and rolling vineyards on either side. "These roads! Why did they not build them straight?"

"What sort of place is this anyway? It's all old and feels dusty," asks Cheryl, her face smooth and expressionless from too much botox and cosmetic surgery. She's not talking about the house, we are not there yet, she's talking about Italy in general. She doesn't pause. "I thought Italy was high fashion, and why do they grow all these sunflowers, there's only so many bunches of sunflowers you can bring home, right? And they attract insects. Why would you want that?"

"For the oil."

There is a blast of laughter from Bill and Cheryl.

"Can you imagine?" says Bill, laughing harder than Cheryl.

I am not good at hiding emotions on my face. I am sure I have a look of confusion. "Yes, sunflower oil. Have you never heard of it?"

"Yes, of course I have," says Bill regrouping himself. "But I didn't think it came from actual sunflowers..." He pauses, sees I am not laughing, and stops laughing himself. He's looking at me suspiciously waiting for me to say 'only joking'. "Are you serious?"

Thankfully, we are pulling into the driveway and saved by the dogs coming to greet them.

"Puppies!" Cheryl calls out.

All is forgiven, I like people who like dogs.

"Are you looking forward to the wedding?" I ask, making small talk as Ronan and I help them up the stairs with their many pieces of luggage.

"Yes, I am!" says Cheryl. "How do you say I am excited in Italian?"

"Actually, there is no word for 'excited' in Italian, the concept doesn't exist," I say, struggling with her massive suitcase.

"Italians do not get excited?" she says looking concerned for the Italian population as a whole.

"They express it by saying they are 'very happy' or they are 'emotional'."

"But it can't be, it's not good enough. I say I am excited all the time about everything, lots of Americans do."

Ronan does not like seeing people distressed and so gives Cheryl his solution to speaking Italian.

"You can say you are excite-e-o."

"Excit-e-o? Will that work?"

"Yes, any word you are not sure of, just add eee-ooo on the end of the English version. The Italians will understand you. It is what I have done for the last five years and it works fifty per cent of the time."

Ronan leaves to make coffee-oo while I show Cheryl and Bill around.

"Your husband is so cute and Italian," says Cheryl.

"Ehhh..."

"This whole place is sooo cute."

I'm glad she hasn't called it old and dusty like Italy.

As soon as they have freshened up and are ready, I drive them to La Dogana to be with the other guests for the welcome night.

"Oh my, is that the ocean?" asks Bill, who is much more relaxed after having a shower and a coffee-oo.

"Eh, no, Umbria is landlocked. That's Lake Trasimeno. It's the fourth biggest lake in Italy. It's nearly the same size as Lake Como but less well known."

"I don't know that one either. I've never been outside Florida, it took Cheryl quite some time to persuade me to come on this trip but the bride is her ex-husband's godchild so I felt I should. He was my cousin."

I zone out trying to make the family connections to the bride and groom.

"This is a really beautiful area," coos Cheryl. I'm glad they can now see beyond the dustiness.

"The area around the lake has been inhabited since Stone Age times. The Etruscans were here, then the Romans until they were defeated by Hannibal's army and the Celts," I state, practicing my information dumps for future BnB guests.

"Is that what brought you here? Did you trace your Celtic heritage ancestors to here?" asks Bill.

"Eh, it was 200 BC, so..."

"We have traced our ancestors back two hundred years haven't we honey?" Bill says to Cheryl, taking over the conversation again from the back seat.

"Anyway, the story goes; with brilliant planning, Hannibal and his army and his last elephant trapped the Roman forces, and fifteen thousand Romans were driven into the lake during the battle here, turning the lake waters red for three days with the blood of the soldiers." I enjoy telling this story to visitors.

"Oh my God, is that why the lake is the colour it is?" Cheryl says.

I glance towards the lake and sure enough it is the colour of a blood orange. "Eh no, that's the sunset."

I walk them to where the pizza and gelato night has already kicked off and see the two Swedes have settled in well, surrounded by a group of male guests. They must have got lucky, as they never made it to our house the entire weekend. So the rush to dry the mattress and wash the sheet was unnecessary, but we still got paid.

Looking after Cheryl and Bill was a full-time job though. So much so that when we dropped them to the train station, Ronan and I took a simultaneous deep sigh and said in unison; "I never want to run a BnB".

11

"Your property tax bill of €196 needs to be paid," texts my new fabulous commercialista.

"But I thought there was no property tax on a primary residence?"

"There is if it is a luxury villa."

"But it's not luxury," I protest.

"There are different levels of luxury, yours is one category of luxury because of the square meterage of floor space. But it was due mid-June so there will be a fine."

"How much?"

"I will find out and get back to you."

I don't know if the fine will be tens, hundreds or thousands, I have no experiences to compare it with.

But how unluxurious my luxury villa is, is not my primary concern at the moment. Ronan has heard about his Tessera

Sanitaria—he needs to complete forms and jump through some hoops with an Irish government department. I can't wait for Ronan to organise himself. That's not said with excitement, I literally can't wait, I need to get an appointment to see what is happening with my liver and this water baby I am carrying. Getting down two dress sizes for Christmas is a very attractive carrot on a stick.

So I go to Lucia.

"Can you give me a part-time job?"

"Me give you a job?"

"It's so I can get a Tessera Sanitaria."

"I can employ you for September to do your own weddings if you wish?"

It's ridiculous, but it gives me the paperwork I need to go to the admin of the local hospital to get my own Tessera Sanitaria.

It's the derelict hospital near us, not the derelict one up the hill where Ronan was with his pancreatic thing, it's the derelict one where we first brought Luca to when his arm was cut and he nearly bled to death while I ran around the empty hospital corridors searching for someone, anyone.

This time I'm going during the day and it is still deserted. The walls are painted emerald green with a thick plastic orange padded border around the middle. I'm not sure of the padding's purpose—perhaps to stop patients' heads being whacked off the walls if the person pushing them on a trolley loses control?

While I wait for my number to be called, I can see from the signs this is a rehab hospital for checkup appointments and physiotherapy. There are no overnight wards or an emergency department. Now it makes sense as to why we couldn't get Luca's arm stitched here.

The woman behind the admin desk takes my paperwork and talks to me in Italian, of course. My heart speeds up but I ask her to talk slower, she simplifies what she says and I muddle through. She then types for the longest time, prints out a cert, stamps it and gives me the precious piece of paper.

"It will last until your temporary employment is over in October."

My heart plummets, they have foiled my plan. I hadn't consider them putting an end date on my temporary TS.

My plan has not quite worked but at least it is something and by the time it runs out I will be able to get the TS as the spouse of a pensioner.

I call Doctor Fab Chicken, "I got the Tessera Sanitaria, but it is only temporary, for a month, is it possible to get the doctor appointment for when I get back from my holiday?"

"Sure. Come tonight to the hospital to collect the prescriptions."

I don't understand why I need a prescription, but go along anyway. In Ireland if you need to see a specialist or get an x-ray, the doctor's office applies for the appointment for you and you wait for a letter with the appointment date from the hospital or clinic. It is a waiting game and you have to trust that the doctor's office has remembered to make the appointment. But not in Italy.

At the hospital, the derelict one up the hill with an emergency room, Fab Chicken leads me to an empty doctor's room and gives me six sheets of paper, "Here are your prescriptions for appointments. You need to take these to CUP and they will make the appointments for you."

I pretend I know what he means. I think I know what he means. I know what CUP is, so that is a start. It is an admin person with a computer and desk in some pharmacies. It's where I made the appointments for our vaccines and where I tried to get our vaccine green passes from. I've seen a room with CUP written on it here at the hospital but it is closed for the day, so I'm guessing there is a CUP admin area in hospitals too.

Of course, the prescriptions are all in Italian and I don't understand what the three separate appointments, each with a bar code, are for exactly. I have no clue what to do with them and I can feel anxiety rising. Needing medical care was my big fear about moving to Italy without being able to speak Italian. So I do what I do best in stressful situations, procrastinate. I decide I'll wait until I get back from holiday to tackle the tasks.

A few days later, I get a text from Lucia saying the national health system called her and they have scheduled an ultrasound for me for next month. "You cannot eat for six hours and you need a full bladder. You are now on the Italian health system, congratulations!"

I'm guessing fasting and having a full bladder is not some inauguration ritual everyone has to do on the day they get into the health system in Italy but something I need to do on the day of the appointment.

I message Lucia back and say, "Thanks, but I have no idea why they are contacting you about this and not me or my doctor. Okay, I still don't have an Italian number but I didn't give your number to them either."

"Maybe I am still down as your point of contact since you were trying to get the vaccine?"

"But is it not odd they would tell a neighbour all the details for my hospital appointment?"

"There is no privacy in Italy," says Lucia. "You need to go to any pharmacy, give your name and fiscal code and they will print out the booking to show the hospital and pay the ticket."

12

While I don't like the idea of running a BnB, I do like when people come to stay, such as Ben and his family who come to celebrate the approaching end of us working together on weddings for ten years.

Even though they arrive at sunset, I am glossy from the lingering heat of the day and argue against the hugs they insist on. They say they are hot from the clammy heat too. But they've brought sweaters... It is past mid-August after all and even though we are just at the end of a heatwave, it is officially autumn, so it's better to be safe than sorry in Ben's Italian mind.

Mosquitoes are still around but not as many and the little green shielded stink bugs are beginning to appear in the house. Juno jumps on them, releasing their pungent, bitter smell.

'Made in Italy' is stamped on the plastic bottles of bubbles I give to Ben's kids. It's something I have noticed here; everything from toilets to bubbles are made in Italy with few imports, the same with the food and wine.

Ronan has strung a set of lights over the patio and dragged a table out under the persimmon tree. Covered with a blue check cloth and some pillar candles, it looks picture perfect. The tinkle of glasses meeting in wishes of good health, sharing stories and laughter and the warm night carrying the scent of rosemary and lavender allow me to forget the sadness of the last nine months and bask in the memory of what happiness feels like for a few hours.

Two weeks later, Ben and I have our last wedding together. It's a couple from the United States and seventy guests have flown in to celebrate their wedding at one of my favourite venues; the amazing roofless gothic ruins of the eight-hundred-year-old San Galgano Abbey.

I love doing weddings here as its tall, stone cathedral walls open to the sky offer the most fantastic photography backdrops for an outdoor legal wedding ceremony in Italy.

Built by the Order of Cistercians, away from towns and villages so the monks could live with little contact with the outside world, this place was ideal for a humble monk self-sufficient lifestyle for one hundred years, until the Black Death hit.

To survive, one abbot sold the lead from the roof before the remaining monks were moved to another location by the head of the order. The roof without lead collapsed, and the abbey fell into ruin. A hauntingly beautiful windowless and roofless stone structure remains.

Once the couple and guests are inside and the ceremony starts, I leave it to Ben to look after. I walk around the ruin once and listen to the vibration of the string quartet's moving rendition of 'Hallelujah', before walking up the hill behind the abbey to the small circular chapel where cats laze on the smooth stone floors away from the afternoon sun. In the centre of the round chapel, a thick glass panel in the floor protects a sword encased in the ground underneath. This is a very special building, the place of incitement of one of the most famous medieval legends.

The revered sword stuck in a stone belonged to Galgano Guidotti, a twelfth century nobleman known for his violent and hedonistic approach to life. Galgano had a vision of a round temple in honour of God and the Archangel Michael. He climbed the hill and was so inspired by the vision he thrust his sword into a stone.

So Archangel Michael's intervention did a PR makeover on knight Galgano's image and he became better known as the Knight of God rather than his hedonistic and violent pre-makeover self.

Galgano went on to live there as a hermit. After his death in 1182, they built the round church, 'Rotonda di Montesiepi', with the sword in the stone as the centrepiece.

The stories of Arthur and his Knights appeared decades after Galgano's canonisation into sainthood. And so it is very probable that the accounts of Tuscany's sword in the stone and its knight-turned-saint influenced Britain's Arthurian legend when travelling merchants and pilgrims recounted the story back home in Britain; a Christian knight who started his path by the guidance of a powerful magical figure, a sword in a stone as the symbolic central item, a dangerous path to take and a round temple. And to top it all, one of the Knights of the Round Table was called Sir Gawaine (Galganus).

As I walk back down to the abbey, the musicians are playing 'Oh Sole Mio'. I pause for a moment, looking over the undulating hills of Tuscany dotted with the last of the sunflowers. The umbrella pines and conical cypress cones guard distant burnt-orange villas. Above, a single cloud is encouraged along by a welcome tingling breeze in the bluest azure sky.

It's the last day of working in my twenty-year wedding business, life is short it's time to move on to another goal and adventure. But I'm thankful for the business that allowed me to find and explore the most beautiful and hidden gems of Italy and Ireland. I got to spend time in really cool old buildings soaked in history, mystery, myth and legend.

Buildings like Johnstown Castle in Wexford and Castello Vincigliata in Tuscany, both of which have since closed their doors to weddings.

Castello Vincigliata was one of the most popular castles for weddings in Italy. Sitting on the hill above Fiesole, with a view of Florence's Duomo in the distance, it made an idyllic romantic venue for a wedding. But it closed for business some years ago. I heard it was because of a family squabble. Maybe Bianca–the castle ghost–wasn't happy.

 Legend tells that in the thirteenth century, Bianca, the daughter of the family living there, fell in love with an opposing noble family's son. The girl's father refused to let them see each other, but during a battle with militia from Lucca, the guy saved Bianca's father's life twice and so the father agreed they could marry.

On the day of the wedding, Bianca watched as her betrothed rode towards the castle. As he approached, his jealous brother, who was also in love with Bianca, ambushed him and Bianca watched helplessly as he fatally stabbed her love. Another version says the murderers were from Bianca's family who despised the other family.

The distraught seventeen-year-old either died throwing herself from the castle tower or the other version is she died of heart-break a few weeks later having not moved from the window. It is said, on warm summer evenings the ghost of Bianca, still in her wedding dress, roams the castle protecting lovers, especially those whose union is difficult. It is also said this story was the inspiration behind Shakespeare's Romeo and Juliet.

I only heard about this bride ghost after I had spent many evenings walking around the haunted walls lighting candles, setting up weddings and taken many photos of happy couples at Bianca's window, unaware of the heartache the walls had witnessed.

Maybe Bianca's broken heart could not take looking at all those happy couples passing through her castle and adjusted things to force its closure.

Another favourite venue which closed for weddings for years is Villa Vignamaggio–a rose-coloured vineyard villa in Chianti. I was told originally that it was the birthplace of the Mona Lisa, Lisa Gherardini. But it turns out Lisa was born in Florence on Via Maggio on the fifteenth of June 1479.

Lisa Gherardini's ancestors, a noble Tuscan family, built a castle on a dominant hill at Montagliari near Panzano. From it, they could see the river valley of Greve which was an ideal position for them to rob merchants on their way to Florence. As one's noble family does when living in the Middle Ages.

In 1302 (over one hundred and fifty years before Lisa was born) the Florentine authorities put a stop to them and after a long battle, besieged their castle. The family were not killed or imprisoned but moved to the other side of the valley to Vignamaggio where they built the villa.

The Gherardini sold the villa to the Gherardi family (similar name but a different family) in 1421, over fifty years before 'Mona' Lisa was born.

She may not have been born there nor lived there, but there is still a strong connection.

Everywhere in Italy, every building with its unique and fascinating history continues to send ripples of creative ideas into the world generations after, whether it be stories or art.

I think back to The Sighing House and what it has experienced in the last one hundred years; wars, fascism, the joy of the 1920s, family. And now us. It needs love, stories and creativity springing from it.

As I drive back home from Tuscany to Umbria, swallows and swifts are swooping with the air drifts, strengthening their wings for their long-haul flight back to Africa. Cicadas are singing their last songs and the lavender is giving off its last blast of natural air freshener.

When it comes into view, Lake Trasimeno with its darts of blues, emeralds and greys, looks so beautiful I need to pull over and just observe it for a few moments. A break in the cloud shadowing the hills illuminates the big island and Passignano, bathed in evening sunlight, it changes from amber to apricot. My town.

I still can't believe I live here, surrounded by this beauty in the heart of delicious Italy.

By the time I am on the last stretch of road, the full illuminated white moon has created a silver path in the lake towards my home.

Walking into our clean and shining kitchen the following morning makes me smile, I don't know why. It just looks perfect. A dreamy kitchen with cabinets my favourite shade of blue; the kitchen we designed with its corner hob, black sink, black marble worktops and silver-cup door handles I got from an expensive shop in the UK before Brexit and customs charges.

The water boils in the kettle, the one we bought on Christmas Eve two years ago–the day we moved into the house. The only one in the shop. Taking my cup of tea, I walk to the French doors to let the dogs out. Paddy is curled up on the teal green palatrone I lovingly upholstered, he beats his tail before slumping out the door. My first Italian love–he has got fatter since we found him at the dog kennels. Of course, there were my other Italian fur babies–Moonface and Spooky–my cat twins, and Juno the newest baby, but they are all girls. Paddy is my Italian boy.

I close the door after them and open the dining room shutters. The sun shines in and instantly sends a rush of warmth to the butter cream walls and brick fireplace where the uneven towers of fat pillar candles sprinkled with the dried heads of orange and red roses from the Christmas table nine months ago make it look like a scene from a gothic music video.

A streak of light hits the long dining table and highlights the details of the ornate gothic pew we bought from the guy possibly making a quick getaway from a church the previous year. The long trailing vines of my Devils Ivy plant, free of building dust, traverse the walls, giving it an indoor jungle courtyard feel.

It all comes together before my eyes for the first time. I inhale so fast it's audible; it has all come perfectly together to look like a room that belongs to me. A cosy room with witchy touches. A room I now love; the table has memories of dinners shared for two Christmases, New Year, Jim and his family, jigsaw puzzles, house history discoveries and novels written. It's part of the house and part of me.

I don't want to sell this house. There has to be another way.

13

T he first day we ever stayed in the house, which was Christmas, a wiry guy with a grey beard, tanned, wrinkled weathered skin and flying grey hair cycled by. He was the first person to say 'Buongiorno' to us when we moved in, with a kind smile on his face and even at the reasonable speed he went by I could see he had a twinkle in his smiling eyes.

I see him go by often. But it's becoming freaky... every time I look out the kitchen window or I'm working in the front garden, he cycles past. No matter if it is six o'clock in the morning or ten o'clock at night, he is cycling either up or down the road. If we drive somewhere, fifty percent of the time on our return, we will see him cycling. It's not for fitness, he is wearing work clothes, rain gear or just casual clothes.

"I'm beginning to think we are on the Truman Show, remember the movie with Jim Carey?" I say, bringing him to Ronan's attention. "It's like someone is saying to a production company; 'she's looking out the window, cue the cycling man'. Or 'she is talking about taking the trash out, have cycling man on standby'."

Ronan has begun to notice him too. So we have nicknamed him Truman the Cycling Guy.

Over the years of dereliction, ivy vines have twisted their way around the front railings on either side of The Sighing House's gates. The thick ivy stems have met up on the other side and welded together into a solid mass of roots, creating the perfect strong base to weave its way around the tree, back to the railings, back to the tree, down the wall and up the lamppost, back into the tree and back across to the lamppost, winding around it. The determined plant has decided its new goal is to edge towards the mains electric cable on the street.

Its growth on the public light pole alone is one hell of an achievement. I admire its persistence and strength, but Italian law can be complicated and weird and I am not sure where the responsibility would lie should ivy with roots in our garden pull the cable down or block out the light and cause a road accident.

At my request for a tree surgeon recommendation, Alex is sending a cousin out to give us a price to lop the tops of our magnolia trees and the conifers at the driveway gate and get rid of the ivy. The magnolias are towering above our house at the other smaller unused ornate gate entrance. True to form, Truman cycles passed just as I'm opening the driveway gate for the tree guy.

I was told the tree guy is Albanian but speaks English, so I tell him we just need to 'top' the trees.

"Chop them down?" he says, nodding his head in agreement as we look at the one-hundred-year-old magnolias.

"No, just the top. I just want them lopped."

"Chop down from the top," he says, doing that nod again.

"No, just the top."

"Why you chop them?" he then says with a furrowed brow.

"I don't want them to become dangerous."

"For who?"

"For us, for anyone."

"Not dangerous to cut them down. I will be okay."

"I don't want them cut down, just trimmed."

Eventually he gets the message.

"And these?" he points to the Leyland Cyprus either side of the driveway gate. They should have stayed low tidy shrubs, but after years of neglect they have lost the plot of themselves, trying to be trees and failing. Instead, they are sprawling, patchy shrubs with a thick carpet of brown fallen bits underneath held tightly together with ivy.

"These are dirty trees. Cut down and plant a nice shrub like this," he says showing me a picture of a very un-inspiring freshly planted tree.

"For me to do the work you need to go to the comune and get permission to set up traffic lights to work from the road. We need to stop the cars coming on one side of the road."

This is all sounding expensive. And I was right. A few days later he comes back with an estimated cost of €2,500 to tidy up the magnolias and cut down the 'dirty' Leylands.

The price does not include chopping up and taking away the wood, Ronan had said he'd do it and keep the wood for the fire. It would also be up to us to do all the legwork with the comune about getting the permissions, which is like asking me to pinpoint buried treasure on a map with my eyes closed.

"We just need to do the conifers and we can do them ourselves," says Ronan, repeating what he said when I first insisted we get a professional to do it.

"The magnolias have been there a hundred years without causing problems. If they come crashing through the roof, we have house insurance and it is cheaper than his pruning quote. But with the amount of concrete and reinforcement the lads poured into the roof, I don't think a nuclear bomb would get through it. So we'll leave the magnolias alone and tackle the trees at the gate ourselves."

There's no time like the present for me. Armed with loppers, shears and a rake, within three hours, there is a mountain of ivy with roots as thick as my arm piling up in the driveway. I had started cautiously, unsure of what life forms lived in ivy jungles. I expected rats and snakes or at least some scorpions. But a thick ivy abode appears not to be an attractive option for such creatures. Instead, I just get a lot of snails, a few spindly spiders and a variety of small beetle like creatures that scurry away as soon as they are uncovered.

With so much going on in my head about Jim, Mam and my water baby, I find tiring myself out doing physical work the best therapy. I work until dark, clipping, cutting, pulling, reefing. It frees me from thinking about the future, instead I focus on the moment and what I can control–making the house feel better.

The next day I arrive back from yoga to see Ronan standing inside the gate, his face and t-shirt covered in sawdust and wood chipping, holding his chainsaw.

"Don't worry, I've left enough of height in the stump for Jim to carve a totem pole when he comes over." We both smile at the thought. Jim and I have often talked about the carvings he'll do when he gets over. We have enough ideas and pictures exchanged to fill a fifty-acre park with Jim's speciality–carved totem poles, usually made from old telegraph poles.

But my heart is low. Jim's old neighbour, who he helps, has Covid. Jim was just on the phone telling me the conversation he had with the old guy who asked him to go down to the village and do the lottery for him.

"I can't go near you, you have Covid," Jim had said to him.

"Ah don't worry I am feeling grand."

"No, I don't want to catch it."

"I'll go down myself then and do it," said the old guy.

"You can't, you have Covid."

"I'm feeling fine don't worry."

"That is not the point, you have to stay in so you don't spread it."

"Sure, I've had it a week and seen you a few times and you don't have it." Alarm bells have gone off for both of us.

Covid is still around, and people have become complacent about its dangers to people like Jim going through chemo and with compromised immune systems. Jim is not worried, but I am for him.

I'm also getting concerned about my Mam. Living on her own started out well for her but then letters about house, car insurance renewals came in, forms to be filled to change things from dad's name to hers, bills and all the things dad used to deal with kept coming at her.

She worked through them, calling the numbers, being put on hold, then being told to go online.

"I don't know what a www is," she'd tell me she told them. Mam worries. She is always terrified someone is going to arrive at her door and legally be able to walk in and tell her to get out or send her to prison.

Jim is trying to help but there is a complication with her tax number. The tax office is saying she doesn't exist. Jim has spent hours on the phone, I have spent hours on the phone. I have an accountant involved, and no one seems to be able to get around the computer saying our mother doesn't exist. Until it is sorted, emergency tax is being taken from her pension.

"I think I need to talk to Ma about her coming back over here soon," I say to Ronan.

Ronan pauses brushing the wood chipping out of his hair. It's a big ask, having your mother-in-law move in for a second time.

"I don't think she's doing well and Jim needs to focus on his own care," I continue. "I can't do much for him, but I think if Ma was being looked after, it would be one less thing for him to worry about."

"Absolutely," Ronan says without further hesitation. I am lucky to have such a kind person in my life.

"I'll book my flight to Ireland for when we get back from Greece."

14

E xtract from 'A Rosie Life In Italy 1'

As kids, when we drew our dream houses... My houses always had shutters even though shutters didn't exist in Ireland. Shutters were the hallmark of the perfect house in my mind. I also needed a courtyard with a long table for family dinners. This idea was inspired by watching TV with my family when I was nine. There was a movie with a huge family dinner under the sun, with profusions of food being passed around and wine being poured. It was a celebration, everyone was laughing, kids were playing around grape vines or olive trees. I can't remember who said it, but I remember the words 'Mamma mia' being said. Staring at the TV it was my idea of Heaven.

I went to Mass on Sunday and, as I knelt in my rain-soaked trousers, I prayed someday I would live in Mamma Mia Land with my family; happy and in the sun. The following Monday my teacher gave us pen-pal forms with all the countries in the world listed on them. We were to tick the box of the country we wanted to have a pen-pal in.

"Which country do they say Mamma mia in?" I asked my teacher.

After some thought my teacher answered "Greece".

So I ticked Greece.

My Greek pen-pal Ria and I wrote to each other religiously every second week for ten years without her ever mentioning her long candle-lit, olive-strewn family dinners, even though I often asked how dinner was with her family that week. One evening I happened to see the scene on TV again I had watched all those years ago and realised my teacher was wrong; Mamma Mia Land was not in Greece but Italy.

When I was growing up 'This is Your Life' presented by Eamonn Andrews was regular viewing in our house. He always kept the most special guest until last. At eleven years old, I used to imagine myself on the show when I would be a famous author and at the end, after introducing all the interesting people I had yet to meet and yet to share fabulous life experiences with, I already knew exactly the person Eamonn would keep to last.... "You started writing to each other at nine years of age and here she is, forty years later, your Greek pen-pal, Ria."

My eyes would well up so much thinking about the moment, my eleven-year-old self would have to leave the sitting room.

She lived in an unpronounceable place I could never find on a map and we wrote to each other regularly. It started off about school and family and then over the years about dreams and love until we were eighteen before losing touch. She was my first writing buddy. Years went by. And then social media was invented. Twelve years ago, I got a Facebook message, "Are you the same Rosie who had a Greek pen-pal?" Ria had found me.

We had a lot of catching up to do; she was a mental health nurse, had married a doctor and had a son.

With work ending the week before our holiday, three books with deadlines, and a house to prep for our dog sitter guests, after more building work finishing the day before their arrival, I had not been on social media much in the last month. But when I did click on it, a post from Ria popped up... "Going away for a few days." with a picture of her dog and a backpack. It prompted me to respond... "We're going away next week too! To Crete."

"You are going to CRETE?"

"Yes."

"WHERE IN CRETE?"

"Chiana?"

"That is where I live! Tell me we are going to at last meet?!!"

So I was going on my first real beach holiday and I was going to have my 'This Is Your Life' moment with Eamonn Andrews' voice in my ear... "You started to write to each other forty years ago and here today to meet you for the first time is your life long pen-pal ..."

My cousin's two adult children happened to be planning a tour of Italy and offered to come to our place in Umbria to dog sit.

The night before they arrive, I am scrubbing down the kitchen; I open the pot drawer and not just one but three mice scurry for cover. I'm not afraid of mice, Jim had mice living in my sister's dollhouse when we were little and we always had at least one hamster. But when something springs at me unexpected from a drawer like a Jack-in-the-box, it does make me scream.

It's a scream of surprise followed by a scream of frustration. "Bloody hell not now."

Ronan comes galloping into the kitchen.

"Hate to tell you this, but I think I just saw a mouse in the sitting room," he says, seeing I'm not dead.

"I've just seen three in the pot drawer. We are being invaded. What are we going to do?"

"Leave the back door open and maybe they will leave?" Ronan says hopefully.

"Or they'll bring in the rest of their mates."

There was nothing we could do at this late date, other than empty the pot drawer and write a sticky note, 'do not open'.

I pick Teresa and Joe up from the train; I haven't seen them since they were little and here they are as fabulous adults. We drive home through the area where the fire was three weeks ago. The olive leaves are brown and withered, and the knotted trunks pitch black. So sad to see.

Joe is a chef in a Michelin star restaurant, he is immediately out in the garden after dropping his bag into his room.

"Can I use what you have in the garden to cook with?"

"I'm afraid there are only weeds in the wilderness out there."

"No, you have so much! The hazelnuts, bay, rose hips, the grapes are delicious and fig leaf sauce is great with fish or chicken."

"How do I make that?"

"Just whiz them up in a blender with some olive oil. One part fig leaf to two parts olive oil."

I don't have time to talk recipes as we are already running late for our two-hour drive to Rome but I keep it in mind for the future. Eventually we are driving out the gate, waving goodbye to the dogs on our way to our first ever non-work-related beach holiday in our near thirty years together.

As soon as I'm in the car, I am Googling uses for fig leaves; 'regulate blood glucose levels, prevent heart disease, lowers cholesterol, strengthens bones, possesses anti-cancer properties, prevents wrinkles, helps diabetes and skin conditions such as eczema, psoriasis, and vitiligo. Fig fruits contain a high amount of vitamin C which helps lighten sun spots, scars and hyperpigmentation, leading to bright and even-toned skin. Its seed oil has superb moisturising and hydrating properties and stimulates the skin's natural collagen production.'

The fig leaf rabbit hole I have gone down is quickly interrupted by a weird noise from the front of the car. Only out the gate and two minutes down the road my Googling changes to finding a new phrase in Italian. In all the years Ronan and I have been together I have never needed it in English nor any other language but just as we are on our way for our first proper holiday we have... Una gomma a terra. A flat tyre.

We're looking in the boot for a jack but there are just lots of useless bits.

"This will take ages to figure out, we don't have time. There's a garage down the road, maybe they'll be open and can help," says Ronan who must be far more observant to me as I don't have a clue where he is talking about.

Our car hobbles down the road and into the mechanics court-yard. Within twenty minutes, the guy has identified and extracted the culprit nail neatly skewering the centre of our tyre. Our spare tyre fitted and with the mechanic gladly taking the €20 we offer for his trouble, we are back on the road. Four hours later and we are sitting on a plane to Crete.

Ronan hasn't left Italy in three years, he hasn't been able to because of Covid and the pre-Covid incident with the mafia police. Our friend Helga had warned him it might be best to only travel through Schengen countries in case his criminal case pops up on the system and they stop him getting back in. Travelling between Schengen countries means there are no pass-port checks. Neither Ireland or the UK are in Schengen but Greece is, so he feels safe to leave.

Flying over the Greek islands outlined with gold sand and emerald and turquoise sea gives me the urge to explore them all. 'Maybe we should have moved to Greece instead of Italy,' is a sneaking growing thought as we touch down on the cliff edge runway beside the sea.

"This reminds me of when I flew to the Aran Islands in a tiny plane," says Ronan, leaning over me to take a photo we'll never look at again. "I was sitting beside the pilot and they had a slope at the end of the runway like a skateboard ramp to kick the plane into the sky before it ran off the side of the cliff."

I'd heard this story before, but living with someone is like living with your favourite movie or book, you don't mind experi-encing the story repeatedly. I'd also heard the story of how he refused to fly to the Aran Islands again after that and went by boat the next time. Thirty years ago, there was no harbour for the boat to dock, so the last section of the journey involved climbing down a rope ladder into a curragh–a traditional Irish fishing boat–and getting rowed to shore. Ronan shared the boat with a nun, a sheep and a Honda 50. A winch lowered the last two into the curragh. Not the nun, she climbed down the rope ladder like Ronan did.

As soon as we step off the plane, the smell of salty air carried in on a warm breeze from the crystal blue sea makes me inhale deeper. I miss the smell of the sea. Doctor Fab Chicken told me some people who live in Umbria and never leave it need iodine tablets as it's landlocked and their intake of seafood is lower than other regions. Living near the sea is good for you.

"Maybe we should have moved to Greece and lived beside the sea," I say to Ronan before we have even left the small airport.

"Maybe... we have a week to figure out if we like it more than Italy."

15

W e are starving so once checked-in to our hotel, we immediately go to Pergola, a restaurant recommended by the front desk. The guy serving in the restaurant has non-fashion-statement torn jeans and an 'Eat, Sleep, Ride' t-shirt. His wife serves us. It turns out they are the owners.

"Is the chicken stroganoff good?" asks Ronan, impressed by the huge choice of dishes with heavy cream sauces.

"You like chicken?" asks the woman who has reached that glorious age in life where she doesn't take bullshit from anyone.

"Yes."

"You know what stroganoff is?"

"Yes."

"Then you will like chicken stroganoff."

"This is so delicious," Ronan says. "I don't want to eat anywhere or anything else all week." He has found the Greek equivalent of his spaghetti bolognese. "I don't understand why Greek food isn't high in the ranks of world class cuisine the same as French or Italian."

I agree with him; the Greek salad I have is nothing like anything I have ever tasted before. I note to add pomegranates and figs to future salads.

We spend the first two days lazing on the beach reading between swimming and floating in the clear water.

"You have to snorkel while you are there," insists Jim when I call him. "I had the most amazing time of my life while teaching wind surfing in Greece," he recalls. Like Ronan's stories, I have heard Jim's summer in Greece story at least once a year for the last thirty-five years. But the joy he experiences recalling swimming and snorkelling; the fish he saw, the stray dogs and cats he befriended on the Greek island, makes you feel you are living it again with him.

So I buy a snorkel. I want to anyway, to see what Ronan is talking about as he says fish nip him every time he steps into the water.

"Ouch! Bloody hell! One took a chunk out of me."

With my snorkel on I can see the shoals of flat disk-like fish swimming around people without them even realising they are there. Except for Ronan, who they seem to have mistaken as an enormous piece of bait. Laughing at your husband being fish food while wearing a snorkel doesn't work and I am soon choking on seawater.

Ria and I arranged to meet on day three of our stay. I go alone as I'm not sure how I am going to react.

And there she is.

We hug a lot and cry a little.

"Come on, get your car, we are taking you to lunch," she says as soon as the husband introductions and general chatter is out of the way. We follow their car through villages dotted with wrinkled smiling grey-haired widows hobbling along in black dresses and cardigans even though it is nearly thirty degrees out.

And then through the Grand Canyon of Crete. Its jagged sponge-textured, milky-tea-coloured rocks contrast with sheer smooth cliffs streaked in purples and black with the odd goat precariously perched, munching on some tasty scrub. The dry rounded rocks where a waterfall once cascaded into the gullies running on either side of the road, waiting for rain to tumble again. Greece has had an extremely dry hot summer too.

We stop at a traditional taverna. Platters of roasted wild goat, smoked pork, Greek salad, sausage, chunks of lamb and grilled vegetables fill the centre of the table.

"You are in Greece, here we eat everything together. It's not like Italy where you get the first plate then the second, everything is served together and we share."

So all those years ago, my nine-year-old impression of Greece was correct after all! They are the ones who sit at long tables with family and pass the plates around.

"I see we settled on the same taste in men with the same taste in cars," I say, as our husbands bond after dinner away from where we are sitting, standing by the cars having a cigarette.

"Our car is held together with screws." I am referring to the piece of the boot Ronan pulled off our Irish car and then 'neatly' attached back with screws. Their car has masking tape stopping their car boot handle falling off, almost in the same position as our screws.

"Yes, we don't care for cars but our son wants a Ferrari of course... It is hard to believe we were his age when we started to write to each other," says Ria, nodding towards her nine-year-old son who is feeding goats through a fence. "And now we are sandwiches."

"Sandwiches?" I ask hesitantly. Her English is much better than I expected and I don't want to insult or embarrass her by pointing out her misuse of a word.

"Yes, we are the sandwich generation. Have you not heard of this? We are the first generation in history where women have children to take care of while also having aged parents needing our assistance, all while going through the menopause."

"I had my kids young but I get it... heh, I've never heard of the term," I say, trying to fit in another morsel of delicious food to my already overfull belly.

"I am considered an old Mum at the school gate but I am glad I am, I see those in their twenties and thirties going through so much. I see it in their faces and as a mental health nurse I see it in the clinics I work. Women trying to do everything because that is what the stupid influencers and media make them believe they have to be–perfect. Whereas me, I am older, I don't give a shit!"

We're both laughing about our aged wisdom and how the joy of not giving a crap must be an international feeling shared between women in their fifties, while I send the photos I took of the food to Jim who made me promise to send pics everyday, especially of the food.

Jim calls later, to get a blow by blow account of what we ate and how it was cooked. "I hope you ate the octopus?" says Jim.

"You know I don't eat octopus, they are too intelligent and elegant."

"Not when they are in a freezer." He's a creature lover, but he's also a caveman.

"They are too alien looking... At least I am eating all the other fish on offer, not like Ronan." I defer the heat and pass the video call to Ronan who is having his second cup of coffee of the evening on the balcony watching the sunset.

"Ronan, you have to eat fish, you don't know what you are missing. You can't live in the Mediterranean and not eat fish, that's criminal," begs Jim.

It's the second time today Ronan has been chastised for not eating fish. Ria had told her mum we were going to the tavern as it did a lot of meats rather than the fish restaurant her mum had suggested because Ronan did not eat fish and her mother's response was:

"Why you go to dinner with someone who does not eat fish?"

Jim stays on the phone and has a virtual coffee with us and the three of us watch the sunset together. I wish he could be here; he appreciates every detail of every new moment no matter what it is.

After nearly a week of beach lazing and swimming in the sea, we have our last night at our favourite Crete restaurant.

"So would you live here?" Ronan asks me, tucking into chicken stroganoff for the third time this week.

I think about it. "Swimming in the sea has been great, the food amazing–But I don't know what it is... I don't feel like it could ever feel like home. And you? Could you live here?"

"I'm looking forward to returning to the pets but I am wondering what it will feel like... will it feel like we are going home or just back to Italy, do you get what I mean?"

I completely understand what he means. I have been back and forth to Ireland and the UK several times since we moved, whereas this is Ronan's first trip away in four years. And it's the first time we will be returning together to The Sighing House... will it feel like going home? Everything still needs to find its place and personal touches added to brand it as ours. But will the house have the sense of peace and comfort felt when entering your familiar 'home'?

When I fly back to Ireland, I always think how much greener it is than Italy. Ireland is usually awash with rain splattered wind and a coldness that soaks into my bones, so I am happy to return to the warmth of Italy.

Now, flying home to Italy together for the first time, Ronan and I are admiring how green it is compared to the grey barren rocks of Crete.

"That's it, that's why I couldn't live in Greece, it's not green enough. I need lushness in my everyday life," I say, finding the missing piece.

"But it has the turquoise sea and golden sand?" responds Ronan who is already missing the cream sauces.

"So has Italy, I am sure. We just haven't explored the coastline enough. That's what we need to do... find a place with warm clear aquamarine coloured water within driving distance. It should be on our list of to-dos next summer. Then we will have everything."

16

———

Back home and the dogs go wild seeing us again. Teresa has taught Juno to 'High 5' and a few other tricks. She learns fast, although she is impossible to walk on a lead. She goes hysterical and spins like crazy not from excitement but fear of cars. She knows she is not to go out on the road and yet here we are dragging her out on a lead to the place she is not supposed to go–it goes completely against her nature of wanting to do the right thing. Between weddings, writing and having had Mam with me I just haven't had the head space to train her properly and trying to dog walk the three of them together has become an impossible task.

So I take Looney and Paddy out for a walk on their own, leaving Juno with Ronan. After such a hot dry summer, the lake is the lowest it has ever been. It's fairly shallow at the best of times, averaging only five metres in depth over the past decade.

The combination of mild winters and long, warm summers means the lake warms up to bath like temperatures. There are kids jumping off the pier in town having their last summer swim before school and autumn kicks in. I walk under the shadow of La Rocca; the ruined fort where I have organised many weddings. Tourists gaze up tat it like it's an old wise person who has so much to share.

Walking through the old Italian town's ancient passageways and cobbled streets, its overwhelming to think of all the scenes from individual lives and historic events gone before; and how many sinful stories the church confessionals of Pieve di San Cristoforo have heard during the thousand years it has stood in the old centre. If only recordings of the conversations could be wrung out of walls and wood, like water from a wet sponge.

The sun is on its way to setting, throwing a peachy glow across the town and the lake switches to the opposite of the colour wheel to jewel blue.

Across the water, there is an opposing fort dominating the walled town of Castiglione del Lago which juts out into the lake. The home of the summer outdoor cinema and the adjoining palazzo with fresco-covered ceilings.

It was there I first fell in love with the lake, watching the magical murmurations of starlings dance on the invisible air currents while hot air balloons and colourful kites dotted the sky. It looked like something from a fairytale. I wondered if it was always like this but I had arrived during the annual kite festival, Coloriamo i Cieli ('we colour the skies'), which attracts thousands of kite flyers every year from all over the world.

"Welcome back! Fancy an aperitivo?" greets Shelly, spotting me on the street.

She didn't need to ask twice.

"So how was Corfu?" she asks.

"We went to Crete. Don't ask. I got confused. Now that we are back, I'm going to start working on the garden."

This immediately has Shelly's attention. She has developed their bare building plot to a lavender-infused butterfly and bumblebee paradise. "Oh, what are you planning to do?"

"We need to create an income from the house so it can sustain itself. So I am thinking of ideas... Maybe we should plant more vines and make wine?"

"You'd need more land. From one acre of vineyards you can harvest five tons of grapes, and five tons of grapes produces thirteen and a half barrels of wine," Shelly rattles off, "which is four thousand bottles or sixteen thousand glasses of wine. So, if you make €4 per bottle of wine, after all the expenses, and sold all the bottles, that would be sixteen grand."

"Bloody hell, that's a lot of work for that... And how do you know all this?"

"We considered it."

"What about olives?"

"Blodwyn and Ivor are the ones to ask, but you see how many trees they have and all the pruning they have to do. You'd need more land and it would be a long-term project. Like a generation or two long term."

"Truffles?" I say, getting desperate.

"If you can find them, they would probably be the easiest option. But finding them is the difficult thing."

"Paddy has a good nose, I think he could be a truffle dog... or maybe he just enjoys digging holes." Paddy is splayed out under the tree beside where we are sitting, Looney is using him as a pillow. He knows I am talking about him and whacks his tail up and down in acknowledgement.

"When you bought the house," says Shelly, "didn't the estate agent say there is planning permission for a house on the space between you and your neighbour? How about selling it as a plot? It has its own well and is close to town, you might get €100k for it?"

I hadn't thought of the plot beside the house as an option. €100k would go a long way to giving Izzy back her money and finishing the renovations.

"It may have been all sales talk from the estate agent, I'll ask Alex if his geometra can figure out with the comune what we can do with the site."

Shelly orders us both a second Aperol Spritz. It's too beautiful a sunset not to celebrate living here. "Let's get back to what you are going to do with your garden. The first thing you need to do is get rid of the pampas grass so you are not giving out the wrong message and attracting strangers calling to your door."

"What has pampas grass got to do with strangers calling to our door?"

"My parents had pampas grass in their front garden in the Eighties, and they had a few couples call to their door smiling and asking for directions or some excuse just to chat and they eventually heard the reason," says Shelly, enjoying her spritz. "Having pampas grass planted in the front garden is a secret signal the homeowners are swingers. It's supposedly an urban legend, but it happened to my parents."

"Bloody hell, we have it at the front door and it's at the back-door too so it can be seen from all the slowing trains passing.

First, I thought the house was a Nazi headquarters, now it might have been a den of iniquity for partner swapping?"

"If only walls could talk, hey?" laughs Shelly. "I was just saying that to myself walking through the town! As soon as I have time, I want to learn the history of this place as much as possible."

"What about the history of the house? Have you found any more discoveries?"

"I want to, but it's difficult. It's one hundred years old next year, so it has been through the roaring Twenties and World War Two. I often imagine how it must have been for the family sitting in the kitchen eating their pasta listening to the radio," I say.

"Probably more likely eating rice, as they were trying to ban pasta in Italy around then."

"Ban pasta? Can you imagine them trying to ban pasta in Italy!" I laugh at the idea.

"It's true! Mussolini had a personal vendetta against Italians eating pasta. He wanted them to eat home-grown rice instead. And then some leader guy in the early Thirties had a crusade against pasta, he said it made Italians heavy, brutish, slow and pessimistic so there was a pasta prohibition. Here look I'll show you." Shelly works in TV research, making her a mine of useless but interesting facts and a whizz at research.

"Here it is look," she says, reading from her phone, "The Italian writer Marco Ramperti said '[Pasta] puffs out our cheeks like grotesque masks on a fountain, it stuffs our gullets as if we were Christmas turkeys, it ties up our insides with its flabby strings;

it nails us to the chair, gorged and stupefied, apoplectic and gasping, with [a] sensation of uselessness' ..."

"It sounds like he had a gluten intolerance," I say, finishing my second spritz.

Back home I look into this further. In the 1920's when the house was just young, Mussolini made the first of November National Rice Day to make Italy less reliant on imported wheat.

He never went as far as banning macaroni but he was an anti-pasta.

And then, in the 1930s the Futurists believed pasta weighted Italians down and prevented them from achieving greatness. They believed that, in the future, all food would be replaced with supplements in the form of pills and powders, but in the meantime Italians should eat rice.

The Futurist Movement founder, Marinetti, in the Thirties, gathered recipes and produced La Cucina Futurista ("The Futurist Cookbook").

An example recipe is Libyan Airplane, made from candied chestnuts steeped in Eau de Cologne and milk, then served on a purée of bananas, apples, dates and peas "shaped into the form of a slender aeroplane."

Eau de Cologne also featured in The Excited Pig recipe where "a whole salami, skinned, is served upright on a dish containing some very hot black coffee mixed with a good deal of Eau de Cologne."

. . .

Marinetti wanted to rid the Italian language of any foreign words, so he included a glossary of neologisms at the back of his cookbook. A cocktail was a polibibita ("poly-beverage") and a bar was a quisibeve ("here-one-drinks"). Instead of going on a picnic, you'd go on a pranzoalsole ("lunch-in-the-sun").

But with all the disasters the 1930s brought; the Great Depression, a war with Ethiopia, the Spanish Civil War and Adolf Hitler's growing influence eventually leading to World War II, the people of Italy became more focused on just being able to eat rather than on what they were eating.

Pasta becomes a discussion topic in my next Italian class.

"Pasta is very much part of our culture now, we even have a verb in Italian for cooking pasta; 'Cuocere' is to cook the pasta. 'Scuocere' is to overcook the pasta," explains my Italian teacher. "To say anything is overcooked is scotta or scotto. But telling someone their pasta or anything else is 'scotta' is offensive, so I advise to not use it."

And like all the other 'bad' words I shouldn't say to people, 'scotto' sticks in my brain like cooked pasta sticks to wall tiles, but verbs and tenses still make a speedy exit.

17

Mail arrived while we were in Crete. Two letters look like appointments. I figure out one is for a mammogram–haven't had one of those before. And the other is for a pap test. A package also arrives for me from the health system in Umbria; with a test tube, a return envelope and instructions inviting me to take part in free colon cancer screening which they are offering to people aged fifty to seventy-four.

All this since I got my temporary TS less than a month ago. Once you are in the health system, they like to give you a full MOT and get your life in Italy off to a good start. All I need now is to be issued with a designer cashmere neck scarf with the dates from September to May it needs to be worn so I don't get 'colpo d'aria'.

Seeing the routine appointments remind me of the prescribed appointments I have procrastinated going to the chemist about. The procrastination is firstly because there's the whole language barrier–I don't know what I am doing. And second, I am afraid it might turn into a full-on showdown like with the shouty woman at the bank, or turn into a whole tangled mess because of my lack of a health card. I just don't want to deal with hassle straight after my holiday, so I come up with every excuse to put it off for another week.

Eventually, after some further nagging by Ronan, I pluck up the courage and go to the desk at the back of the pharmacy where I've seen the CUP notice on the door.

"Bisogno fare appointamenti," (I need to make appointments) I say.

I know this is not perfect, but she answers me in Italian with a smile and gets busy at the computer scanning the bar codes.

"For this appointment you can choose between towns where to have it as we don't have it here," she says, holding up one of the appointment sheets and lists towns I don't recognise.

"Can I have a town nearby please?" I ask in Italian, and she suggests one to me with a choice of afternoon appointment times.

It is made for three weeks' time. I don't know what it is for; I think it is the specialist.

After scanning the other two bar codes she says, "Unfortunately they have both expired."

"What do you mean?"

She points to '20gg' printed in the top right corner. "It needed to be made within twenty days. They expired yesterday. The other I have made has 30gg written on it, so that was okay."

I can't believe I have missed them by a day because of my stupid procrastinating, it makes the whole getting employed by Lucia thing a pointless exercise.

But then I show her the text Lucia sent me about an appointment. She types in my name into the computer and says, "Ah yes, it is the same procedure as one of the others that has gone out of date. Do you need two?"

"I don't think so," I say, even though I don't know what it is two of that I don't think I need. So she confirms the appointment, prints it out and staples it to a sheet. I see the word 'ecografia' which is obviously the ultrasound.

The other out of date 'prescription' is for an MRI scan. As my temporary Tessera Sanitaria has expired, I'll need to go private. My stupid procrastination has cost me dearly.

I pop into the main part of the pharmacy to pick up some nail varnish remover. I can't find it at the supermarket and the only other shop I've seen it in keeps it in a locked cabinet right at the back of the store. The faff of finding an assistant, thinking of how to explain what I want, waiting around while they fetch the key, and then taking a ruddy expedition back to the nether regions of the shop would have seen at least twenty minutes down the drain.

I didn't have time to spare that day so I just painted over the chipped paint for the fifth time. The same Italian shop had gallon-sized bottles of near one hundred percent alcohol freely available on its shelves, but women could not be trusted with what they might do with nail varnish remover so it was kept in a locked cabinet.

"Excuse me, are you English?" A tall woman with dyed black hair is standing beside me as I'm browsing the shelves, waiting for the queue to subside.

"No Irish," I smile.

"Do you live here?" She looks desperate.

"Yes, I do, are you okay?"

"Yes, well, I moved here a year ago ago and well... can I ask where you get your HRT?"

"My HRT? Oh, hmm, I'm not on it... Haven't quite got to that stage yet."

"Good luck when you do. No one in Italy seems to be on HRT. I nearly had to fight my doctor here to prescribe it, she eventually did a few months ago, but last week my pharmacist told me it has gone out of production."

"Can your doctor not prescribe you a different one?"

"She prescribed me an Italian brand, the only brand available in Italy, I've been taking it for four months, all my horrible symptoms have just started to ease. I'm down to my last week's supply and I've gone to nearly every pharmacy from here to Perugia to find a packet of it but none of them have any left."

"What did your doctor suggest?"

"She suggested I buy HRT on the internet! There are so many types I don't know what to buy or if they are genuine medicines. Italian women don't take HRT. Can you believe it?"

"Maybe go back over to the UK as soon as you can and go to a Well Woman clinic and ask them to give you six-month supply?"

"Do you think it would work?"

"It's worth trying and they would probably give you something more specific to your hormone needs rather than just a generic one size fits all?"

"I really can't go back to the way I was. I'd rather throw myself in the lake. Anyway, thanks for listening and the suggestion, I'm going over for a visit next week so I'll book an appointment."

"You are welcome! Best of luck."

I love women in my age group, they just know what they want and ask for it. They don't care what people think. Older and wiser and less bullshit taken in or being given out.

Note to self; find out why Italians don't do HRT and what women, with bad menopause symptoms, do instead. Good to have this knowledge in case things get rough in the menopausal years to come.

"I'll do the ultrasound first and then see what the specialist says," I rationalise to Ronan back at the house. He's as impressed as I am about the speed of appointment dates and I hear him tell his friend in the UK about Jim who has spent five hours sitting on a plastic chair waiting to be seen by his cancer consultant.

I'm madly impressed too. I know some things are complicated in Italy but their appointment system through the farmacia works really well, and is amazingly quick. Getting appointments for non-urgent scans, MRI and a specialist within two weeks of joining the health system would not happen in Ireland where waiting lists go on for years never mind months.

It's a pity the Italian court system isn't as quick though, and we didn't have Ronan's gun-running hanging over our heads. All we can do is sit and wait for the court date and for Ronan's future or non-future in Italy to be decided.

18

It's late September and it's getting chilly in the mornings.

I've been a full-time author officially for a week now. My narrator has sent me the first two chapters of my first audio book to review and, with a push, I could get my third book in my rom-com series finished by the afternoon.

"So did you get it done?" texts Shelly late morning.

"Nearly, I might leave it until later."

"If you can get it finished by the afternoon let me know, I want to take you somewhere you will love. A mystery trip. Ronan is in on it, so let him know when you are finished."

So I push on. Nothing like a mystery trip to motivate me.

"DONE!" I call to Ronan, as I attach the file and press send.

"Okay, grab your swimsuit and get into the car," he says. "We're going to the hot springs with Shelly and Sherwin."

"Ohhh. Nice!" I've been meaning to go to hot springs since we arrived in Italy, but have never got around to it.

Ronan, who hasn't changed out of his long sleeves, jeans and woolly socks he resurrected from his winter wardrobe suitcase, is sitting waiting for me in the car.

"Aren't you a bit overdressed for the hot springs?" I ask wondering if I had completely misunderstood where we were going.

"I've had enough of water and swimming and being eaten by piranhas for this year so I'm not getting in. Hot springs are up mountains, aren't they? I'll go for a walk and take photos, it will probably be chilly and I don't want to be savaged by mosquitoes so I think I'll be the one best dressed for the excursion."

As Ronan drives like Evel Knievel, rather than driving in convoy, Shelly and Sherwin have sent me the Google link to the location but my crappy phone decides to have an internet off day and refuses to link to my data. So Ronan uses his. I am trying to ease off being an angry control freak, so I resist the urge to check what he has put in.

After a while, I start to see signs for Terme Felice. My phone is working again.

"The thermal baths are in a Saint Francis Theme Park?" I ask curiously when I read the description.

"Are they?"

"That's what the website of Terme Felice is saying." I am trying to imagine what a Saint Francis Theme Park will be like... "Perhaps all the rides must be animal themed? Maybe a roller coaster going into a tunnel the shape of a wolf's mouth? Or maybe it's a water park but all the water is holy water? Or perhaps everything will cost a fortune to go on so we all end up the Franciscan way of living in poverty?"

I know all about Saint Francis. He was mine and Jim's favourite saint growing up, Jim still is a massive fan of his. We both wanted to be him but Jim, being seven years older, said I could be Saint Clare as she was the female version of Saint Francis. I accepted reluctantly but grumbled as she wasn't the one that tamed the wolf and there weren't statues of her like Saint Francis. His statues made him look like a bearded version of Snow White with birds on his fingers and animals around his feet. I wanted to be him, but Jim, being the oldest and with the capability of growing a beard someday, had first dibs.

When Jim visited us before his chemo started, we took him to Assisi, which is Saint Francis Land. Jim was in his element. He chatted with the monks, visited the saint's tomb, lit candles and bought himself a Saint Francis cross to hang around his neck. "Don't wear that to work, if it got caught in the machines in your workshop, you could end up strangling yourself," I warned, hearing our mother in my voice.

"No, it's just a momento, not something I would wear. Well only on special occasions," he grinned. "I'll hang it on the wall beside the little statue you got me of Saint Francis and the wolf a few years ago."

The statue I got him is the size of half of a thumb, I'm impressed he still has it. "I'd have lost it ages ago... It's weird both of us have given each other statues of wolves, the only other gifts I remember us giving each other is food or plastic animals when we were kids."

In the little side street shop of Assisi, Jim was also tempted to buy a medieval crossbow and a BB gun which were on sale alongside the Saint Francis and Pope paraphernalia. He and Ronan were like two kids talking to the shopkeeper about the medieval weapons. But Ronan had been warned, no more guns or crossbows.

The Saint Francis theme park was disappointing; no roller coasters or holy water splash pools. Just a hotel spa with a thermal swimming pool and a formal garden with the typical Saint Francis garden statue; peaceful and serene, covered in small animals. The real Saint Francis was so much more interesting than that.

Before his conversion, his wealthy partying buddies called him 'Dominus', because he was the King of Partying, hosting lavish parties full of food, wine and women. He loved the stories of King Arthur and wanted to be a knight like him. He fought in two wars; a civil war in Assisi and as a horse-back soldier against the city of Perugia. During the Perugia war he was captured and held as a prisoner of war for over a year.

The ex-party-animal soldier then renounced his wealth to live the rest of his life in radical poverty and to serve God's creatures.

While Ronan is trying to find Shelly and Sherwin, I surprise myself at being able to translate an information notice about the spa we are at; In the seventeenth century, the historian Fausto Dear Weasel narrated the beneficial properties of the springs in the area, saying: "l'acqua perfetta e per uso dei bagni et hoggi ancora serve detta acqua per chi patisce di male di fegato e di difficoltà ad urinare."—The water is perfect for people with bad livers and have difficulty urinating.

While my liver can probably do with a boost, the idea of the warm waters giving relief to people who have difficulty urinating is off-putting.

"Crap. We are at the wrong terme place," says Ronan, coming back to me.

"Why am I not surprised?" My controlling brain wants to shout, but I bite my tongue and we follow Ronan's GPS to a roundabout in a small town when it announces 'you have arrived'.

So we drive around the roundabout and follow the brown signs for 'terme'. As often happens in Italy, the signposts then abandon us and the GPS kicks in again. She directs us to take a right down a white dirt track and then a left under a narrow railway tunnel leading us to a walking path amongst heavily laden vines with plum-purple grape cones ready to be picked.

"Do you think it's a hole in the ground around here?"

"I don't know but let's take this in for a moment... This is where we live," I say, looking at the spectacular scene we have driven into.

Although we have been through the driest summer in history, the recent rains have turned the parched earth into lush green valleys.

Across the rolling hills of vines, farmers are busily unpacking crates from the back of tractors, ready to gather the harvest in the following morning, backed by hills sprinkled with creamy stone villas and orange-red roofs.

Shelly is texting. They have arrived and she sends us directions from the roundabout. 'Go over the railway tracks and take a right.'

She has pinned their location.

"Ahhh, we were supposed to go over the railway tracks rather than under," says Ronan as if that made any sense. We trundle down the track only fit for tractors and walkers and find a spot to turn around in the vast beauty. We eventually find Shelly standing in front of a large stone modern looking building, surrounded by a big car park with few spaces left.

"It must be a big hole," says Ronan.

"Oh, wow look at the colour of it," I say, pointing to a small brook running through the car park. Steam rises from the aquamarine water slowly flowing through a white calcite base.

"Is that it? Is that where you are going swimming?" asks Ronan.

"I doubt it." But I'm not sure.

"Come on!" Shelly says as we follow her through to a reception desk and changing rooms.

"There's a coffee shop, I'll go for a coffee and I suppose follow you after you get changed?" says Ronan.

I'm not sure what to expect.

Shelly is barefoot, and the woman is shouting 'ciabbatta' at her. I proudly know she means slippers and is not stating what bread she had for lunch.

Ronan follows us outside and for the first time in all our years in Italy he is more overdressed than any Italian in sight.

Women are walking around the well-maintained fields of grass in thong bikinis while older and more discrete men and women are wearing towelled robes and ciabatta on their feet. Dotted around the lawns and terraces are sun loungers with umbrellas similar to those we spent our days lazing on in Crete only a week before.

"I feel like a perv fully dressed with my camera hanging out of me. I thought we were going to a mountain not a swimming pool place. I'm going back to the coffee shop," Ronan says.

The hot springs are not the hole in the ground up a mountain either of us were expecting. Instead, there are four large pools set out in a park with sun loungers and tables. It's only by the time we are in pool four, that we discover each pool has a different intensity of heat, with the hottest near the door. Logic would determine that you go there first, but being the pasty-bodied Irish and English we are, we go to the furthest pool with the least amount of people in it.

"It's not very hot, is it?" We twitter at each other. "I thought thermal pools were much hotter than this."

Of course, we weren't saying this by pool number four. The Italians ended their sessions in the cooling pool and strutted back into the changing room looking calm and refreshed. Whereas we ended our experience in the steaming-hot pot starter pool, looking flushed and blotchy. But I still felt relaxed and ready to take on my next life challenge; the ultrasound on my water baby.

19

I arrive with a full bladder at the hospital on the hill ready for my ultrasound scan. I've had four pregnancies, so I know what to expect from an ultrasound. They smear cold gel on your tummy and then move a thing like a computer mouse over it, like they are playing an escape room challenge game and trying to find their way out of your insides.

Having a full bladder pushes everything forward, so it's easier to view the heartbeat, fingers and toes. Except this time, I am not looking for fingers and toes, I just want to make sure this cyst is just a water balloon and nothing potentially malignant.

It's the hospital beside the ancient castle with the summer outdoor cinema. The frescoed palazzo attached to the castle houses a small museum and has a terraced entrance facing the square the hospital also faces. On the other two sides of the square are the lake vista and the start of the cobbled main street.

Usually we can park outside the hospital entrance, but today it's blocked off. A microphone stand and speakers are set up on the museum palazzo terrace, and a small crowd has gathered.

Even though it is a small hospital, and everything happens in the arteries off the main entrance corridor, finding my way around still makes me feel like I am an alien landed on earth and given a human-looking body. I know how to ask things like 'where?' while handing the guy at the admin desk my appointment sheet. But on the inside I am panicking with the anticipation of not knowing what his answer will mean. Luckily I understand some of the words; "Porta' is door and 'Sinestra' is left. Phew. I understood his simple directions but not the added instruction he has given me. I'll just follow the directions and then deal with the next instruction.

I take the corridor on the left where there are six chairs against the wall with a sign reading 'Ecografia' and 'Mammografia' on the wall facing them. I sit and wait two minutes, ready to watch what other people do but there is no one to watch. So I get up and walk down the corridor to find an office with two guys in red pull-ups looking out the window at the crowd growing in the square. I want to ask what is happening, but even if I knew the words, I would not understand the answer. One turns and sees me standing there. "Aspetto qui?"—'I wait here,' I ask, pointing at the chairs outside while he looks at my sheet.

"Ah yes," he says in Italian but then says 'prima devi pagare.'

He used a modal verb, my brain is doing a happy dance, giving me High 5s for recognising it–this is what happens when you are older learning a language and only getting to grips with verbs and articles that washed over your teenage school brain when you were more interested in whether Sinead O'Connor was going to knock Kylie Minogue off the number one spot that week.

I'm so caught up in recognising the sentence structure, I have paid no attention to what he was telling me to do. So I ask him to repeat it and he tries to say it in English but I'm saying 'no in Italian', I don't know how to say 'I just wasn't really listening to you'. Eventually with hand signals and a mix mash of bad language skills on both our parts, I figure out he is sending me back out to the main corridor to the CUP office near the front door. The 'porta sinestra'; the door on the left of the admin office.

It's the woman who bashed my passport off the table when I got residency in the CUP office at the other hospital, and also the same woman who said the system was down at the CUP desk in the farmacia when I was trying to get our vaccine green passes. "Ah, you are from Ireland! I love Ireland. That is €60." I'm not sure why I am paying, I thought x-rays were free. Perhaps because my TS has expired I am back to being considered an alien.

I glance out the front door where the crowd is much bigger. An elderly lady with a wooden walking stick and a guy with his teenage son has joined my waiting area. Both are called in for their appointments. That's good, things are moving along. I'll be next.

I hear applause coming from outside and a man's voice talking over the speakers.

I text Ronan who is waiting for me outside, "What's happening?"

"I think it's a politician. Some guy arrived in a new Merc with what looks like three bodyguards. He's not talking yet. I think it's the Lord Mayor talking at the moment. There is an election in a few weeks so I think it's a political rally?"

After about fifteen minutes, the lady with the walking stick who was before me walks out of the scan room, linked on the arm of a woman in a white coat, who I am guessing is the doctor. She is listening intently to the old woman and walks her slowly past me and around the corner. I'm thinking how nice the Italian health system is, here's the doctor taking time to walk this old patient out to the person waiting for her and listening carefully to her.

I text Ronan, "shouldn't be too long, I'm next."

I wait five minutes but there is no sign of the doctor returning. Maybe she had to walk her to the front door and is waiting on someone to pick her up? My full bladder is becoming increasingly uncomfortable.

Another five minutes goes slowly by. It's now forty minutes past my assigned appointment time so I get up and walk to the front door to see if I can see where the doctor has gone. Maybe she doesn't realise there is another patient waiting for her?

The sun is so bright outside it bleaches everything four shades lighter. There's a guy in a very nice suit speaking from the palazzo terrace. And there she is, the doctor I saw come out of the ecografia room, standing at the railings of the hospital along with a few other white coats and ambulance crew, intently listening to the man speaking.

In the crowd in the square, I spot the old woman who was before me sitting on a bench under the shade of the large leafy tree. A man in his thirties shouts towards the politician. I can hear her growl something in Italian at the heckler. He turns and says something to her with a smile on his face and then shouts louder at the politician. She's up on her feet behind him and then she does it.

Lifts her stick and starts bashing him on the back with it. The guy covers his head and skulks off further into the crowd, glancing back to make sure she isn't following him. She retakes her seat, and no one around her bats an eyelid at what just happened.

I give it another few minutes. But my bladder is calling, and this is ridiculous, you can't ask a woman to sit with a full bladder for more than an hour.

In preparation for my scan, I have learnt all the names for my inside bits: Gall bladder is a cistifellea. Kidneys - Reni. Liver - Fegato. Cuore - heart. But not for bladder.

"Scusi, penso ho un appointmento con Lei?" I say to the doctor at the railings.

"Ah sì! Salve!" she says, smiling. And then, still smiling, says something in Italian like; "I will be with you shortly this is important." And turns back to listen to the speaker.

I don't know how to say my bladder is full and I'm about to pee in my pants. I know gall bladder is cistifellea. So maybe I could say 'my fella is full' or 'my cisti is full'?

When you want to say full the word is pieno. And I know the word for liver. So I'll go for a combo of those two and hope she gets the message that one of my internal body parts needs attention.

"Ho un fegato 'pieno'," I say pointing to the area below my belly button with my open hand like a true Italian.

When I look up the translation later I realise I said "I have a flat liver", but it seems to have done the trick. She turns to her colleague, they laugh a moment and then she says 'va bene' and leads the way back to the scan room.

She asks me a few questions in Italian and I struggle to understand but answer the best I can. She finishes quickly and then
releases me to visit the long-awaited bathroom.

On my return, she hands me a printed sheet with the regional
health website address on it, with a code and a password.

"Your results of the ecografia will be ready tomorrow," she says.
"You need to go on to the website after tomorrow and get your
results. This code will expire in ninety days."

"I understand," I say.

And then she says, "You need an MRI."

Outside the crowd has dispersed and Ronan is waiting for me
in the car. He's looking at his phone concerned. His pension
payments have been put on hold for the last couple of months
as they needed an admin form completed.

"They still haven't sorted out my pension. They say that verifi-
cation form they sent out to me which I sent back, never
arrived."

"It is such a waste of government money to send out a verifica-
tion form to ask if your circumstances have changed just a
couple of months after you started getting your pension. What
were they verifying? That you have not got younger?" I say. I
can't imagine what someone would do in Ronan's circum-
stance if they didn't have an earning partner.

"I posted it weeks ago. Luckily I scanned it and I sent it by email
to them but they have come back to say they need the paper
form. So I'll fill it in again and give it to Sherwin to post from
London when he goes back next week. It has more chance of
arriving from there than Italy."

We can't get the S1 form which we need for the Tessera Sanitaria until this glitch with Ronan's pension in Ireland is cleared. If this was happening in Italy, we would be grumbling about Italian bureaucracy.

The following evening, I go on to the website the doctor gave me, and I follow the clear directions, even though they are in Italian and find my results and prognoses by the doctor. She starts with 'there was a language barrier'. She confirms it is a large liquid-filled cyst and an MRI scan is needed for a more accurate picture.

I send the diagnosis to Fab Chicken, and he writes back. "Just what I thought! No need to be worried. I will make you a new appointment for the MRI scan."

"But my temporary Tessera Sanitaria has expired, so I'll need to make a private appointment I don't want to wait until our health card is sorted."

Doctor Fab writes me a prescription for an MRI at the private clinic only twenty minutes from us. It's a small modern clinic with five MRI machines. No need to go to the CUP, as it's a private booking I can go directly to the clinic and make the appointment.

The woman at the admin desk is perplexed as to why I don't have a TS.

"But you are a permanent resident?"

"Yes."

"Why do you not have a Tessera Sanitaria?"

"They won't give me one."

"Why?"

"I don't know!"

With a furrowed brow she takes my prescription, types the content of it into her computer, prints it out with other pages, including an instruction sheet of how I have malfunctioned, stamps it, takes my payment, prints out a receipt, staples the smaller card roll receipt to it, paperclips them all together, puts them all in a folder and hands the small forest's-worth of paper to me. Then hands me back my original prescription. 'Ciao!'

The appointment is for the following week and the cost is €295.

I always impressed on Ronan that we needed to learn Italian in case either of us needed medical help so we understood what they were saying to us. I thought it would be him in need of it not me. But here I am.

20

I get a message from Shelly to be outside my gate at ten. I love Shelly's mystery tours. Her parents are visiting, "We are going to Margheriti Piante–the garden centre I told you about near Chiusi."

Arriving through the gates of Margheriti Piante is like entering a potted Jurassic park. Enormous fully grown trees in massive pots ready to be shipped to landscaping projects of hotels, parks and wealthy property owners who want to see a finished garden appear in a matter of days, or young new money who have no interest in watching a tree grow.

Shelly tells the assistant she wants to buy a nut tree.

"Where are you planting a nut tree, your garden is full already?" I ask.

"I don't really need or want a nut tree, but they keep the nut trees the furthest away so they'll take us there by golf cart and you'll get to see the whole garden centre on the way."

Within a few minutes, Shelly and I are on the back of the golf cart with her parents in the front, whizzing through the lanes lined with giant ferns, cedars, pines, past the hot houses bursting with banana trees, tropical ferns, jasmine, wisteria, and every type of flower and shrub you can imagine. Eventually we swerve into an aisle of Virginia creepers dressed for autumn in burnt orange and crimson red.

"Did you see anything you want to go back to have a look at?" Shelly asks.

"Everything! I could happily work here as a volunteer just to hang out with the plants all day."

"Nuts."

"Not really, I really like being around plants."

"No, I mean we are here at the nuts. Hop off and help me choose a plant for Helga."

Once Shelly selects a small young hazel nut tree, we are back on the back of the golf cart, her parents in the front chatting to the driver. It is nearly lunchtime and I guess the driver is in a hurry to get back to start her three-hour lunch break. As our bums hit the seat, she slams her foot on the pedal and is reversing at high speed, just as a forklift truck turns into the aisle driving towards us, its long lifting prongs empty but at the perfect height to skewer us.

"AHHH freno, freno!" I roar, immediately remembering the word for 'Brake'.

The driver looks over her shoulder and swerves to the right and swings around the human-sized barbecue prongs just in time. She's laughing and so is the driver of the forklift. We're laughing out of relief and Shelly's parents are still chatting, oblivious to our near death jousting experience.

Back to the starting point after our high-speed golf cart ride, we explore the greenhouses and bump into Karen and John.

Karen is a part-time landscaper for hotels and luxury gardens in Italy but often her projects grind to a halt when they find a buried ruin and have to wait months for archeologists to come and check it out.

"Just the person I need to give me some advice on what to plant in my garden," I say hugging my old friend. "I'm not buying anything today, we still have a lot of prep work to do, but I want to create a flower garden and I'm not sure what will grow here that I'm familiar with in Ireland."

"Okay so in your garden, you have the sturdy supports the vines used to grow on, so you could grow wisteria on them," says Karen. "Its drooping clusters of purple flowers in spring would kick off the year with a good display. Then jasmine could take over for the summer and if you built a dining area under it, it would fill it with its scent in the evening. Roses are classic for Italian gardens and can put up with being forgotten about."

Karen talking plants is like a Michelin star chef talking about food. I'm taking notes on my phone while walking behind her and John as they place potted plants on a trolly.

"Lavender is great for attracting bees and butterflies and of course gives off a nice scent and keeps mosquitoes away, so does rosemary. I know irises are one of your favourite flowers, they do really well in Italy. You can get them in shades of blue, purple, yellow and white so plant some bulbs in a sunny spot soon and they'll spread each year by themselves. You could, of course, plant some more vines."

"What about bougainvillea? I would love to have a bright pink or purple one in a terracotta pot against a white wall. Like they do in Greece," I say, recounting the inspirational beauties I saw on our recent holiday.

"They are hardy and drought-tolerant but they need to be kept out of the wind and they often don't get through the winters where we are. Oleander is tough and durable shrub, maybe try that?"

"Okay next question; where do I buy paving slabs? The DIY stores have a very limited range and there are none here."

"You need to go to a building supplier. I don't know any near you but just google it and you will find one. But before you start gardening, don't forget to check your trees for processionary caterpillars."

"Have done already and we have none. I don't think they are as common in Umbria as they are in Tuscany so no chance of being blinded thankfully," I say, recalling the story behind Karen's warning.

John winces. His experience with the little beasts may have been about ten years ago but the memory still hurts. A white silken nest the size of a football had formed in the pine tree of the house they were renting. It wasn't like anything they were familiar with in the UK so a kind neighbour came over, had a look at it hanging in the tree as requested, went back to his own house and returned with a shotgun.

"This is how we get rid of the caterpillar nest in Italy," he said, before shooting it out of the tree. "But be careful they are dangerous to dogs, if they investigate the caterpillars the stinging hairs stick to the tongue of a dog, it makes the animal's tongue swell and they can suffocate to death." As he talked some of the surviving white-haired black caterpillars were already forming a line behind each other for a hike across the garden.

"This is how they get their name; they walk behind each other head to tail in a procession, they look cute but do not let your kids near them their hairs can blind. Dopo!" And off the neighbour walked with his shotgun.

"We can't keep the dogs and kids indoors until the caterpillars decide to bugger off or turn into moths or whatever," exclaimed Karen.

"John, go out with the lawn mower and vacuum them up into the bag, we can then dump them at a careful distance away from where the dogs and kids play."

So John got on his lawnmower and cut the grass while it sucked the caterpillars up. It wasn't a good idea. The caterpillars released their hairs into the air around him and soon were in his eyes. It took six weeks of medication and eye baths to get the irritation and poison out of his eyes and back to normal.

"Come visit us before you go back to Ireland," Karen says hugging me goodbye. Shelly had disappeared back to the car with her parents.

Back home, as Shelly drops me off at my gate she shouts, "Hang on, I got you these to start your garden with." And she offloads three little vines and two wisterias. She is such a generous soul.

21

I t's difficult to plan a garden when you don't know how much garden you have to plan. Alex's geometra has already been out to the house and made initial enquiries to the comune if it is possible to build something in our side garden or was it all sales talk by the estate agent.

"You are very lucky people," says Alex when he calls with the results. "You have one of the few sites available in walking distance of the town where you can build a house the size of your own. Two hundred square meters over three floors. You will get a lot of money for it. Perhaps €150k."

We're excited. That sounds very promising.

The geometra needs to come out again with Alex to do some measurements and to advise on how we will need to divide the garden to sell it as a site.

So Ronan is out with his new strimmer to get the grass down on our 'spare' garden.

I can't watch Ronan strim. This is the third strimmer he has had since we moved in, I don't know what he does with them but he breaks one per year. I have warned him this is the last one, so he has gone all out and got a model with a metal blade. He says he 'kind of' read the instructions. He obviously skipped the pages on safety as he is out there strimming in his shorts and sunglasses and the work boots that I have thrown out several times. It's a warm day and his naked torso is gloss-varnished with sweat.

That's not why I can't watch him. I can look at a working man all day when they are doing something that will make my life easier. It's because it's a metal blade spinning around at Looney Tune leg speed and he is practically naked. It will just take him hitting a rock or a something metal and I could be calling emergency services. So I can't watch, but I keep my phone in my hand and jump to look out the window every time the strimmer stops to check if he is lying beside a limb that should still be attached to his body or to see if there is a new fountain feature in the front garden made of Ronan's arterial blood.

It's not like he doesn't know what he should wear. He has watched One Spot Charley enough in a neighbouring house. We don't know who this guy is as he is dressed head to toe in protective body wear including a full visor and boots. Three times per year he starts strimming the garden next door at 7am and doesn't finish until 8pm for three days in a row. Every blade of grass is not just cut, but ploughed into the ground by his technique of strimming in the same spot for at least five minutes without moving. That's why Ronan named him One Spot Charley.

"You build or you sell?" asks Alex when he arrives with his geometra. "If you sell you will need to square off the end of the garden and give them this section," he says, standing beside the vines and waving his hand to the side, translating what the geometra is saying, looking at his notes.

"What the vines and end of the garden?" I ask perplexed.

"Yes, you need to give them a certain amount of space. Eight hundred square meters."

"You mean get rid of the vines?"

"Yes, of course. And you will need to destroy the end building as it is illegal and you can never sell the house with it there. Unless the people are like you and don't care."

"How much will that cost?" asks Ronan.

"About eight or nine thousand," Alex says matter-of-factly still translating. "And then you could get one hundred euros per square meter for the site. Start at eighty thousand and you will probably get sixty thousand."

"Sixty thousand? I was hoping more like one hundred and fifty thousand or at least one hundred thousand?" I say, feeling disillusioned. That's less than half of what we initially thought and then the cost of destroying the illegal buildings, the real estate fees and taxes would probably leave us with a fifth of the initial estimation.

"But first you must offer it to your neighbours, to give them first option."

"Really? Ugh this is sounding messy and complicated," says Ronan.

"Of course, that is how it is in Italy... Why not build on it yourself as then you have control of what we will build here?" says Alex in his usual doesn't stop for an answer manner. "Why you not sell the house with the land, you sell it and I find you something smaller to buy, why not? It is too big for you and Ronan. I know a real estate guy who sells to the foreign market. You could get six hundred thousand from the right buyer for this house, of course they will come and rip out everything you have done, that is the type of buyer who will buy your house."

He hasn't stopped for a breath.

"Because I don't want to sell I want to–"

"Six hundred thousand?" says Ronan nearly frothing at the mouth.

I don't feel it appropriate at this moment to remind Ronan it was Alex who had put the estimate of one hundred and fifty thousand in our heads and since the geomatra has been involved that has already been cut by two thirds.

"Why you sell the land anyways?"

"To pay for the roof to be finished and to do the garden and all the other jobs to be done." I don't tell him about wanting to give money back to our daughter, it would be too complicated.

"What? You need money? I give you money."

"No. Thank you but no."

"I do the roof for you and you pay me over time. And then I do the garden for you, I will do up a design we put down paving and stone and make a big car port, get rid of the grass."

"Get rid of the grass?"

"Yes and the vines, they are old. Get rid of them, I make something nice there. We get rid of all the grass and we put stone.

Get rid of the cement supports for the vines, do completely clean."

"Oh no!"

"Why you want grass? You want to have the sheeps?! Come on, Rosie, get rid of the grass and then less work for Ronan."

"But he has a ride-on lawnmower!"

"Yes, but he breaks them. You know this. Less grass, less stress for you about Ronan breaking things and less space you need to store tools."

He has a point, Ronan has also gone through three lawnmowers since we arrived, but I needed a bit of green, I am Irish after all. And the suggestion of getting rid of the vines was nearly worse.

"You can do the roof but hands off my garden," I say with a grin.

Alex looks hurt.

"We will think about whether or not to sell the plot, but we will definitely do the garden ourselves, we love gardening. Getting back to the roof, while you are here, will you come up and have a look at it and give us a price?"

Up in the attic space, now cleared of the gramophone, broken chairs, old baths, bottles and magazines, Alex re-examines the beams the first guy hacked lumps out of two years before. I feel we have done so much since then, but still have so many odd jobs to do before we can say it's finished. The small roof is the last big project in the house. "I want to turn it into a useable room... with a secret door behind a bookcase."

Ronan looks at me as if I have ten heads.

"What's your problem?" I say to him. "Everyone wants a secret doorway behind a bookcase into a hidden room and this is the perfect place to build one."

"Yes, it can be done," announces Alex. I know when it comes to it he will say his classic 'why you do this?' line, but for now, his agreement makes me happy.

"What's that?" I say noticing something move behind Alex's head. We all step closer at the fig-sized golden thing stuck to the beam. It's moving. In the half-dim light seeping through the loose terracotta roof tiles we watch two wasps regurgitate mud and realise what's happening. "Wasps... building a nest!" I exclaim.

"They are only starting, I'll get rid of them later," says Ronan casually, but I'm already out the doorway where my secret bookcase is going to be someday.

I call Jim later, "I'm getting a secret door behind a bookshelf. Into the attic room."

"Great idea!" he says chopping up vegetables for a stir-fry.

"And we found a wasp nest."

"Do you remember the one in the attic of Abbeyfield? Me and Da dressed in plastic bags with Terry next door going up and spraying it? And then we had the empty nest, it was like an intricate maze built with tissue paper. Do you remember it Rose?"

Memories flood back of our childhood home and how everything in nature was amazing to Jim and me. Birds, stray neighbourhood dogs, insects, fish, wasps in the attic, hedgehogs under the hut.

The following morning before breakfast I have dug the holes for the new vines. I am off to Karen's for a catch-up night before I go back to Ireland to bring my mother back for the winter so I go upstairs to pack.

"The roots on the vines are surprisingly small. I thought they would be bigger," says Ronan as I come back down to the garden with my bag.

"Well, they will grow down and..." I say before stopping. "Hang on, how do you know they are small?"

"Because I saw them when I was planting them. Look I'll show you." I watch in horror as Ronan wraps his fingers around the vine stem and lifts it by its neck out of the pot leaving all the clay around its roots behind.

"Bloody hell Ronan, that is not how you plant something. We have had four gardens before this have you never watched me plant anything? Just leave the bloody plants to me."

I feel like a complete control freak. The garden is completely out of control so even Ronan's yellow fingers would help.

"This is how you do it," I say, tipping the pot to the side and gently easing the pot-shaped moulded clay into the deep hole. Granted, the clay is very loose, not like the other pot-bound plants I have planted previously.

"We need to find a builder's merchants for patio paving so let's find one and order the paving for the terrace," I say quickly to keep Ronan away from the potted wisteria. Cement and bricks are more his thing than plants and clay.

22

Online, I find a builder's merchant near Perugia with rows of lovely paving on display to choose from. So off we go.

I haven't been able to find the same paving slabs as the ones we put down the previous year in what is now called the hammock area, so going for something completely different is the best option. We both choose a terracotta stone in four different shapes and sizes that integrates into a rustic mismatched pattern.

The guy in the shop doesn't speak English but his kind eyes encourage my efforts of Italian while Ronan just tells me things in English for me to ask about. It isn't helping my concentration.

"You need to learn Italian. I can't be managing every simple thing. If the two of us tried, we might have more chance of making sense of the language."

His lack of effort because he is 'too old' is starting to really frustrate me.

My Italian classes each week are beginning to make sense. I've become better at reading and with some thought and time I can write sentences in the past and present tense.

Sometimes when an Italian is trying to talk to me, it is more understandable for me if they say it slowly in Italian rather than me piecing their broken English together. I am sure it is the same for them as my Italian has reached the standard of English most Italians have.

"I can get by," says Ronan.

"Okay smart ass, you order what we need," I say, standing back.

Ronan turns to the guy at the desk, "We need sand-eeo for the paviment-eeo and cement-eeo."

"Well, you got the 'pavimentio' right," I say trying to be encouraging but knowing by the look on the guy's face, no matter how confidently Ronan made his request, the guy did not understand.

"Vogliamo la sabbia per questa pavimento nel giardino," I say, showing the guy a photo I took outside of the paving slabs we want, and handing him the size of the area we have carefully measured five times, argued about, and then guessed the amount needed.

He takes our order and tells us the price.

He asks in Italian if we have a car and then says to follow him. We think he is just going to ensure it's the right paving he is ordering for us but no.

"Andiamo."

"I know that means 'we go'. Does he think we can put the four sacks of sand and four pallets of paving in the back of our car?" asks Ronan as we walk behind him. "We want it deliver-ooo," states Ronan in his best non-Italian.

"Andiamo la sabbia."

"Isn't sabbia beach? We are going to the beach with him?"

"No," I say trying to be patient. "That is spaggia, but you are close. Sabbia is sand."

Down the track and around the back of the building we reach mountainous heaps of sand and gravel.

"Which sand do you want, white or grey?" the guy asks in Italian.

"Okay," I say, translating to Ronan. "Apparently in Italy we need to make a fashion statement about the sand under the pavement."

"This one is better for drainage." He lifts a handful of the grey gravel which, on closer inspection, is courser than the white.

"We have cemento," says Ronan.

"No you cannot have cemento," he says smiling at Ronan's stupidity.

"But we do have cemento."

"No cemento without permission-io," the guy says, answering Ronan in Ronan's version of Italian.

"The cemento is already in the garden, this will go on top of it,"

I say in English and then as best I can in proper Italian not Ronan Italian.

"Ahh okay. Then grey is better for you," he says in Italian. I translate for Ronan, "He thinks the grey stone suits your skin tone better."

We go back to the building to make the payment. One computer on a desk provides us with the invoice. The second computer across the other side of the shop takes our payment and the third computer across from that desk gives us a receipt. We did of course have to provide a codice fiscale, as well as full name, address, telephone, date of birth. Not sure why a date of birth is needed for buying paving. Is there a legal age limit for buying paving in Italy?

Of course, I'm talking to Jim regularly about our garden plans.

"You have to have a pond," Jim states yet again.

"I can't have a pond, it would be a perfect breeding ground for mosquitoes and the fish would cook in the water on a hot day."

"Come on, you can get a fountain or waterfall going to keep the water moving to cool it off and mosquitoes won't breed in moving water."

"I have a bloody big pond out the back, called Lake Trasimeno, and don't forget I have two wells." I love ponds but I am very aware mosquitoes love them too.

"Talking of which," says Jim. "Have you checked how deep the wells are and if there is anything dead down them? Maybe you should climb down into one and have a look?"

"The chemo must be affecting your head, do you think there is a chance in hell I am going to climb down into a well?"

"At least throw a weighted string into it and test the depth."

To keep Jim happy and figure out what to do with the wells, I get a ball of wool, tie a lump of metal on the end and Ronan and I go to explore the wells.

A circle of rusted, jagged metal weighed down with broken blocks and bricks and the tangle of rusted wire we pulled from the vines sits on top of the ugly cement well wall in the middle of the spare garden. Ronan pulls off one brick and the thin rusted sheet with its mangled wire and brick topping threatens to give way and plummet into the depths of the well.

He peels back the rusty panel and I immediately see a huge cockroach-like thing and spider scramble up the inside side wall towards the light and towards me.

"Ouuu, I hadn't thought of creatures living in it... only dead mafia victims or one of the cousins who stole the last inheritance or maybe Paolo himself."

Cringing and wanting to get this over with as soon as possible, I cast my wool line into the abyss until we hear a plop. I ease it down until I feel the resistance of the bottom of the well.

"I've reached the end."

"Or a dead body... move it around a bit to get around any potential limbs or skulls."

I'm still keeping an eye on the large ugly black beetle thing which has evolved to live in the dark innards of the well.

I draw up the line and find where wet meets dry.

Stretched out on the measuring tape the water depth is 2.5metres." Is that good?" I ask Jim on video chat.

"How the hell would I know?"

"You are the one hassling me to measure it!"

"Yeah well I am more interested in knowing what creatures are in the well. Get a microscope, and test the water, you might find a new amoeba... Tell me again about the beetle."

23

"This is the first time I have come into the house through the front door," Lucia says standing in the hallway looking around as if she has never been there before. Maybe she hasn't. We use the back French doors as they are the same distance from the front gate and just what we are used to since the renovation work.

It's so good to have her over for dinner as she has been crazy busy developing her agriturismo into an amazing yoga retreat venue and she has moved in with her boyfriend so we, her 'Irish parents', have rarely seen her outside of weddings for the last year. But she is always there if we really need her, like a true friend.

"You are missing a scarpiera. A garage for your shoes, you know? Italians don't wear outside shoes in the house, I walk in socks but a lot of people put on slippers for inside the house.

"You need to become more Italian, first to speak it... but that is my fault for speaking in English to you all the time." She tuts at herself, walking out to the dinner table set up in the garden.

"What are you doing here?" She asks, seeing the Halloween skull and crossbones plastic decoration tape roughly sectioning off the site.

"We are thinking of selling the site."

"How much would you get for it?"

"We had originally thought one hundred or one hundred and fifty but Alex said sixty would be more likely. And it would have to be a very skinny house apparently as it needs to be five meters from our neighbour's border and five meters from our garden border."

"Don't forget you will need to pay high taxes on the price you get. It will also devalue your house having something possibly big and ugly built there. Maybe they start it and don't finish and then you have to live beside a building site for years." These points had crossed my mind but hearing them reinforced the niggle; I really didn't want to sell the spare garden.

"Why not keep it and maybe build a small house there for yourselves someday so you can rent out the entire big villa? Or just make a really nice garden fit for a villa? It would add value to the house rather than take it away."

The guest season has been good this year for Lucia, it's the first full season since pre-Covid years. All has been good except for a disgruntled distant relative who has it in for her and keeps making anonymous official complaints. Health inspectors, police and the council have made regular calls to Lucia's agriturismo to do checks throughout the summer.

"They have never done so many checks before, it must be my relative, actually I know it is her. Only a month ago, I was issued with an order from the road authority to resurface the entrance to my agriturismo. They gave me fifteen days to do it or I get a fine."

"Surely they can't do that, it's private property?" I say, dishing Pasta alla Norma onto her plate.

"I had to get my lawyer–Fabrizio Rana–involved, telling them I had guests and this is the only entrance, so we cannot plough it up until the season is over. And I cannot find someone to price it and schedule the work and have it done within fifteen days when there is a building boom-boom. So they came back and said 'okay you have thirty days'."

"Gosh, it was still very short notice."

"It was!" Lucia says exasperated.

"I was lucky, when they arrived, your friend Alex was there giving me a quote to redo some of the guest bathrooms and he helped me. He looked at the order and had it done for me within a week.

"Then when it was done, they came out to inspect it and said it needs to be done in concrete. I said, 'I have done what was ordered. There was no mention of concrete, concrete would have been cheaper and I would have had to get permissions to pour so much concrete, but I have resurfaced the track with compacted stone. So if your boss doesn't like it he can bring me to court.'"

"So what happened with all the other inspections?" Ronan asks.

"When the health inspector came with the police, they checked everything and I mean everything. And the guy says to me, near the end, 'We need to check the oil mill room upstairs' and that is when I knew it was her who was trying to cause me problems. I said 'that is interesting you call it the oil mill room, as she was the only one to call it that!' And he went red with embarrassment. Even though people make these complaints anonymously triggering inspections, at the comune you can find the name of the person who made them. And I went, and I found out it was her."

"There's not much point in making it anonymous so," says Ronan. "So did they find anything they could fine you for?"

"They could not fault me on anything, so when they were finished after hours, I said 'okay you now need to call the gynaecologist to come finish the inspection as you have checked everything else'. They found that funny."

The conversation about comune rules and how they differ from town to town leads us to talking about the new fines introduced in Venice for tourists eating while sitting on steps.

"I agree, they should not do it! Italians never eat on the street, while walking along and they never eat in their cars or on public transport like I have seen in other countries. How can you enjoy eating food in this way?" Lucia asks perplexed.

"When not at a restaurant, we only eat outside when there is a food festival, you know, a sagra? Or sometimes there are roadside food trucks serving porchetta sandwiches, but you eat the food there like at a bar or take it home to eat. Of course, gelato does not count, but we would sit down to enjoy it, not eat and walk. And why would you walk with coffee in a paper cup? Coffee and food are supposed to be savoured!" she says, finishing her plate of pasta and automatically taking up a slice of bread to clean the plate of the remaining sauce.

"And this," she says pointing to the piece of bread. "This is the other Italian way you need to learn, when we use bread like this to enjoy the last of the sauce it is called a 'scarpetta'. A little slipper. Do not get it confused with scarpiera that goes in the hall or the scarpe I gave your mother for Christmas."

"You mean ciabatta?"

"A scarpetta can be a piece of ciabatta. And scarpe and ciabatta are the same thing when they are for your feet."

There's little point in her telling me this, as I will be lucky if I remember even one of the words, and if I do, I will inevitably use it incorrectly.

Conversations with Lucia about her business remind me of the huge amount of bureaucracy there is running a business in Italy and the high taxes involved. It's complicated and off-putting to start a business here. But I need to think of some type of business so we don't have to sell the garden... or the house.

24

B y the time I get back from yoga, Ronan has chopped
down a stray bay tree in the front garden whose seed
wandered in to where it was not supposed to be,
blocking our view of traffic coming around the corner. It didn't
seem that big when standing, but when horizontal, it's much
bigger. Ronan gets working on chopping it into logs and
stacking them under our new fireplace.

"Have you taken care of the wasp nest?" I know I could take
care of it myself but... I have a Ronan.

"I had a look at it. It's still tiny, it won't cause us any problems.
However, the six or seven others up there might though. And
the one I just found in the van."

This is the second time we have found wasps building a home
in our camper van. We haven't used the van for camping since
Ronan kicked out its insides to bring home a bed we bought for
Izzy. It is now used for DIY shop runs for the materials we need
for different projects.

However, I am refusing to travel in it again until Ronan clears out all the random items he has left in it. It's too embarrassing to slide back the door and a store assistant be exposed to the variety of odd items such as the chainsaw chain, empty bottles, a shovel, work boots and bin bags strewn around the van every time we go to buy something. It looks like we have just returned from burying a body in the woods.

This year our preparing for winter projects include adding a gutter and drainpipe to the main bathroom extension and replacing the ugly green corrugated roof on the sunroom we were supposed to destroy with a new Perspex roof. As my Mam is returning to Italy for the winter, we have decided to extend the life of the doomed structure so she can enjoy the winter sun. But I can't bear looking at the cobweb-ridden, corrugated roof for another six months.

Another thing I can't bear any longer are my dogs barking at anyone walking by the house. It was Juno who decided running to the front gate yelping was one job she needed to do, and Paddy likes this new game too. Looney also joins in, but her bark is so small it doesn't count.

The solution we have come up with is to put forty metres of fencing along the cement vine posts down the centre of the garden to stop the dogs getting out to the front of the house until they learn that barking like maniacs is not something we want them to do.

The last thing on our winter prep list is to find a solution to stop the rain coming in through the old French doors of the dining room under the old small roof waiting to be replaced. Ronan enthusiastically removed all the guttering the first week the scaffolding was first put up two years ago. And Antonio's lads didn't think of putting it back in place before they took the scaffolding down.

"How about a pergola with a Perspex roof the same as the one we are putting on the sunroom?" I say to Ronan as we both toss around ideas of makeshift gutters, ledges and all sorts of rain shielding devices.

"That could work, and it would look good too," Ronan says after we both stand and stare at the back wall several times with cups of tea.

So once Ronan clears out the van with lots of grumbling, off we go to the DIY shop. They have pergolas, yeaaaa!... but there is a twenty day wait and the delivery fee adds nearly fifty percent to the cost. So while in the shop, I order one from an Italian online company which will be delivered within five days with no additional delivery charge.

Next is the fencing. A ten-metre roll of plastic-coated wire fencing is €30. But they only have one roll. We need four. We search the courtyard for an assistant to ask if they have more but there is no one. It's when we return to the spot of the one roll I look up.

"There are more up there," I say, pointing to the storage shelf above, about seven feet up. As there is a stepladder leaning up beside the shelf Ronan doesn't hesitate, he unfolds the ladder and goes up two rungs and starts handing me down the rolls we need. Of course, as soon as he does this, a store guy walks out to the courtyard and starts saying 'no, no you can't do this' from a distance.

"Just keep going before he gets here," I urge Ronan. By the time he gets to us, Ronan is handing me down roll number four.

"This has never happened before, no one does this," he shouts at us in English as if we have killed his mother's cat.

"First time for everything," says Ronan, a little guilty, but he's never been one to wait for someone to wait on him when he can do something himself, and we had been looking for someone to help us for a while. The guy is so disgusted at us, he ignores Ronan asking him where he can find ties to fix the fence to posts. The guy just walks off shaking his head in despair repeating, "no one does this."

So we go in search of ties with no assistant around to help again. "Let's just hope they aren't on a top shelf somewhere," mutters Ronan.

We eventually find the ties on our way to the cash desk with our fencing and six sheets of Perspex suitable for conservatory roofs.

"With all the winter prep jobs we have to do, how about we put the delivery of the paving slabs off until spring?" I suggest to Ronan. "We've enough to be doing and the chances are we won't get around to it until spring and so we'll just have pallet loads of paving and mounds of sand blocking up the driveway for the whole winter."

"Good idea, better to be sitting in the builders' yard rather than ours."

By the afternoon, I've postponed the paving delivery until March and we have the fence up just in time for Patricia our postwoman to deliver yet another bill.

"Why are you putting a fence in the middle of your garden?" she says, inspecting our work.

"To stop the dogs barking at passers-by."

She's surprised. "It's very considerate of you, Italians would not bother. They even leave their gates open with barking dogs."

Italians criticise their fellow Italians a lot.

Within a couple of hours, both Paddy and Juno have found a gap under the fence to get through and are back at the gate, barking at everyone who passes. We spend the next day pegging the fence down, blocking holes with bricks. But they wait until we are not around and magically appear on the other side.

"I give up, I can't figure out where they are getting through. Every inch of the fence is secured along the end, there are no gaps," Ronan says, after another round of checks along the barrier.

"Grab a cuppa and follow me," I say, leaving the back door open for the dogs to get out to the garden. Ronan follows me to the back bedroom balcony. And, sure enough, they go out to the garden, stop on the patio, look around to see if we are out of sight and then as quickly as anything Paddy climbs the fence like a ladder and hops over to the other side when he reaches the top. Juno follows his example. "Well, that was €120 well spent," says Ronan dragging on his cigarette. "The kennels weren't exaggerating when they said Paddy was an escape artist."

Of course, when it comes to putting the roof on the sunroom Ronan and I disagree about how it should be done. I want it done my way; prep and paint the supporting metal first. It will be so much easier than when the Perspex is in place. He wants to put the Perspex up now and 'we'll' paint around it afterwards. Which means, it will never be painted. As he has the height and strength to do the labour, he gets his way. As usual he is too impatient and wants to get it done quickly; he grabs a rickety chair from the porch to stand on rather than getting a ladder.

"I can't watch this," I say, leaving him to it while I go up to paint the railings on the balcony before I erupt.

It turns out I don't have to watch Ronan do it his way after all.

I hear him moving the roof sheets into place and then a thud as I get into the room above.

Running to the balcony, I look out and there is Ronan lying flat on his back, like he should be chalked around in a crime scene. There's a chair around one of his knees and the bottom half of his leg is sticking through the wicker seat.

I could say 'I told you to use the ladder, that chair wouldn't hold your weight,' but that would be mean. So I opt for ignorance. "What happened?"

"I had a fall."

"You mean you fell over. You are too young to have had a fall. Are you okay?"

"I'm just winded, I'll just lie here for a minute... The house is quite nice from here, I've never seen it from this angle before." He looks serene, like he's sunbathing but still in the crime scene position with the chair around his leg. I get on with my struggle of trying to open the tin of paint and he breaks the silence; "At what age does falling over change to having a fall?"

I can't resist any longer. "I told you to use the ladder as that wonky chair wouldn't hold your weight."

Ronan eventually gets up, gets the ladder and finishes the roof, his way.

When the pergola arrives, we work on it together. Ronan again uses a chair rather than fetching the ladder which is inside the shed twenty steps away. At least he's using a sturdy chair this time. It only takes a few hours to put up the pergola and we have the Perspex roof on it just in time for the first autumn downpour.

We take our morning tea and coffee outside and sit under the pergola. I'm on the rickety chair I have patched up with a piece of wood and Ronan on the more solid chair.

We watch with satisfaction as the length of guttering Ronan has added to the bathroom extension and the pergola work a treat as the rain pounds down. "I think I have found the spot where I'll be having my morning coffee from now on," says Ronan, kicking back and taking a deep breath.

He's done a good job.

"And it's the perfect spot for me to patch up and paint the shutters. That is the next thing on my to do list."

Working on them and getting back to my online Italian classes will keep my mind away from worrying about my impending MRI scan.

25

I arrive for my MRI scan on the assigned appointment day. The information desk woman talks a lot in Italian and points me in the direction of an admin desk person. I have prepared for this like a final college exam, with everything in the folder including some helpful words and phrases I might need written on the inside. I like the word 'cistifellea' but I don't think I'm going to need it.

The admin woman is very welcoming, takes the folder and scans everything then hands it all back to me, before sending me over to a waiting area.

I am not sure what I am waiting for as the MRI area is sign-posted in a different direction, but I go and I wait until a doctor comes out and calls my name. He's a jolly-looking man with a neat grey beard.

I say my usual, "I'm Irish and my Italian is cattivo." I am getting tired of hearing myself say this. I wish my brain would just learn the language and let me get on with things without the major obstacle.

The doctor, who talks in a mix of Italian and English asks, "How long are you here?"

"Two years," I lie.

"And you don't speak Italian?"

"I am learning, but Covid made it difficult and so does my brain."

He looks sympathetic, I think I have said or implied I had Covid and it affected my brain, whereas I am just using the lame excuse that Covid lockdowns stopped me talking to Italians, something I hadn't done much of anyway before or after.

"You need to read and watch TV."

I can't imagine what he would prescribe if I told the truth of being here nearly five years.

"And so you had stones?" he says, getting back to the subject of my prescribed scan.

"No."

"You had pain?"

"No. Nothing. It was discovered by accident."

"Why were you at the doctor?"

"Hmm..." I don't want to say, 'just for a go on his new scan machine toy.'

"A check-up." I've completely forgotten to blame my recovering frozen shoulders as an excuse.

He nods.

"This is an important scan. We will scan your kidneys, liver, aorta, gallbladder and colon. You need to stay very still when we say 'breathe in' then 'breathe out' then 'hold'... Inspira. Espira. Presa."

None of the words stay in my head, even though there are just three to remember. All the words have left me. I am doing that rabbit in headlights thing again where even if he asked me my name I would find it difficult to remember the answer.

He goes back to filling in a form on his desk.

"What is your doctor's name?"

"Fabrizio..."

I can't think of his second name. I only call him by his first name.

I am trying to think of the word for chicken but it's gone. As the doctor is a friendly chap, I consider standing up and doing an impression of a chicken. I can do a really good one, but I don't think he'd be impressed and would probably refer me on to a psychiatrist rather than a liver specialist. Instead, I start to sweat as I scan through my phone looking for something with his proper name on it, rather than his contact details in my phone which I have listed as 'Doctor Fabulous Chicken'.

"It doesn't matter, you can send it to me if I need it," he says, smiling and handing me another piece of paper to add to my growing file.

"Follow the green line to the blue, then follow the blue and sit on the orange chairs."

I do as he says and sit and wait and check my messages. Jim has the results from his CAT scan checkup and his count has increased a little so they are not giving him 'a holiday' from his chemo treatment. He's still positive and joking, "when they said they might be able to give me a holiday, I thought they were going to send me to Amsterdam or somewhere." He sends me a pic of the new project he's working on; a totem pole with carved butterflies. On it, painted in calligraphy is a line from a Spike Milligan poem; 'Oh what beauty, oh what grace, who needs visitors from outer space'.

The guy operating the MRI machine asks, "Have you drunk anything?"

Well, I think that is what he has asked. Or was he asking me out for a drink? I'm trying to figure out the tense. I can tell by his professional face it is not the latter.

"No," I say, wondering if I had, would it have been a problem. I had told a friend I was going for an MRI and she said she went on a two-week detox after the chemicals they put into her. They mentioned nothing about chemicals being ingested when I made the appointment. He returns from his office and hands me a carton of pineapple juice, he is just being nice, it is a private clinic after all.

"Thanks... do I have to drink it?" I ask, he just smiles. He doesn't speak any English. I leave it on the shelf as I'm not a big fan of pineapple juice and I don't want to deprive him of the lunch his Mamma probably packed for him.

I'm lying on the plinth when he asks me if I drank it.

"No... do you want me to?"

He sighs, he's just short of rolling his eyes at me.

I struggle to get back down off the plinth as my back has been aching lately and go drink my pineapple juice. When I am back on the plinth, he gives me a squeezy thing for an alarm and moves my arms above my head and then I begin to move into what looks like a plastic tube; I haven't thought this through. I don't know how to say "I can't leave my arms like this for long because my frozen shoulders are still not fully functional." Having them in this position is already causing discomfort.

The machine is telling me in Italian to breathe in, breathe out, hold your breath and then relax. Except I don't understand what it is saying, I thought I had rehearsed these commands but I'm faltering; I can hardly hear the commands with the noise of the machine. I know I am getting it ass ways.

And then the commands switch to English. He must have found the language setting. Forty minutes later and my shoulders and arms feel like they are about to crack off, both arms have pins and needles and I'm not sure how much more I can take. Every time I think it's nearly over, it goes again.

I have to move my arms; I don't care the pain in my shoulders is beyond torture at this stage. Just as I move them down to my sides, it ends.

Four days later, I return for the results. They give me a CD and a written prognosis, so I sit in the car using a translation app where you take a photo of the text and it translates it. There are a lot of 'normales' throughout, which is good. It confirms Doctor Fab's diagnosis; I have an 11cm by 10cm beverage reserve across the front of my liver. It's not causing me any harm just taking up space and increasing my waist band size by two notches.

Perhaps it also acts like a built-in buoyancy aid? Maybe that is why I kept floating when I tried scuba diving years ago.

I send it to Fabrizio when I get home at 7pm and he texts me back by 9pm. "Nothing to worry about! When you have your TS, I will organise a visit to a surgeon to remove the cyst, it is just taking up space. Or you can get it done in Ireland."

I'd be on a waiting list for about three years in Ireland for a non-urgent procedure.

"No, I'll get it done here," I text back, relieved it is nothing sinister. I don't think my family could take any more bad news at the moment.

"Let's go to the cinema," I text Ronan, having spotted Top Gun 2 is showing tonight on a leaflet with cinema dates on the floor of the car. "I'll be home in half an hour to pick you up."

We haven't been to the cinema in Italy yet; I don't particularly like going to the cinema as I find it very uncomfortable to sit in the same upright position for an hour and a half and even with the discomfort I usually cannot keep my eyes open. But we have said every summer we would go to the English open air cinema night within the walls of the castle beside the lake in Castiglione del Lago.

It's a beautiful night, the star-speckled sky stays midnight blue with a big yellow full moon creeping above the ancient stone walls. The permanent chairs are set in an amphitheatre-style, facing the screen on the stage. The theme tune transports me back to the Eighties when life was equally complicated but in different ways and I had all the hopes and dreams of my future ahead of me.

Now here I am, with all that future I looked forward to behind me; love, children, travel, career. It has all happened. My four-teen-year-old self expected her fifty-year-old self to be an estab-lished, best-selling author with copies of her books in airport shops. She believed she would have finished travelling around the world having saved indigenous tribes, the Amazon and several species of animal, met her Tom Cruise and had a large brood of adopted and biological kids who would all speak several languages, be martial arts champions, musical, artistic and entrepreneurial.

She never envisaged her fifty-year-old self sitting on a warm summer night under the stars and a haloed moon surrounded by ancient Italian castle walls listening to the same movie theme tune. She also didn't imagine she would have to wait thirty-five years for the sequel to her favourite movie.

I imagined life would be fabulous. It has been. But something is rising in me. For a moment, I forget my current worries. What happened to the fourteen-year-old full of dreams? Now that all those dreams are memories, my fourteen-year-old self is asking fifty-year-old me; What's next, Rosie?

26

I blast Pavorotti as I write; it stops me over-thinking. Juno is intrigued, her head going from side to side, Paddy comes and lies beside her, both looking fondly at the speaker. Looney is not bothered. Of course they like Pavorotti; they are both Italian dogs, whereas Looney is the Irish one.

But Pavarotti isn't doing it for me today. I'm concerned about Jim's count being up, and about Mam–she's not doing well living on her own, I can see it in her face when we video chat. I would go now and take her back to Italy but my brother Peter is travelling from New York to Ireland for our Dad's first anniversary, so I've booked flights for mid-November, after his visit.

I'm also secretly stressed at the idea of bringing Mam back to Italy. Her previous stay had joys, but was stressful for us both in different ways. But I need to get her back here, no matter how stressed she makes me, I love her to bits and don't like to see her looking drawn and tired.

In the meantime, all we can do is keep her upbeat on phone calls.

"The supermarkets will be happy to see you back, they all increased their stock on shelves to two rows of Jameson just before you left and I'm sure they are wondering why sales have plummeted," says Ronan joking, but actually what he is saying has truth. All the local supermarkets had increased their Jameson stock from one or two bottles to two rows of Mam's favourite whiskey.

"I've fixed your electric chair..." Ronan says as he shows her by video chat the progress we have made in the house since she was last here in July, "...I've upped the voltage."

She laughs hysterically. "I am looking forward to getting back."

He shows her the free-standing bookcase we are putting together which arrived in a hundred pieces. It's my dream book-case, covering the end wall of the Tranquila Room. It's the perfect way to celebrate our fifth anniversary of moving to Italy. I never thought I would have given up weddings and become a full-time author within five years of being here. But it's not Italy that has made the magic happen, it's this house.

The bookcase finishes the room perfectly. Unpacking the dust encrusted books stuck in boxes since we arrived from Ireland five years ago gives me so much satisfaction and, even more importantly, I can dust off the set of encyclopaedias and other books of Paolo's we found in the house. The shelves fill up fast and having my books on shelves makes me feel more complete in the house. It makes it feel more finished, more like home, although we still have a lot to do.

The following morning as I wrote my word count for the day, the earth moved for me. The bed shook for about eight seconds and there was a low grumble. I thought it was Juno underneath scratching herself. I hung over the side of the bed and looked under, but she wasn't there or anywhere in the room. The house wasn't moving, just the bed. Experiencing an earthquake was on my 'then I will be integrated into Italian life' list.

I quickly google and yes, there it is, an earthquake out in the Adriatic; 5.2 with slight tremors felt as far as Perugia.

Ronan and I are on our way to the clinic to try to sort out our Tessera Sanitaria. After my liver cyst confirmation, I am even more anxious to get into the health system.

"Did you feel the earth cake this morning?" asks Lucia when we bump into her in town.

"I did! I wasn't expecting to feel one around here, I thought the lake protects us from earthquakes?"

"The lake is so low, perhaps its magic powers are drying up with it," she says, thinking about it.

 "I hope not, I wouldn't like 'earth-cakes' to be a frequent thing."

We arrive at the clinic and queue to go into the room with the small hatch. We're wearing the required anti-covid face mask. The woman behind the desk is wearing hers as a necklace. Things are definitely getting more relaxed about Covid.

"We would like to apply for our TS," I say in my best Italian, pushing the S1 form Ronan has at last received from Ireland, our marriage cert, our passports and our residency certs through the gap under the window.

"Not here, you need to take these to the office in Panicale."

"But we already were in communication with Panicale as you instructed and we got the S1 form."

She must have seen the desperation in our eyes.

"What I can do is send them from here if you wish?"

"Yes please, that would be great," says Ronan.

"You will need to fill out this form." She pushes a blank version of the same form we filled out on our first and second visits here. I am getting fond of these forms.

We step aside to fill out the same form again and as she photocopies all our documents again, Ronan does that thing he does of talking overly loud about how great and helpful the person is. He believes this makes people more helpful.

"She is so helpful and nice, she doesn't have to do this you know?" his voice raising an octave to be heard over the photocopier.

"She is very busy, but she is doing it for us because she is so helpful and nice," he continues.

I'm trying to talk about something else as I am sure it looks like he is shouting at me for criticising her and he is coming to her defence.

The form needs our Codice Fiscale. Ronan has his on his phone but I've lost the ever so handy CF card Ronan made me out of a cornflake box.

I wonder if we will ever get the official CF cards. It's been five years, maybe it will be on our TS cards, that would solve it. That's if we get them before another five years pass.

We complete the form and give it back to her. "When they have finished, you can come here to collect your card," she says, smiling.

I'm beginning to understand the system; The CUP places can't do the official checks to do the initial processing, they just issue the renewals. An appointment booking and collection point of sorts.

Ten days later, Ronan comes down to me in the kitchen after checking his emails. "I heard back from the office in Panicale, everything is okay with my application, but you are not on it so we need a new S1 form with you added as my wife."

"But there was no section to put me as your wife."

"Bernie in the Irish office said I need to add you onto the form as a dependent."

"But I'm not a dependent, I pay a lot of tax in Ireland and Italy."

"It doesn't state financially dependent... You could be emotionally dependent on me?... And you are dependent on me to get the health card?"

"True." I love Ronan's twisted logic sometimes.

Two days later, Ronan strolls into the kitchen with a look of smugness. "Veronica got back to me, my health card is in and ready to be collected."

"Veronica?"

"Yeah, the woman at the hospital. She's very nice. She must have used my old application, as she said when the paperwork is through for yours, I can just email it on to her and she will sort it out from there. No need to go to Panicale with it. She's so helpful."

The fact Ronan was already on first-name terms with someone who could do something in Italy and get results without speaking a word of the language, made me realise I was doing it all wrong. "That's it. From now on, I am leaving it to you to deal with all the bureaucracy in Italy."

"You know Rosie, when you try to get something done in Italy and they say 'no', you just need to go back again a few days later and the same person will give you a different answer. You have to take into consideration they may not have had enough coffee, or maybe they found out their partner is having an affair again with someone they don't approve of. The Italians are an emotional bunch. You just have to take their emotions into account."

He was joking but I think he had a point.

"Let's hope mine gets through."

"Ah, it will if Veronica and Bernie are looking after it. It will be bizarre if you don't get it and I did, after going to so much trouble when I don't want the bloody thing. I just wanted to drive my van and live under the radar."

"Live under the radar? Let's not forget, you have a court case for gun and rocket launcher possession."

"Oh, yeah..." he gulps his coffee. "Now I'm in the system they'll be sending me for all those bloody health checks they sent you for automatically."

"I don't think so Ronan. You are missing a few items."

"No, Veronica says she has everything she needs, so they will I bet."

"I mean you are missing the anatomy items, not the paper-work... boobs and a cervix? I don't think they will send you for a mammogram and a pap test."

"Oh, right yeah. But I bet there will be others."

I am not sentimental for dates but on the day of Dad's anniver-sary I wake up thinking about him. My body is feeling the loss, I feel a piece of my soul has been wrenched away and discarded. Maybe it is the word 'year' that makes it feel so long and final. And with worrying about Jim and Mam, I haven't given myself time to grieve for the little big man.

I work as usual, writing a chapter on my laptop; I don't even realise it but tears are rolling down my cheeks. Juno is over the other side of the room, her eyebrows raised and head tilting from side to side like she did listening to Pavarotti, but her face holds concern rather than joy. She can't hold back any longer, she bounds across the room, jumps up on my bed where she's not allowed, licks my tears and then puts a paw on either shoulder and rests her head on my heart. Hugging her eases the pain growing in my chest and temporarily patches up the gap in my soul.

27

"Have the Al-Qaeda stopped yet? They make an awful loud racket in your garden." Mam hasn't left Ireland yet and is already complaining about Italy.

"The Al-Qaeda?" I say, confused.

"Yes, those grasshopper things."

"Do you mean cicada?" laughs Jim.

"Whatever they are, the noise of them! You wouldn't believe it James."

"I do know them, and I love them! They make me feel like I'm somewhere tropical," Jim says, looking up from the recipe he's reading. "Do you remember Rosie when we had the pet geckos, and some grasshoppers escaped from their tank? It sounded like we were in the rainforest for weeks."

He has found a recipe he can tweak to his strict dietary needs, which includes lashings of the huge wedge of parmigiano I have brought him from Italy. "Lucky you brought this, otherwise I would have sent you back for it, I'm down to just smelling the last sliver of the chunk you brought over the last time."

Taking a suitcase half full of parmigiano, pecorino, olive oil, coffee and mandolin dates over to Jim and filling the space left when returning to Italy with tea bags, vitamins, stock cubes (Italian stock cubes are very salty) and Bisto has become the norm.

"You didn't bring over that mozzarella crap, did you?" says Mam. "It is very stringy, it's like eating a piece of elastic. I'm going to take my Kinsale Cookbook with me this time. It has some good basic recipes which even Rosie could follow."

The Kinsale Cookbook is one of Mam's go-to recipe books. Published in the Eighties, the promotional pic on the cover is of a full cauliflower in a pot of water on a stove top that isn't switched on. There isn't a cauliflower recipe in the book, the publishers must have just thought this mouth-watering image of impressive Irish cuisine would pull in the readers.

"Ma, you need to appreciate Italian cooking if you are going to live in Italy," says Jim. "I'd be there at the drop of a hat if I could." A silence falls between myself and Jim, but I break it, we can't let ourselves think it's going to be a long time before he makes it back.

"Next time you come over, fly into Naples and we'll go to Pompeii and then we'll drive up to our place."

"Aw yeah! Pompeii and its graffiti!"

While he's been doing chemo sessions Jim and I have been texting each other samples of Pompeii's graffiti. Our short-lived fascination started when one of us heard how archeologists in

Pompeii had uncovered the oldest record of graffiti. It simply read 'Gaius was here'. Dated 78 BCE.

We learnt the city had lots of interesting graffiti on its walls and soon samples of Pompeii's two-thousand-year-old graffiti statements and outcries were bouncing between us:

'Phileros is a eunuch!'

'Cruel Lalagus, why do you not love me?'

'I made bread on April 19th.'

'Epaphra doesn't play football well.'

And then Jim found an absolute gem, he texted; "You wouldn't want on your Trip Advisor reviews: *'We have wet the bed, host. I confess we have done wrong. If you want to know why, there was no chamber pot.'*"

However, we discovered most of the graffiti was of a much more indecent nature, but had us crying with laughter:

'Floronius, privileged soldier of the 7th Legion, was here. The women did not know of his presence. Only six women came to know, too few for such a stallion.'

'Chie, I hope your haemorrhoids rub together so much they hurt worse than when they ever have before!'

'My lusty son, with how many women have you had sexual relations?'

'Weep, you girls. My penis has given you up. Now it penetrates men's behinds. Goodbye, wondrous femininity!'

'Restituta, take off your tunic, please, and show us your hairy privates.'

Ronan agrees, as soon as Jim has a break from his chemo and is in recovery, we will book his flight to Italy to see Pompeii and its graffiti, even though we won't be able to understand it in its original Latin form.

"He'd probably like to go back to Assisi again too, we should schedule enough time for a day there," says Ronan, who on our last trip to the basilica in Assisi pointed out; "it's strange neither of them are lying about in a glass box." He was referring to Saint Francis and Saint Clare and sounded genuinely disappointed he hadn't seen his monthly quota of saintly body parts.

It was a good observation. Human parts are often on display in church cabinets around Italy as holy relics. Thankfully, there are no bits of Saint Francis lying around. The Patron Saint of Italy is kept together, neatly stored in his tomb.

There are, of course, his simple tunics made of rough burlap brown cloth. These can be seen on display in the crypt below the altar of the basilica.

Saint Clare of Assisi, also known as Saint Chiara, followed in Saint Francis's footsteps renouncing her worldly, wealthy life and founded the order of the Poor Clares. She cut her hair as a symbol of rejecting her previous life. Someone collected the cuttings and they too are on display at the basilica... along with her fingernail clippings in a crystal container. But that is as far as the displays go with body parts.

When visiting a church in Italy, I am no longer surprised to see a body laid out in a glass sarcophagus. Actually, it's one of the things I used to check for when scouting out churches for weddings. A dead body, even if it was a saint, was always a no no and the church would be blacklisted as a wedding ceremony option.

Saint Anthony has multiple bits of himself in his basilica in Padua, including his jaw and tongue. As he is the guy who helps us find lost stuff, I suppose he'll be able to find his body parts if he needs them.

Saint Catherine of Siena is another who has bits of herself spread out around Italy. She died in Rome and was buried at Santa Maria in Minerva. Knowing how much it would please the people of Siena to have the remains of their great fellow citizen among them, her confessor went to her tomb, popped her head off and sent it to the church of San Domenico in Siena, as well as one of her fingers. Other parts of her can be found in a convent in Rome and a church in Venice.

Rome has the most holy relics per square mile of any other city in Italy, including several severed saint's heads. The head of Saint Agnes is there, as is Saint John's in the church of San Silvestro.

Saint Valentine's head is there too, the rest of him is in a town in Umbria while his heart is in Dublin. I know this as I was taken to see it as a childhood treat.

Crusaders pinched the head of John Chrysostom from Constantinople and took it to Italy. However, the smuggling paperwork got confusing and now there are at least four skulls supposed to belong to John Chrysostom dotted around the world. While Russia and Greece both have one, Tuscany boasts having two of his four heads.

It's not all about bones and heads and organs though. The 'doubting finger' of Saint Thomas is also in Rome and there are some Papal innards in a church near the Trevi Fountain. The feet of Santa Lucia are in Venice.

After he died of exhaustion, Saint Francis Xavier's (not to be confused with St Francis of Assisi) body was put on display, where thousands travelled to pay their respects. One devoted woman bent as if to kiss his foot, and promptly bit off one of his toes, walked away unnoticed with said toe in her mouth, which she took back to display in her private chapel in Portugal. I can't imagine how she got through airport customs with a toe in her mouth. The toe attracts crowds of devotees to this day. His forearm somehow ended up in the church of the Gesù in Rome, while a village in Goa has a less impressive display of one of Xavier's fingernails.

Naples has the blood of its patron Saint, Saint Gennaro, stored in its cathedral. His blood supposedly liquifies on his feast day on the nineteenth of September or the sixteenth of December or the first Sunday in May. This is believed to be a miracle and protects the region from calamities such as Mount Vesuvius erupting.

The strangest for me was a withered penis of a saint or martyr in a glass case amongst a vast array of relics. It was at the church of a villa that wanted to work with me. Needless to say, with my strict no-dead-bodies-or-bits-of bodies-at-the-venue rule, I never did a wedding there.

Talking of which, the Holy Foreskin–yes, the supposed skin from Jesus Christ's circumcised penis–was kept for centuries, until it mysteriously disappeared in 1983, in the town of Calcata in Lazio, also fondly known by Italians as the Village of Freaks.

As if it wasn't revered enough, the Holy Foreskin was apparently worn as a ring by the previously mentioned Saint Catherine of Siena. None of my brides had such requests from their grooms at the weddings I'd planned. Can't imagine why not, maybe they weren't devoted enough to their beloved.

While the Foreskin was one of the strangest, the most... I'm not too sure what word to use... creative, perhaps?... is the Capuchin Crypt of Santa Maria dell'Immacolata Concezione in Rome. Let's say there may have been a very OCD monk put in charge of it, or maybe he was just very bored, or in need of a creative outlet.

In the Capuchin Church of Santa Maria dell'Immacolata Concezione the bones of over four-thousand monks who died between 1528 and 1870 decorate the walls and ceilings of the crypts. You might think my use of the words 'creative' and 'decorate' are wrong when writing about human remains... but there are lamps, arches, a clock, chandeliers and floral arrangements all made from the bones of the monks. Some of the complete skeletons are in various poses, mounted on the walls, hanging from the ceiling or having a wee rest in a nook.

The names of the five decorated crypts will give you a clue as to what to expect the decorations to be made from when you go inside; There is the Crypt of the Skulls, The Crypt of the Leg and Thigh Bones, and The Crypt of the Pelvises.

The message the monks wanted people to take away from the display was;

'Noi eravamo quello che voi siete, e quello che noi siamo voi sarete.'... "We were what you are; and what we are, you will be."

However, I think they meant we will all end as simply bones. Not a fancy chandelier.

28

The visit back to Ireland was quick. Seeing Luca settled and content, long walks on the beach and enjoying meals with Jim and his family was fabulous.

I was eager to get Mam back to Italy as I could see how nervous she must have been living by herself. She'd leave the radio on in her room all night–and I am not talking about calming whale music, I am talking Duran Duran and Queen on full volume–music she shouted at me to turn off in the Eighties. They blocked out potential unnerving noises she might hear otherwise. Tiredness and lack of motivation to cook just for herself, after years of cooking for others, was showing on her face. Any anxiousness about having her living with us dissipated, I was glad to be able to hug her and care for her again.

However, while pushing Mam in her wheelchair through the shopping mall to buy the last of her essential-non-essentials for her trip, my back goes into spasm so badly I have to stop, bend and stretch.

"What's wrong with you?"

"I'm fine. My back is just twinging. I'll see an osteopath when I get back to Italy."

"You need more exercise girl, I'll have you fit as a fiddle when we get back."

"Ma, we are not starting this way again. Things will be different this time," I say, slowly standing back up straight, alarmed at what has just happened.

"Aye, I think you are right, our expectations of each other are much lower this time," she says with a laugh.

Mam has the biggest suitcase from the last time she emigrated to Italy. And she had filled it again, even though half of her belongings were already in Italy. I unpacked it and re-packed it, leaving out all the non-essential essentials she felt she needed to bring; a bag of buttons, needles, a statue of Saint Anthony, a dictionary, a back scratcher, a thirty-pack of batteries, a box of drawing pins, a pack of panel pins and a hammer.

I've also ten cuttings from a Mexican Orange plant Jim has carefully wrapped for me. "You have to grow this, wait until you smell it. It will be great in your garden."

Even though he'd just had chemo the day before, Jim drives us to the airport. With four weeks to go until Christmas, I arrive back to Italy with Mam after ten hours of travelling from her door to ours.

It only takes a couple of days before I see her face back to the content way it used to be.

While she knows Jim has cancer, he has not mentioned the word 'incurable' to her.

"Sure, he'll be grand. I survived breast cancer, and he's a stronger man than me." The chances are he'll long outlive her. Thanks to the plenty of greens and a no sugar or carbs diet, he was defying the cancer specialists and staying well and strong. Like Dad, I think he's living by the belief that if he ignores it, it won't take over his life–it works for him.

Jim tells me he gave Mam a lecture on not telling me what to do in the airport and in my house. "Leave it to her, she knows what she is doing, don't be telling her what to do," he says, recounting the conversation he'd had.

"I have to tell her what to do, I'm her mother," she joked back but must have taken his advice as travelling was so much easier this time.

Two weeks later, we get a speeding ticket for the date Ronan collected us in Pisa. "This always happens when we go to Pisa, no matter how careful I am about the speed limit," says Ronan, reading out the two payment options from his translating app.

"If you pay it in ten days, you pay €139 or if you pay twenty days, it is €195."

In Italy there is no rebuke or a way to question a speeding fine. You pay up or it just keeps increasing.

But I'm not bothered about it, I'm more bothered about my back as I am finding it difficult to stand for more than a couple of minutes at a time and walking and sitting have become increasingly painful. I feel I am turning into my mother.

Ruth, my yoga teacher and friend, gives me the number of her osteopath who she highly recommends. Within minutes of texting him, he responds.

"Good morning. Today (Friday) would normally be by appointment only but since I don't have any, you can come from seven to eleven tonight."

It's bloody cold out but dry. A guy about ten years younger than me opens the small clinic's door. He reminds me of someone. After ten minutes, I realise it is 'Tom' a cartoon drawing from the kids' game of 'Guess Who'. When we finish the general health questionnaire, I stand in front of him without four of the five layers I am wearing. He steps back, looks at me, and says with a smile, "You have scoliosis."

"What?" The word scoliosis brings images of crippled, bent over old women who were neglected as children.

"Have you never noticed one of your shoulders is higher than the other?"

"I'm fifty and have just finished rearing two children, I haven't looked at myself in such detail in about thirty years."

He takes my photo with a specialist camera from the front and the side and shows me on the screen. "Look. You can see how one shoulder is lower than the other. Lots of people have it. I have it. There is no manipulation I can do to help so I won't waste your money. But I can refer you to someone who can help build your core strength which will help."

"But what about the pain?"

"Strengthening your core will help."

That sounds like it's going to take time.

I limp out of the clinic and I'm happy to see Ronan waiting for me with the heating on in the car.

"He had a look at me from across the room and said I have scoliosis." I'm looking in disbelief at Ronan.

"You mean you are a hunchback without a hump?"

"I don't think that's what it means, but I'm not sure... scoliosis means a curved spine doesn't it?"

"Yeah, I think so. Where's the curve?"

"I didn't ask. He must be wrong. Am I going to be a hunchback?"

With that, the church bells bonged their usual evening bongs.

"Well, there is one question you need to answer to find out... Do you have an urge to climb a bell tower like Quasimodo when you hear the bells?"

He has me laughing about it already, there's no way I could have scoliosis, it would have been detected earlier in my life.

"He's got it wrong, there's just something inflamed or in spasm from pushing Ma around," I decide on the way home.

The following day, I wake up with a new sense of determination. It's time Rosie started looking after herself. With online research I construct a fitness plan for myself of twenty minutes intermediate walking and running on the treadmill, a dance app and some lightweight arm and shoulder exercises and floor exercises aimed at strengthening my core.

Keen to get started, I'm down early to make Mam her breakfast.

"What are you doing today?" she asks as usual with the Irish news blaring from her Alexa.

"I'm going to do exercises for my back and then I am going to do some Italian."

"Who is he?"

"What?" Did my mother just make a dirty joke?

"Never mind. I'll help you. I was looking through the big dictionary in the sitting room last night and I found some good words."

She picks up her diary where she keeps note of everything and reads; "New words for today are Bozzo. Do you know what that is?"

"A name for a clown?"

"No, it's 'bump' and do you know what 'gonzo' is? I'll give you a clue; you are one if you don't know what it is."

"A muppet?"

"No a fool, you fool!"

"I think I'll stick to learning the verbs and writing a journal in Italian." And off I go back upstairs to start my new exercise routine and to do an Italian as my mother would like to believe.

By the end of the day, I couldn't remember any of the verbs I had learnt that morning but I remember 'bozzo' means bump and 'gonzo' means fool. Maybe mother does know best.

29

M am is determined to be independent in Italy during her stay this time. Besides walking across the street once per week to get her whiskey in the supermarket, she sometimes goes for a walk down to the lake path, pushing her wheelchair ahead of her. But even though the place is dripping in too much scenery, she finds something to complain about. This time it's about people not complaining.

"Why doesn't anyone complain about not having a path outside your house? It's disgraceful," she says as she carefully makes her way down the garden after one of her 'escapes', as she calls her walks. Ronan and I are down near the vines patching up holes under the fence to contain Paddy and Juno as they are back to ninja crawling underneath it rather than climbing over it. It's the perfect opportunity for us to remove more of the dangling lengths of rusty wire interlaced through the vines, no longer holding the vines up, just threatening to poke our eyes out.

"Probably because no one cares that there isn't a path outside our house other than you?" I say, trying to tame an out-of-control length of rusty wire.

"That's a massive shed you have there. You don't know how much space yous have." Mam's tone sounds like she should finish the sentence with 'you unappreciative gits' as she points at the illegal building covered in ivy at the end of our plot. Luca, Ronan and I had tackled the ivy during our first spring in the house but I learnt when you cut back ivy, it grows back twice as vigorous.

"I thought you were supposed to knock it down?" scoffs Mam, referring to the agreement when we were buying the house that the shed had to be DESTROYED.

"When we have the time and the money to knock it, we will," I say, mentally adding it to the end of my to-do list, hoping some form of illegal building police don't arrive at our door before we can afford to do it.

"I'd love to get in there and do a good clear out," Mam says dreamily. While I just see it as a mammoth task full of scuttling creatures, my mother romanticises it for the treasures she would find. "Before you tackle that Ma, maybe start by taking your breakfast dishes out of your room?" I joke.

"I'll get chickens and keep them in it," she announces. "And maybe goats. We could get a few goats, they'd keep your grass down. I love goats."

"When we moved over first, Lucia's dwarf goat had twin babies, she called them Rosie and Ronan. They were gorgeous."

"Yes, delicious meat," she says, smacking her lips together.

"Noooo, not gorgeous in that way. They were cute gorgeous! And we are not getting goats or chickens, we have enough to be thinking about at the moment! And at the moment I want a cup of tea, want one?"

"I met a woman today with a dog who speaks English," Mam says as we walk back up the garden arms linked.

"Wow, talented dog," says Ronan from behind us.

Mam ignores him and continues.

"She's Dutch, and she has a horse."

"Oh, I know the woman you are talking about. A tall woman," I say remembering her from one of our yoga classes.

"Yes, tall and looks like a horse herself," Mam still doesn't understand body shaming is not a done thing anymore. "I don't know where she got her dentures from, great big lumps of teeth, they don't suit her at all."

"Ma, she looks like Julia Roberts, they are her own teeth! And very healthy teeth by the look of them."

"No, I can't believe it, nothing grows naturally like that. She has too many teeth, God love her. So has Julia Roberts. Having teeth like that is not natural."

Mam, like a lot of Irish in her generation, had all her teeth gone by fourteen and her first set of dentures by fifteen. She often says it is one of the best things to ever have happened to her. "Everyone should have their teeth pulled out and get dentures. No more pain and horrible dentist visits."

Cooking is the other thing that keeps her busy the first weeks she's back. She doesn't open her Kinsale Cookery Book but she makes shepherd's pie, quiches and a favourite of ours; her potato cakes. Ronan and I savage them with lots of Irish butter and salt.

But after two weeks, the walking trips stop and so does the cooking. The adrenaline from arriving has subsided, she can't keep up the pace she has set herself and tires quickly.

Mam is back to giving mixed messages of what she wants me to deal with to make her more comfortable here. "Does that dog ever stop barking?" she'll say as I'm trying to fix something.

"Paddy stop barking," I shout out the window at our Houdini hound. We've given up on the fence being anyway effective.

"Don't stop him barking, he needs to communicate," she tuts.

She's knitting. There is something comforting about watching her knit, it brings back the feeling of me as a child watching her create crafts at Christmas, birthdays or just beside the turf fire with the TV on and a black and white fuzzy image talking in the background.

I help her find and pick up a dropped stitch. Her eyes aren't what they used to be, waiting for a cataract operation for the last year isn't helping.

"Where's your ring?" I say, suddenly noticing the yellow gold ring with the diamond set in a tall steepled four claw bezel setting was missing from her ring finger. The ugly thing had been part of her hand all my childhood as much as her fingers and thumbs were.

"On me finger."

"No, not your wedding ring, the ring. Aunt Kitty's ring."

"That old thing? I haven't worn it in years."

"But you always wore it, it's part of your hand, like it was part of Nanny's since Aunt Kitty died. The only family diamond."

"Ugly old thing in a Victorian setting. I gave it to Jack last year."

My mind does some sort of forward and backward flip. Mam had given our great aunt's engagement ring to my sister's son Jack? He did get engaged last year so maybe it was a nice senti-mental gesture, but I hoped he got it remodelled before giving it to his fiancé. That's what I had planned to do with it one day when my time of inheriting the only family diamond arrived... it was a joke between me and my sister Eileen, which one of us would inherit the diamond in the ugly monstrosity of a pedestal-like setting. Eileen surrendered her dibs on the inheri-tance after Nanny gave her opals to Eileen–she had them made into a necklace and earrings.

"He needed a holiday, so I told him to pawn it."

"You did... he did WHAT?"

"Will you ever relax Rosie. Sure, what would you be doing with it? You don't wear diamonds or gold."

My gasket blows. "THAT'S BECAUSE I DON'T HAVE ANY DIAMONDS OR GOLD! Are you serious? Did he pawn it?" Please say no.

"Sure, it wasn't worth anything–"

"I know it's not worth anything, but it's been on all the women's hands that I've loved and–"

She's not listening, talking over me. "–a few hundred euro, he only got a week on the Aran Islands out of it. Nothing special."

I had to leave the room. I've never punched a pillow before from rage. It's quite satisfying.

Mam knits and buys a book every three days from my Kindle account, blasts all the bad news from the Irish news stations from 7am to lunchtime and then watches endless reruns of English comedies from lunchtime to evening.

For the first couple of weeks, I stay in the sitting room to keep her company. While she knits, I switch between learning Italian and trying to learn to play the tin whistle.

"What are you doing with that?" Mam asks, looking over her glasses at the offending whistle.

"You should have sent me to better music classes," I say, trying to follow the YouTube channel about finger placement.

 "I've always badly wanted to play an instrument."

"Well, you are doing well playing an instrument badly." She chuckles and goes back to her knitting.

However, I break this routine as I need to get back to work and there are only so many hours of 'Only Fools and Horses' and 'Dad's Army' I can watch, so I work upstairs most mornings and afternoons, coming down to have lunch with her. This works out better for both of us as we have something to talk about over lunch and dinner, even if it is just about preparing the lunch and dinner.

Jim had obviously said something to her about Ronan and I needing our own time together. So she goes to her own bedroom at about eight to read or watch the Catherine Cookson DVDs I bought her for Christmas but she savaged all twenty-four of them before Christmas had arrived and she doesn't see the point of watching something a second time no matter how much she enjoyed it.

After a few weeks, she gets bored of her bedtime routine. "It's too early for me to go to bed, I'll sit here and watch something with yous if you don't mind." We don't mind but it does mean we have to go back to restricting our TV viewing to things that won't be laced with tuts and comments from a disapproving mother.

She still disapproves of Italian shops closing from 12.30 to 4pm. She's not ready to go anywhere in the morning and by four she wants dinner and to relax with her whiskey and knitting. Instead, she'll write lists of random items she needs me to get for her; Gesso for canvas, a darning needle, super glue, rubber gloves, hair spray. In Italy this requires visiting at least four different stores spread out over a fifty-mile radius.

But I make sure I get her the darning needle so she can finish the very nice jumper she is knitting me for Christmas. "There are mistakes, but they are on purpose," she says. "In case you fall into the lake and drown, we will be able to identify you... like what the women of the west of Ireland used to do for their fisherman."

"How many women wearing Aran jumpers are you expecting to fall into the lake who look so like me, that a dropped stitch will be the only way to tell us apart? Anyway Ma, I think you are mixing up Aran sweater patterns with Persian rug flaws?"

Fishing from curraghs (small Irish fishing boats) was a precarious occupation in the old days and the original knitters of the Aran islander sweaters each had their own identifying cable passed down through generations which was used as identification if tragedy struck.

"Ask that Persian friend of yours when you go to hers for dinner," Mam says, referring to Julie, our new friend from Iran who has moved to the area. While Julie is super clever, I am not sure if she will have insight into the minds of the women of the Aran Islands when they were knitting their jumpers.

Mam has decided she isn't taking Julie up on her kind invite to her joining us for dinner.

"It's bad enough having to eat Italian food, can't imagine what she'll be cooking, lovely and all as she is. I am fine by myself."

I am no longer tense about leaving Mam on her own like I was during her last stay; she feels safe here with the dogs.

Around the table at Julie's dinner party, there is an eclectic mix of Iranian, American, Scottish, English, Irish and Italian with an equally eclectic mix of professions; Italian author, opera singer, architect, yoga instructor, software engineer, ex-TV presenter, ex-war reporting cameraman, cosmetic surgeon, olive farmer and us. We feast on Persian food and discuss how one of the best things about moving to another country is the immigrant community you get to hang out with. I'm lucky to have met such a great group of people.

30

While Mam doesn't make many phone calls, except to her 'three lovely sons' every day, she still makes full use of her phone. She uses it like an intercom. The random calls I get from her always make me jump as I immediately think she has fallen over, but it's; 'The telly has gone off', 'The cat wants food,' 'I need another book on my pad thing,' 'There's a noise outside my bedroom door, I'm afraid to open it to look.'

She has also discovered the joy of scrolling on her phone. "She's seventy-two-years-old but with this makeup she only looks forty-two, click here to know her secret," she reads off her phone screen. "I'm clicking, but it's just showing ads. I can't find her secret to looking forty-two anywhere... Here, find her secret for me I want to look forty-two," Mam says, handing me her phone while I am trying to trace fifteen missing invoices for my end-of-year accounts. This is followed by, "That reminds me, I need you to go to the chemist and buy some new Max

Factor creme puff for my face," as she jots it onto her random must-have-object list.

"They don't sell a big range of beauty brand names in the chemist," I say, trying to think where have I ever seen makeup for sale in Italy other than the duty-free shops at the airport.

"Where do they buy makeup then?"

"I honestly don't know... I don't wear makeup."

"You should, your face is very red these days. Are you getting sunburnt?"

"Ma it's December and I'm fifty, so I'm probably just having a hot flush... or high blood pressure from dealing with you." We say these sort of things as jokes to one another but with a slight serious tone. "And anyway, they probably wouldn't have the light tone you like, they have darker skin here."

"That's ridiculous."

"I'll ask Izzy to bring it over when she's coming." The thought of Izzy and Luca arriving for Christmas puts a smile on my face. "We'll have to get the Christmas decorations out soon."

"Your face is probably red from the cold. You should put the heating on and warm up the house before the kids arrive."

The house isn't cold, and the weather is still dry but there is a bite to the air and giving Izzy and Luca's rooms a blast of heat for an hour or two each day isn't a bad idea.

"Good idea," I say, flicking the switch on the thermostat in the hallway just outside the sitting room. But nothing happens. I try turning it off and turning it back on again. Still nothing happens.

"Did you switch something off at the main box?" I shout to Ronan. "I'm trying to put the heating on."

Ronan comes out to the thermostat and turns it off and on, as if him doing it would make it work better than the way I have done it.

"Heh, nothing is happening." He sounds surprised. "It's probably air. We'll need to drain the radiators to get the air locks out and top up the system. I'll go around the radiators and open the valves to let the air escape and you stay in the Star Trek room and open the valve when the dial drops below two bars to let more water into the system. Okay?"

"Why can't anything be easy?" I say, not delighted with having to do this with a brand-new modern heating system. I sit for fifteen minutes, balanced on the watering can in our boiler room, and watch the pressure dial. There are lots of shiny new valves, dials and pipes managing the heating and hot water of our three floors. It looks like a control panel wall from a black and white movie spaceship, that's why we call it the Star Trek room. The pressure dial doesn't drop below two like we thought it would if the system had air in it. Ronan comes down and presses some buttons.

"What are you doing?"

"Resetting it," he says confidently.

"You know how to reset it?"

"No."

"Maybe just press the reset button then, rather than all the bloody buttons," I say, annoyed he yet again refuses to read instructions.

"Stop telling me what to do."

"I have to, as you don't know what you are doing."

"Neither do you."

"I know! But I also know pressing all the buttons when you don't know what you are doing is not what to do... I'm going to have a shower, I'm meeting Shelly for a drink."

Halfway through my shower, just as my hair is full of suds, the water runs cold then freezing. "Are you still fiddling with knobs down there?" I shout out the window towards Ronan who's below in the Star Trek room.

"I'm trying to fix the heating."

"You have knocked the hot water off."

"I don't know how, I've tried all combinations. Not sure which one knocked off the water."

"Bloody hell!" I grumble, rinsing off as much of the shampoo suds I can for as long as I can bear before getting out of the freezing shower as quickly as possible.

Dangling my head down, I enjoy the heat of the hair dryer warming my cold head. But I smell smoke. Tossing my head back, I immediately turn off the hair dryer and pat my head vigorously to ensure my hair is not on fire while I make my way to the mirror. Hair is good. Well, it's all over the place, like I've pulled a magpie's nest apart looking for jewels, but at least it is not on fire.

A film of wispy smoke is hanging in the air, making it look like I'm in some mystic scene from one of the Highlander movies. "That's not good," I'm thinking. Maybe trying to turn the heating on has shorted a circuit somewhere and caused a fire.

As I run down the stairs, the smoke screen lessens. "Look!" says Ronan, grinning, as he has lit the first fire in the beautiful fireplace Alex renovated for us. It looks magnificent, but there's no smoke in the room, so the smoke upstairs can't be caused by it billowing out of the fireplace.

"We won't need the heating on downstairs at all with the pellet stove in the sitting room and this in here," says Ronan, delighted he has come up with a solution to the defunct heating system and has an open fire to play with again.

"There's smoke upstairs. We must have a crack in the chimney somewhere."

"... or maybe there were more electric wires through it," says Ronan gravely. It was not something I had thought off. As we both reach the stairs, the faint smoke wisps have turned into a fog and the thick smell of burning is travelling down the stairwell.

Like the time we discovered the doors were missing, we are taking two steps at a time, up our four flights of eight steps, to locate the source of the smoke. But there isn't a source. It's just there hanging in the air around the hallway where the chimney is, spreading into the rooms.

"Maybe the chimney is on fire?" Ronan hangs out of a window to see if he can see sparks coming from the chimney top. The smoke is just somehow magically appearing in the hall with no sign of where it is coming from.

"It is seeping through the walls of the chimney... it must need a new flue," I say. I don't exactly know what a flue looks like but I know it lines a chimney and if a flue is old and damaged or nonexistent it causes smoke. I know this from my Dad who I had many conversations with about chimneys and importance of flues, laced with warnings that you shouldn't buy a house with cracks in a chimney breast, ever since I was a kid sitting beside open fires with him.

"If you contact Alex about the chimney, I will get on to the heating company about the boiler," I say as we watch Ronan's fire burn out and the smoke lessen.

Ronan isn't feeling great, he hasn't for a few days. As the temperature drops to mild winter levels, Ronan's temperature goes up. A blue line confirms his fear—it's Covid.

So that's him packed off to his wing of the house, leaving me to fix the heating. I take a test too, it's clear, but I'll keep my distance from Mam for a couple of days just in case. I just hope she doesn't get it.

I request someone to come to service the boiler and reset it. A guy arrives two days later and with my translation app and patchy Italian I explain the heating is not working. He takes the boiler apart, cleans it or whatever servicing involves and puts it back together again. The service costs €100.

"There is nothing wrong with the boiler. I have reset it and your hot water is working. For the heating it is the pump that is the problem, you need a new pump."

"How do I get one of them?"

"From the installer. It should be under guarantee."

So I contact Danny Boy who says Roberto will call in and fix the problem. However, the pumps were only guaranteed for one year.

Roberto arrives the next day and stomps around in his usual way with a cigarette hanging from the side of his mouth. "There is nothing wrong with the pump," he says. "It is an electrical problem."

We need to pay him €60 for his call-out fee. So I get back on to Danny. He apologies but he can't come he's too busy and not in the area.

"Well, can you recommend someone in my area?"

"No, I am sorry I don't know anyone."

In the meantime, Alex comes to inspect the chimney.

"The problem with the chimney is in the attic, the mortar between the bricks is brittle with age. I will come and plaster it, that will fix it don't worry. I have a cousin who is an electrician, I will ask him to come this afternoon to fix your heating."

I'm going out to get Ronan another heap of Covid tests as he is testing twice a day so he can get out of his room at the earliest possible stage to help find a solution to our heating issue.

"I am running out to the pharmacy," I shout to Mam.

"Wait I need something," she calls back.

I shouldn't have said anything, she has a list of things she needs ready. As she lists them, I'm clocking the time each will take to find;

"Stamps"; Ugh not the post office... Two hours queuing.

"Christmas cards"; Italians don't really send cards, I'll need to go to the mall to find a stationery shop that will possibly have them... Two more hours and in a different direction.

"Ingredients for mince pies. Suet, raisins, currants and sultanas"; I've seen raisins in some supermarkets but not currants and sultanas. The Italians prefer to keep their grapes in liquid form rather than different varieties of dryness. And suet? Isn't that some sort of dried fat from animal organs used in Dickens's time?... Two hundred years back in a time machine.

Alex's cousin arrives and after two hours of work, he says there is nothing wrong with the electrics; it's a problem with the boiler and both pumps are broken.

He doesn't charge us. I'm at my wits end; my elderly mother is living with me, my husband has Covid, the weather is getting colder and no one seems to be able to fix the heating system that is still so new some parts still have plastic wrapping. Christmas is only ten days away and Italy and its workforce are already winding down.

I send Danny Boy another text with a plea of help, but this time he doesn't even respond.

Nearly two weeks after our troubles with our heating were discovered, Ronan's test gives him the all-clear, and he contacts Lucia as a last hope she might know someone who knows someone. "I will ask my boyfriend Davide, he knows everyone. But send me the boiler service guy's phone number I will tell them they have to get their ass down here at the same time and find the problem with the plumber."

The following day, a guy called Bob arrives with his tattooed assistant, just as the boiler maintenance van pulls up at the same time. Hopefully they will be my saviours.

31

"I'm going to park the van across the driveway gates so they can't get out until its fixed," says Ronan. He's not joking. The three guys have been up and down the stairs several times and in and out of our Star Trek control room. Switches have been clicked, covers removed, pipes tapped.

"Italians don't respond well to being captured," I say to Ronan, hearing his plan. "I've a better idea, something they can't resist and will make any Italian man desperate to help."

"You are going to walk around in your underwear?"

"God no, that would just make them run from the house, anyway it's too cold for a tactic like that."

"What then?"

"A Nonna in need. It's time to roll out the Mamma," I say, going into my mother's room where she is still having her early morning cup of tea.

"If you can get up soon and when the guys are in the dining room, walk into the kitchen with a woolly jumper on and this hat," I whisper, not that the lads would understand what I was saying even if they did overhear.

"I'm not wearing that hat, it will flatten my hair... Leave it to me."

In the meantime, Alex has arrived and has lit a small fire in the fireplace to try to locate the problem areas. Smoke fills the first floor and is floating down the stairs. The heating guys are arguing in the dining room and I am trying to work out what they are saying while in the kitchen making them coffee.

Bob's on the phone to Danny Boy blaming him and saying he needs to come out and fix the problem he created, while the tattooed younger guy and the boiler guy are having a heated discussion with a lot of hand gestures.

And then Bob stops mid-sentence. They all do. In the sudden silence I hear scuffing feet and glance into the room from the kitchen to see Mam shuffling out, a fog of smoke following her as she walks into the middle of where they are standing; the tartan fluffy blanket off the sofa over her head and wrapped around her, a hot water bottle gripped to her chest, and the long scarf she is knitting looped around her neck with the knitting needle still attached to the length dangling at her knees. It clanks off the metal walking stick she is leaning heavily on, exaggerating the hump on her back.

"HO MOLTO FREDDO," she announces. (I am very cold).

Bloody hell, she's learnt lines in Italian to go with her acting skills!

Bob hangs up while Danny is still shouting. The boiler guy blushes. And the younger guy glances towards me sympathetically. Bob barks an order at the young guy and the boiler man scuttles out to the Star Trek room again to try something else.

Mam has made it to the kitchen and winks at me. "Give us a glass of water, I'm sweating in this blanket."

An hour later, Bob is on the phone to Lucia's boyfriend, Davide, and hands his phone to me for the translation.

"The heating is now working," says Davide. "But there are a couple of problems with the system that need to be worked out after Christmas. The thermostat on the second floor is faulty."

"Oh, that's the one the first lot of builders poured water into," I say, relieved the problem is just a replacement thermostat not a pump or boiler system.

"You poured water into it?" asks Davide.

"No, the first lot of builders did. And they didn't replace it but the second lot did."

"Ah, you didn't replace it, that is the problem," he says thinking he understood my riddle.

"No, the second lot did. But it was secondhand."

"Sex in your hand?"

"No, it was... yes if he can come and put a new thermostat on the first and second floor after Christmas." I'm getting exasperated at my lack of being able to converse in Italian.

"You want two?"

"Yes, because the second builder changed the one on the top floor too for some reason I can't remember. So we have three different thermostats in the house and I would like them all the same and new please."

"Okay that is the problem then, he will come after Christmas. For now, you turn the heating on and off on the first floor at the electric mains switch."

The heat is on, even though the house is warm enough, but I feel hopeful again and I am decorating the bannisters with ivy and Christmas lights. The younger guy trotting up and down the stairs collecting their tools gives me a smile every time he goes past, probably because I am giving him an encouraging smile each time he passes.

Outside, as I am paying them €100 for five hours' work, he is rolling up the leg of his combats to reveal his tattooed attractive hairy leg. Is he doing this for my benefit? I am staring, so it is working. But really, why is he rolling up his trouser leg? Maybe he is showing the older guy the unfinished tattoo he is getting. But the older guy is not looking, just me staring as I hand over the €100 and he's smiling at me. Maybe he's trying to get a tip. Maybe I should have given him a tip.

"They are in exceptionally high spirits considering they have to run off to another job," I say, making a cup of tea for a plaster-splattered Alex.

"Of course, it is because it is la tredicesima–the thirteenth. People who work for other people in Italy get their salaries once a month–twelve times, but around Christmas, they get their salary a thirteenth time. Not me, as I work for myself."

"It looks like the young guy is going to spend it all on tattoos."

"Did you hear what he said about asking for a photo of you?"

"Eh no!" Was I blushing? I turn away to take the teabag out of the cup even though I had already removed it.

"He wants a tattoo on his leg of his Nonna with your hair. She had the same long grey hair as you, but he does not have a photo of her like that."

Ronan's coffee goes up his nose and he's spluttering.

"I remind him of his Nonna?" I am not screeching with anger exactly, elevated with disgruntledness would better describe my voice.

Even after Alex's thick plastering in the attic, when we light a test fire, the walls still billow smoke.

"You need a flue in the chimney," says Alex.

"I know, I told you that," I say.

He ignores me. "We will come back and do it after Christmas."

We never see Bob and his tattooed assistant again, but the heating works like a dream.

Five days before Christmas, my back is so bad I'm finding it difficult to get up from lying position and walking is so painful I am struggling after ten minutes and getting in and out of the car is a mild form of torture. If I am to finish this house and garden, I need a functional back.

So I go to Doctor Fab Chicken and he gives me a shot to relax the muscle and anti-inflammatories for five days while he tells me about how he doesn't sleep well and while awake last night he counted the number of conferences he has been at this year. Eighteen. I'm not sure how he has time while working in the hospital and running a GP service. I tell him to drink chamomile tea.

The anti-inflammatories offer enough relief for me to go Christmas grocery shopping and buy a 4kg turkey in the local store for €26 and lots of fresh vegetables.

"Buy me extra whiskey just in case," calls Mam as I am leaving for the store.

"Just in case of what?"

"In case they run out over Christmas." She does a loud 'HA, HA' like some crazed scientist making a discovery. She often does this. People find it hilarious. I used to find it hilarious. But not anymore, it's just bloody annoying.

"They don't drink like that in Italy at Christmas. Maybe they'll overdo it on wine and digestivos but not whiskey."

"Well, buy me extra anyway in case someone forgets to buy me a Christmas present and you can give them a bottle to give to me to save them embarrassment." Her logic is amazing. And there's that 'HA HA' again. But I'm okay, my blood is staying below boiling point as it's a great day.

With the house warm, the fridge fully stocked and candles flickering in the fireplace for atmosphere instead of logs, Ronan and I go to the airport with hearts full of excitement and love to collect our kids for Christmas.

32

The evening Izzy and Luca arrive for Christmas, we go out to a restaurant we haven't been to since before Covid. A murmuration of starlings dances above the lake. Mam pushes her wheelchair, using it as a walker and a way to carry her large bag of must-have things. This includes a hammer in case she gets mugged and a pack of cards (in case we bore her?). And, of course, the obligatory bottle of holy water alongside the emergency bottle of whiskey. My back is hurting so bad, I feel she should push me along.

"This restaurant is very popular for their torte and sandwiches," I hear Luca explain to his granny. I like the way he still peppers words of Italian into conversation by accident.

"Tortoise sandwiches?" Mam exclaims. "Oh I wouldn't like that."

At the restaurant. Izzy and I order pizza. Luca says he is considering the tortoise sandwich but has decided to go for cinghiale ragu instead. Mam orders a calzone with cheese, truffle and ham against everyone's advice as we all know it will be too tough for her teeth. Izzy has described it to her as 'a pie'.

"Whoever made that pastry should be shot. It's tough as old boots," Mam says, digging into what looks to us like the perfect calzone.

"It's not a pastry pie Mam... it's more like a sandwich."

"Sandwich? What sort of excuse of a sandwich is that? It's not one of those tortoise sandwiches you were talking about Luca, is it?"

We all want dessert including Mam who has polished off the calzone.

"I'll have that one," she says to the waiter, pointing to the ice-cream picture. He obliges and brings her the novelty ice-cream in the shape of a penguin with a plastic spoon attached.

"Hold on Ma, I'll get you a proper spoon."

"Scusi," I say to the passing waiter. "Possiamo cucchiaio?" The waiter smiles and walks away.

"What the hell, Mum?" says Luca laughing. "You just said to the waiter, "Can we spoon?"

I've gone past the point of blushing about my Italian language mistakes, I'm never going to get it right.

With drinks and desserts, the bill comes to €100 for five of us.

"That's it," says Mam, walking back to the car. "That's my last visit to a restaurant. Don't ask me to come out again, I am happier with my own food at home, rather than their stupid pies, tortoise sandwiches and pizzas without pineapple."

Mam not wanting to go to any stores before 12.30 or after 4pm, or going to friends' houses or restaurants for dinner is really limiting my options of where to take her. But for now, she is happy. 'One day at a time' has not just become a mantra but a way of life for me.

I watch our two kids walking down the cobbled street towards the car, their laughter together sounds like the most beautiful song to my ears. Time is so precious, Luca only has four days off work so he will fly back to Ireland the day after Christmas, Izzy will stay an additional few days.

Having us live in three different countries so early in their adult lives was never how I expected life would go. Their laughter and conversations tell me they are doing better without me trying to over-manage them. But it's so hard to let go. 'One day at a time,' I tell myself and today is to be enjoyed.

Karen comes over with her son Charlie. We haven't seen each other in ages as we have both been so busy with work. We play board games and feast on great food and pull Christmas crackers I brought from Ireland.

On Christmas morning, instead of Mass, Mam is watching Songs of Praise. "I like the singing. Our priest once said to us during Mass, 'I want you all to sing like protestants'. They do it better."

We all busy ourselves in the kitchen preparing the feast. This year Ronan is taking charge of the dessert as Izzy has brought him over the ingredients for what was his Christmas speciality in Ireland: A sherry trifle.

It turns out perfectly. Strawberry jelly with pears and sponge with just the right amount of sherry soaked into it, with cream and chocolate flaked on top.

But before it, we have turkey, gravy, stuffing, carrots, broccoli and potatoes done in three ways. We are Irish after all.

And if we hadn't eaten enough, I can't help snacking on the traditional Italian cakes, pandoro and panettone, we have been gifted. Pandoro is a light, fluffy cake dusted with sugar, while panettone is a denser, fruitier cake with candied fruit and raisins.

A game of cards, gift giving, music, lots of chat and calls to my brothers. No time for Christmas movies this year, I need to just absorb every minute of our time together. But it all passes too quickly and soon Luca is winging his way back to Ireland.

Izzy and I go for daily walks down to the lakeside, having long mother-and-daughter talks, figuring out the world and our lives. The walks are part of my self-created program to help my back.

As Izzy is no longer a child but a fully baked adult with her own wisdom and insights, I find myself opening a stress release valve.

"I'm so bloody angry all the time. Snapping at your Dad, irritated by my Mam, I've even been impatient with you and Luca at times. It's like I'm losing the ability to love. I don't know what's happening to me."

I don't tell her I've already figured out it is not because of the grief for my father but for the grief I am already feeling for Jim. The torturous impending sadness which I can do nothing to stop. It could be a year, five years, eleven years. Whatever length of time it is going to take, it is going to happen. The grief is already here.

I don't tell her my mind sometimes ebbed towards the most horrible thought; the unfairness, the annoyance, the frustration of me having to again be the one to tell our mother another one of us has... "Stay the hell away," I'd scream at the thought. I couldn't let it in... I have created a defence system; if I stay annoyed, there will be no emotional space left for the gut-wrenching sadness to take its place and consume me.

In the last thirteen months, annoyance and anger allowed a glimmer of another weird negative feeling I've never experienced before. Envy poked its head in briefly one day; "Your mother had her favourite brother and sister to talk to, to visit, to enjoy up until she was eighty-five," Envy spat at me from around the doorpost. "You? You're only fifty and your only sister is gone and now Jim's going to go too. And your mother had her husband for sixty-six years. Your husband is sixteen years older than you and let me tell you he's not getting any younger," laughed Envy. "Your mother is a lucky woman, let me tell you."

"How did this thought enter my head about my own mother?" I ask Izzy. "I am turning into a horrible person who even I don't want to be around."

All the anger I have been feeling, the resentment and sadness has me believing this about myself more and more.

But my daughter is wiser than her years, she has been researching podcasts about grief to help us through the past, present and future. "Grief brings up lots of emotions; anger and envy are some of them."

She teaches me something she learnt from one podcast recently; "You are not the person of your first thoughts. In other words, if you have a horrible initial reactive thought, that is not yours, it is not you. It is just an impulse. It's the following thoughts that are you, the ones you are in control of. You are not in control of the first thought that comes into your mind. You are not a horrible person Mam, it's grief you are feeling, that's all."

Our walk around the town leads us up to the old fort with the amazing lake view and then on to the old cemetery full of family mausoleums. I like mausoleums, it must be comforting to know where you are going to end up and your family are around you even if you are dead.

They put photos of the person within onto gravestones here. There is a guy with sunglasses and a moustache from the Sixties, black and white photos of men in uniforms from the war years and women looking like movie stars. All these people who have walked the streets of this town for generations before us makes me wonder where the previous owner of our house, Paolo Legume, is buried.

After a couple of hours, we walk up the track from the lake towards the T-junction near our house. Just as we reach the side of the road, BAM!

"He hit the ape!" exclaims Izzy as we watch the three-wheeled ape spin on the tarmac, toppling away from the car with the squashed bonnet that had edged out too quick.

I stand for a moment, staring at the ape on its side with its front wheel spinning and then realise we were the only ones on the scene.

"Call emergency services," I say to Izzy, automatically pushing her back with my hand as I jog towards the ape.

"What's the number?"

"118... I think?"

There's no movement as I approach the ape and I am thinking I could be about to see my first dead body in Italy besides all the holy ones lying around in churches. But, I am greeted by something more surprising. A man with a gun.

33

The man in the up-turned ape is about seventy-five. He's dressed in faded hunter green combats and hunting vest over a washed-out blue shirt. There's a small cut on his bald tanned head but the blood doesn't reach the tufts of grey above his ears. We're about the same height. His blue eyes look dazed.

"Va bene signore?" I ask.

A woman coming out of the supermarket has arrived on the scene and is checking on the man in the car with the crumpled front. She's on the phone, talking to emergency services. Two men come out of a house and together we help the elderly, but capable man climbs out the top of his ape. He sits at the side of the road on a low wall while the two men in their late forties rock the ape to get it back in its upright position. I grab the front windscreen just as it pops out and is about to fall to the ground. It's then, when I'm there standing holding the windscreen I notice the dog inside the ape struggling to find his footing and the central battery about to fall on him. 'Aspettate!' I shout—wow I remembered the plural form for 'you wait'.

The men ignore me; they are busy doing manly things. I can hear the approaching ambulance siren. "Il cane, il cane," I holler. Izzy is by my side. I throw her the windscreen and I grab hold of the falling battery just as they launch the ape into a forty-five-degree angle and then upright.

The dog stays on the floor of the passenger side, waiting for his owner's command. Izzy opens the door and with a low command from the old man, the dog hops out and cuddles his head onto his master's lap with a slow wag of his tail. The dog's name is Toby—the same name Mam gave our dogs growing up. The man strokes the dog's head, receiving equal comfort to what he is giving.

The police are already on the scene, questioning the other driver, and the ambulance has parked and paramedics are checking out the old man's head. We've picked up the full petrol can from the road and put it in the back of the ape along with his windscreen and a dead pheasant.

We don't want to hang around but being witnesses we feel we should offer a testimonial of some sort. So we go up to the policewoman, "We saw it. Do you need us to stay here?"

"How long you stay here?" she asks in English after suffering my patchy Italian.

"I live here, but my daughter leaves in two days."

"Come at 1pm tomorrow to the station to do a report."

As the following day was going to be Izzy's last full day, we had plans to go to the Christmas market in Florence but we sacrifice it for our civic duty and go to the police station at the required time. It's closed for 'riposa' and there is no notice of opening times. It's sunny and the air is deliciously crisp. "Fancy lunch by the lake?" I say to Izzy.

Wrapped in our overcoats, we sit at our favourite outside bar and have a slice of pizza.

"So, what are your New Year's resolutions?" asks Izzy. "You are always setting goals, what's this year's?"

I sit back and think of what to say. I didn't want to tell her the truth–that I feared what the new year would bring. And for the first time ever with no plan for the future, my life feels like a blank canvas.

In previous years, I usually had weddings as time stamps for the rest of the things in my life to pivot around, including trips home to Ireland to see my parents and brother. Without weddings absorbing fifty hours of my week and my Mam back living with me, I had nothing to use as a fulcrum.

"My New Year's resolution is to take it one day at a time... to stop being angry at everything... To stop facing each day as if I am going into battle."

"Mine is to find three things to be grateful for each day," she says, biting off another piece of her pizza margherita. "And to adopt a word for the year. Have you heard about that? I read it in an article somewhere online. You adopt a word to remind yourself of every day. Mine is going to be 'determination'."

I think about it for a moment and without hesitation I say, "Love... 'love' will be my word of the year."

The next day, after hugging Izzy goodbye at the airport, I'm back in the house. Standing in one of our rain showers with the perfect temperature of water pouring over my head, I get a flashback of the schizophrenic dribble and sticky shower curtain we had in Giovanni's for three years.

Jim is still lamenting my expulsion of the red retro bathroom. I get it. I too was hesitant about removing the kitsch, groovy, headache-inducing orangey-red 1960s bathroom suite and red floral tiles. It was so gaudy it had a striking beauty.

However, my restoration efforts don't go as far as cleaning brown streaks from toilet bowls. Okay, I know the brown steaks were caused by water calcite and I'd read it could be treated with vinegar and some vigorous scrubbing with bread soda, but somehow the idea of it did not excite me in the slightest.

Also, all the lead and rusty water piping needed to be replaced and new sewerage pipes installed so the walls had to be drilled into, destroying the groovy tiling. And we needed a shower rather than a cast-iron half bath.

We found a pile of the red tiles in the shed, left over from the Sixties, so I'll do something with them at some stage. A tabletop or something, in memory of the Austin Powers bathroom.

I think about Izzy's new practice of listing three things she is grateful for and although with her gone back to London I feel lower than my usual low; I think about it...

"I'm grateful to have a hot shower on demand in a nice bathroom," I say to myself. "I am grateful to live in this beautiful house in this beautiful country."

I feel better already.

34

"Did you know the Mona Lisa doesn't have eyelashes or eyebrows? The word for eyelashes is 'ciglio' and eyebrows 'sopraciglia'. Sopra means above. So eyebrows translates as 'above eyelashes'. Isn't that funny?"

Since Izzy brought the requested Max Factor creme puff, Mam has given up trying to find out what the seventy-two-year-old's secret to looking forty-two was, and has gone back to feeding me her scrolling finds of Italian heritage and words.

I'd just finished doing a Zoom yoga class with Ruth. Having removed inflammatory foods from my diet such as sugar and grains and doing yoga daily, my back pain has eased. I refuse to believe I have scoliosis; I just need to get fitter.

Ronan is outside in the damp morning fog constructing a net to catch some of the falling persimmon fruit splattering the courtyard daily, making it as slippery as an ice rink.

"Ronan, what do you want to do in the next five years?" I say, feeling a bit lost at sea without having any proper tickable goals for the year ahead. My brain is a completely blank canvas as far as the next five years are concerned.

"Eh, I don't know, I'm old now. I don't know if I will last five years," he jokes. He's been joking about being old since I met him when he was thirty-six. But I'm not finding the joke funny anymore. A cold sweat breaks across my back making me shudder. "I'm serious, what do you see yourself doing in the next five years?"

"Just a quiet life. Painting perhaps."

"Is that it?"

"I don't know, what do you want to do?"

A sense of panic fills me... I want freedom, I want to escape the suffocating cocoon closing in on us.

"I want a healthy body and to be able to go wherever I want to go, whenever I want," I say.

"Off you go then," he says, going back to fixing his net.

"Right," I say sharply at his dismissive attitude to my profound statement. "I'm going to get fit and travel. I don't know where to yet, but I feel I need to get my body ready for adventure. I'm going to start looking after myself, put me first."

"Good, about time too."

"To start with... I am going to have a bath." I sound like Bridget Jones.

"You mean you are going to use that clothes horse in your room for its actual purpose?" He's sniggering.

I hadn't told him why I hadn't used the beautiful free-standing bath Alex had installed in our bedroom, making it look like a luxury hotel suite. But the truth is, I was afraid it would fall through the ceiling with the weight of water and me in it.

Izzy had given me expensive bath stuff as part of my Christmas present, so I intrepidly fill the bath to a halfway point and gingerly slide in. After five minutes of not plummeting into the dining room below, I relax.

We had a small celebration as we rang in the new year a couple of nights ago. A necessity for Mam as she always loved a new year's party, even if it was just her and Dad and me, the teenage gooseberry, as they danced by candlelight in the sitting room, before shouting out the countdown and singing Auld Lang Syne.

The new year of 2023 marks the house's one hundredth birthday. We know this as 1923 is carved into the keystone above the front door.

I feel I should do something to mark its centenary. A 1920s party would be the obvious choice, but I am not keen on throwing parties, especially at the moment. I'll come up with something, I am sure.

I'm wondering what news would have filtered through the speaker of the 1920s gramophone radio we rescued from the attic. It's waiting for its turn to be lovingly restored in the dining room below, which I thankfully still haven't plummeted into.

So much was happening around the year The Sighing House was built; the fascist party became the ruling party in Italy and King Victor Emmanuel III appointed Mussolini prime minister. It was the same year Adolf Hitler was arrested and later sentenced to prison.

The Soviet Union was formed in 1923 and the Hollywood Sign went up in California. The first issue of Time magazine was published and the discovery of insulin revolutionised the treatment of diabetes.

The family of the house probably watched slapstick comedy movies with Charlie Chaplin, Buster Keaton, and Harold Lloyd. As they were silent movies, I am guessing they were shown in Italy too? Cartoon characters like Felix the Cat, Mickey Mouse, and Betty Boop were created in the 1920s. But it wasn't until 1932 when Topolino Giornale, a new weekly comic for kids, was published that Mickey Mouse's first Italian story came to be.

I wonder did the radio treat the Legume family to jazz for the first time while they walked through the house in flapper dresses and bobbed hairstyles? Did they bask in the Cabaret culture during the 1920s or would it have been gloomy after the First World War. Was there less frivolity in Italy than elsewhere?

Mam hasn't come out with us much since her decision to stay in the house but I feel she is getting bored, in need of conversation with people other than Ronan or me. Mam comes alive with an audience, she lifts people's spirits and has lots to talk about but she has already said it all to us. She finds sitting in normal chairs uncomfortable and needs to keep her legs up.

She is finding it more difficult to walk around and can't stand for any length of time. My plan is to add her as my dependent when I get my Tessera Sanitaria.

"Remember to follow up with the paperwork about the health card," I remind Ronan after my bath.

He contacts the office in Ireland and they message back; 'We are waiting on the front page of the document from you.' He sends it again. Italy isn't the only place with inefficient systems for bureaucracy.

Lucia calls in to wish Mam a happy new year and bring her flowers.

"That's very kind of you," says Mam, always touched by Lucia's kindness.

"Would you like some tea?"

"Yes, thank you," says Lucia.

"Make Lucia some tea," Mam instructs me.

Lucia smiles. "Rosie, you have herbal teas?"

"She does, doesn't she? I've always said that about her," says Mam.

"Said what?" Lucia asks, confused.

"Terrible knees, Rosie has always had terrible knees, they were always knobbly but not so much now with all that fat on her."

"Mother of God!" I say, leaving the room where Lucia is dying laughing.

A few days later, Ronan calls the health service in Ireland again. 'We are just reviewing it. The application is missing a signature.'

He sends the page with the missing signature, and we wait again. My back waits and my water balloon waits.

But then everything becomes a lot more urgent.

35

"Patricia really isn't getting the leaf thing, I just found a flower in our mailbox," says Ronan, referring to his method of leaving a large leaf from our magnolia tree stuck between the lips of our mailbox slot. When mail is stuck through its mouth, the leaf falls out so then we know to check the mailbox. We don't get much mail, so it saves us checking every day.

It worked until Patricia became our mail woman. We discovered she had been delivering mail and then diligently picking up the fallen leaf and inserting it back into the mailbox. It was only when she asked us one day "Why the leaf?" that we found weeks of mail in the box. Ronan explained his reasoning, and she seemed to understand, but today she has posted a flower into the mailbox with a letter addressed to me.

The envelope looked official and serious. Maybe Patricia knows the envelope the department uses and posts a flower to all her female customers in receipt of one on her route, as it is from the mammogram department of Perugia hospital. With my translation app, I read that 'they' have tried calling me many times since my routine exam in November. I need to call them urgently. My stomach tightens.

I call, my insides acidic with anticipation of having to make such an important call in a foreign language. I just hope the person answering the phone can speak English.

She can't speak English. I have learnt new words in preparation including; Seno: Breast. Seni: Breasts–not to be confused with Sensa, which means without.

She asks me to spell my name. The Italians have a phonetic alphabet system based on letters relating to regions.

I'm regretting skipping that lesson.

"Eh per Empoli?" she asks. I am wondering if Empoli begins with an 'i' or an 'e'. "Sì" I say, then follow with "not 'c'." I get to 'D' and try to think of something in Italian beginning with "D per Dada? Dogana?" This is ridiculous.

Eventually she finds my file using my date of birth and I hear her asking someone in the background if they speak English. I hear the word 'Fuori' meaning outside. The person who might speak some English is outside having a cigarette.

"Sono preoccupata," I say. Which means 'I am worried'. I am careful not to say "sono occupata" which means 'I am busy'. I had a habit of confusing these when we first moved to Italy and regularly asked Giovanni, our landlord, if he was very worried.

I'm on the phone that has been left lying on the administrator's desk for five minutes, listening to them chatter before a door squeaks and footsteps get closer.

"Buongiorno," says a male voice. And for another three or four minutes saying nothing and then he says in Italian, "You speak some Italian?".

"A little," I say.

"You need to come for an exam... profondo... I don't know the word in English."

I do. The last time I heard it was when they were describing the cut on Lucas's arm. Deep.

Like the breath I am taking as my heart races.

"We have been trying to contact you. Please come Monday evening at eight to the address on the letter."

I don't know how this will work as I got the initial appointment on my temporary TS which has now expired. I still don't have my health card. I have fallen between the cracks of the European system.

I came to Italy healthy. I turned fifty without ever needing an operation or medication of any kind. In less than six months, they have diagnosed me as having scoliosis, a massive water balloon and now this. All from routine tests. My body is falling to bits.

I'm afraid to do the other two routine exams they have sent me appointments for, in case they find something there too.

And then the awful words jump to attention; 'What if?'

My mind immediately goes to Mam. She's content here. We have both got low expectations of each other this time, but I can't help but feel she's bored. It was particularly when she stated "I'm bored" several times in the last two weeks that has made me think this.

But what if something happened to me... what if I needed hospital care or long-term treatment like Jim?... What would happen to Mam?... I couldn't leave Ronan to care for her and, anyway, he might be in prison by the summer... unlikely but still a niggling possibility... What if she had a fall and broke something and was in hospital without the language and without people other than me to visit her?

It's Friday, and with an appointment looming for Monday evening which could drastically change my year ahead and life, I need to think fast.

As if by magic, Sharon, a friend back in Ireland texts me. "I was just in with my mum and she says hello! You should see her nursing home, it's like a bloody resort, lots of activities, outings, great food, nice rooms. We should check ourselves in! So relieved, she loves living there."

Ever since I was a child Mam had it drilled into me, "Never put me in a nursing home... shoot me before putting me into one of those places." It was often when we were walking back from visiting my great Aunt Kitty, who Mam helped find a better place to live, away from the dreadful so-called nursing homes Kitty had been in. But that was the Seventies, and by the sounds of my friend's experience, things have changed since then.

Hesitantly, I google nursing homes in Ireland; I feel I'm betraying my Mam... but I'm just looking... arts and crafts, live music, bingo, gardening, baking, outings, there's even a home with its own pub! Bloody hell, these are like hippy communes for old people. They sound fantastic! She'd have people to chat to, share stories and laugh with and we'd know she was being looked after should anything happen to us.

So I go downstairs to broach the subject.

"You know my friend Sharon? She went to visit her mum in her nursing home and she said it was beautiful, they do arts and crafts, and all sorts of activities, they have musicians coming in once a week and—"

"I'd love to live somewhere like that. It's been bothering me what I'm going to do, as I can't stay here once it gets hot and I really can't stand the idea of going back and living on my own. It really doesn't suit me. I was thinking of asking Jim if he'd come stay with me a few nights or I go stay in his place."

"Ma, that isn't an option... Jim needs to focus on himself at the moment."

"I'd go somewhere like that place in a heartbeat, but I could never afford it."

"Sharon told me there is a government aid scheme to help with the cost, will we explore the idea together?" I say apprehensively.

Within a couple of hours, I have made a string of enquiries and printed the extensive application form for the government Fair Deal scheme along with applications for several nursing homes. Mam is on the phone, telling Jim she is going back to Ireland in February to get her affairs in order to move into a nursing home.

"February? I was thinking more like May," I say as I overhear her.

"I need to go over and visit places, see what they are like and organise things." She's excited, making lists. "No offence to you and Ronan but I'm getting bored here."

"But Ma, we are doing this because you can't live by yourself. And who is going to drive you around?"

"You will come with me, won't you?"

"Yes, of course I will," I say without hesitation.

I haven't told her about my call-back appointment, and dealing with the nursing home whirlwind decision has distracted me from the ball of apprehension growing in my stomach about how everything might change and spin further out of control after Monday night.

36

I'm usually quite good at living in the moment and not getting stressed about 'What ifs'. However, this time is different. I'm stressing because if anything is found during this examination, I won't be able to ask the rapid questions I need answered to get the information I need to continue to live in the moment and not freak out.

It is difficult enough to decipher medical speak without trying to do it in a language I only have pidgin level of. 'Will they need to operate immediately?', 'how much chemo?', 'will I have enough time to bring my mother back to Ireland?', 'do you have good wigs in Italy?', 'will a wig be too hot during the summer?'... Bloody hell Rosie, my inner voice screams, what the hell are you thinking, a wig is the least of your worries.

I write my full medical history including my Mam's history of breast cancer on an A4 page, and translate it. On a separate page, I list all the possible terminology they might use and questions I might have and translate them. I'll record the answers they give and ask Lucia to listen to them with me, that will be my course of action through this.

Of course, it bloody snows all day on the day of my appointment. It hasn't laid in our garden, the ground is too wet, but up the hill we can see the houses and fields dusted in white. The beauty of it distracts me for a moment from my 'what if' thoughts.

I haven't been feeling one hundred percent for a few months, my energy has been low, my stomach gurgling and bloated... maybe they are all signs of this thing, this thing that has yet to be discovered. Although since giving up grains all these symptoms had improved. But maybe that was all in my head? A placebo.

Maybe my back pain is because of cancer. Maybe I'm riddled with it? Maybe it's messing up my hormones, and that's why I am so angry? A fertile storytelling brain is not a good thing to have in these situations.

I tell Mam we have to go to visit someone. "Well enjoy yourselves," she says but not really meaning it, as she has told me several times it's ridiculous going out on a night like this.

Ronan is driving. As we climb higher and away from the lake, the road conditions get more treacherous.

I am giving the directions. I'm also reading translations of 'reviews' the hospital has received. I read one out to Ronan that is like a short story:

"The flagship of the Eighties, today it still boasts highly qualified staff among doctors and nurses and has outpatient clinics with efficient but somewhat dated equipment, however what clashes is the provincial aspect of the outpatient clinic system.

Let me explain better. My elderly mother had to have blood tests done, I avoid asking for home service because I want, as long as she can walk, to take her to the health facilities. I arrive at the entrance lane and the unqualified concierge man raises the problem of the companion, no more than one.

I answer, but the mother's Caregiver has to do blood tests too, therefore there are two patients and one companion, that is me.

Well, once this obstacle has passed, I take the number '45' from the ticket office and sit down to wait.

I immediately notice that there aren't forty-five people in the waiting room, at most there are thirty people.

At first I think they went for a ride or to the bar given the wait, but then I have to surrender to the evidence.

When the number appears on the display, the patient appears out of nowhere, sometimes alone, other times with a companion.

Strange that I didn't notice it in the room, I tell myself, but the story still repeats itself five or six times.

I deduce that those people have been served better than me and have received the number for eliminating queues even before arriving at the clinic, picked up prematurely by someone compliant directly on the spot.

I don't want to point the finger but honestly the confirmation came by itself when a lady who saw the queue reach eighty units before her, picked up the phone and a person who I will call "togato" or "shirted" arrived to her aid by passing from the preferential lane and conversing in the open with the attendant. In another era perhaps this provincialism could have been there, but in the third millennium and with digital technology just a click away it's implausible, I could have documented everything with images, but it's no use. All that's needed is for the counter to remove the dry branches, alone. So the flowers can bloom again."

The last sentence probably has meaning in Italian when not directly translated, but it is hard to believe someone has taken the time to write so much about the injustice he felt in the waiting room. I am relieved the 'dated' equipment he is referring to is just the ticket machine and not the medical equipment and attention, which so far with all my family medical experiences in Italy, have been wonderful.

The road around the hospital is not well lit nor can we see any sign saying this is a hospital, I just recognise the building from the Google page.

It's difficult to figure out where to park as the barriers do not open when we drive up to them. There isn't even an 'unqualified concierge man' to ask. They must have got rid of him after reading the guy's review and replaced him with barriers.

I can make out from the notice stuck on with Sellotape, the parking available beyond the barrier is just for invalids.

So back out on the road we find parking in a multi-storey car park across the street. The slushy snow is starting to freeze on the downhill ramp to the hospital entrance. My foot goes flying and Ronan catches me.

Although we are outside a hospital, breaking a bone here would not be favourable as this hospital is for outpatient appointments only with no emergency department.

The main large waiting room is empty and there are several reception desks with digital call numbers above their stations.

They definitely read the disgruntled guy's review. Yet another surreal desolate scene to add to my collection of Italian hospital memories.

I follow the signs for the 'Sanologica Department' as I was instructed to do on the call. The signs for the departments are also written in English which is a relief. The department I need is on the 'inferior' floor.

Passing a sign for the 'menopause' clinic, Ronan is rushing ahead of me down corridors. "Just ask someone," he keeps saying.

"Ronan will you just stop. Unlike you, I can follow signs I don't need the stress of following directions I don't understand."

He has gone in the wrong direction towards the mammagrafio clinic. Or the 'Mamma Mia grafico' as he has asked for.

"That is not where I have to go, it is this way. The senologica department," I hiss at him and walk in the opposite direction. Ronan catches up and passes me. He walks past the waiting room and heads down the corridor to find another someone to ask.

I've had enough. "Ronan will you please stop."

He hears my tone and halts.

"Please? Can you just go into the waiting room and wait? I've got this... sit down and wait, you are stressing me out."

He does as asked. I take a breath, compose myself and go to the administrator.

"Hello, I have an appointment," I say in my well-prepared Italian.

"Ah yes, Meleady?"

I am surprised she knows who I am. But then again, maybe I am the only one speaking in broken Italian or perhaps I am the only one scheduled or who came out in the snow for their evening appointment as there isn't anyone else around. She takes up my chart from her table, writes '61' on it and then hands me a cut-out square of paper with '61' printed on it and tells me to go wait in the waiting room. We are ten minutes early.

There is another man in the waiting room, scrolling through his phone, concentrating on the screen intently.

"I'm number 61," I say to Ronan as I hold up the piece of paper and take the seat beside him.

Ronan kicks out his legs in front of him and folds his arms as if preparing for a long wait. "There's no way there are sixty other people in this room ahead of you, you'd think they'd digitise it," he says in a deadpan voice, quoting the crazy review. He has done it. Hit my funny bone hard and an unstoppable laugh starts up behind my mask.

I try to control my laughter by distracting myself, going over the words in my folder. Having my full medical history, all my contact details, an explanation about my Tessera Sanitaria delay on a single sheet of paper translated into Italian eases my stress levels.

I've told Karen about my appointment and have her on standby as my 'phone a friend'. She also had a call-back after a mammogram and, having a creative brain like me, spent a sleepless weekend writing her will in her head before getting the all clear. "Hopefully they just want to test out a new bit of kit they've bought or they want to see if Irish breasts are the same as Italian ones." She likes to keep things light in these situations.

At the exact time of my appointment, we hear footsteps coming down the hall. The waiting man, who has been intensely scrolling, quickly pushes the phone into the handbag on the chair beside him and grabs a different phone from his pocket and sits back as if he has been casually scrolling that one instead.

A man in a white coat arrives at the waiting room door and calls my name, the woman with him walks back to where her husband is waiting and takes her bag while quietly telling him her results. The sly fox has been checking her messages while she was in having a breast exam? Ronan gives my hand a quick squeeze.

"Do you want me to mind your phone while you are in there?" he smirks, having also observed the mini soap opera.

The doctor makes small talk as he prepares the ultrasound machine beside the bed. I block out the usual white noise which enters my head when any Italian speaks Italian to me. I mouth the words he has said back to myself "Dove habita?" means "Where do you live?" I can answer that.

"How long have you lived in Italy?"

Again I repeat the question to myself and answer "five years." He corrects my pronunciation a little in a helpful way. I think I have just said five assholes.

"Do you have friends who are Italian to speak with?"

"Yes, but they speak English."

"And your husband, does he speak Italian?"

"No, he is Irish too."

As the doctor smears gel over my boob with the sonograph tool he jokes "If you had an Italian husband you could speak Italian." Or he may have said if you got yourself an Italian husband you will speak Italian. I need to spend more time on verb tenses.

He is looking closely at the screen; I hold my breath and then he breaks what feels like a forever silence and says the words I have been waiting for.

"Tutti bene." All good.

What a relief.

"I've realised why there isn't a shortage of doctors in Italy," says Ronan on the drive back. "It's because many of them can't speak English. If they could speak fluent English, they would have probably left for better paid positions in English-speaking countries."

"Hmm you might have a point. I've heard they teach English in schools the same way we are taught Irish in Ireland."

While there is a new appreciation for our own Gaelic language in Ireland, if you ask most Irish people who have gone through thirteen years of mandatory Irish language classes in school to speak Irish, most will either say 'An bhfuil chead agam dul go dti on leathrais?' which means 'Can I go to the toilet?' or 'Ta an caca milis'; the cake is sweet. Our command of our own language is abysmal.

I look out at how pretty and striking the old towns look on the snow-flecked hills as we drive home.

"Perhaps it is not a language thing holding Italian doctors back," I say, thinking about it. "Perhaps like Doctor Chicken, they just appreciate their own country, its beauty and culture, and they choose not to leave... Who would want to?"

I didn't know I was soon going to contradict myself.

37

After a gorgeous sleep, I wake ecstatically happy. It's the first time I have felt this light and happy in ages. Last year I was suffering from a long stretch of burnout since Covid wreaked havoc with my business. Along with grieving for my Dad, Luca leaving home, trying to adjust to a new life with my Mam and Jim's diagnosis. Then the last few months, I had one health issue after the next.

Finding out all is clear after my mammogram has put everything else in my life into perspective. I can't imagine how Jim must feel waiting for results after each scan, but I stop myself getting low and instead think about how happy he'll be when he gets to hear it's in remission.

I have a new lease of motivation, within a nanosecond of waking, everything is clear. I know what I want to do in the next five years and it involves making major changes in my life.

"Life is too short not to live it the way you want to live it," I write in my journal. "And with my kids both gone and my

Mam possibly moving into assisted care, I am free to decide what I want to do with the second part of my life. I am going to travel."

Within seconds I am googling working with orangutans in Borneo, learning to scuba dive in Belize, voluntary work with sloths in Costa Rica. A medicinal, spiritual trip to Peru in June pops up. I know the guy running it, well I met him once at a family funeral. A shaman who said 'you must come on one of my trips to Peru sometime'.

There's no such thing as coincidences. This is what I should do. So, with a small deposit, I book it without a second thought. Just the venture, not the flight. I'll book that in a few weeks when I have worked out where I am going. it will be a one-way ticket to Brazil or Costa Rica before Peru. A solo trip.

I call Izzy, excited. "I am going to Peru on a spiritual medicine journey."

"You mean you are going to Peru to do drugs?"

"No, not drugs. Medicine. Medicine for the soul."

"Mam, Peru's spiritual medicine is Ayahuasca. You need to know what you are getting into. Do you know what Ayahuasca does to you?"

"Of course I do!" I say slowly as I google rapidly. "Oh wow," I can't help but exclaim before reading the result out loud as if I knew about it all along.

"Ayahuasca-induces changes in many areas of the brain involved in feelings, memories, vision, and consciousness and allows for amplified introspection and problem-solving related to past and current life stressors, and for powerful envisioning and strategising of solutions for a more hopeful future... bloody hell that's just what I need. I'm definitely going."

"Mam! It's a psychedelic drug!"

"I've never done drugs, it's about time I tried some."

"Mam!" exclaims Izzy.

"And I'm getting a tattoo."

"That's such a midlife crisis thing to do. Are you okay?"

"I am more than okay," I say, jumping out of bed as fast as my back will allow, which is not very fast.

"The Venetians are known to be drinkers. The Genovese are tight with their money," my mother states when I bring her breakfast, after her morning of cultural research scrolling.

"I found that out when I was trying to find the powder that makes you look forty-two on the web thing this morning, and then I saw a picture of a woman in Umbria in front of her birthday cake with one hundred and twelve written on it. I need to get back to Ireland quick in case I catch whatever it is here that makes you live that long. Let's book our flights today and get back for Jim's birthday."

The glaze of morning frost on the grass of the previous two weeks is missing. It's overcast, but the temperature is still fourteen degrees, perfect for working in the garden, but instead I take Mam to the supermarket. It's Martedi Grasso; Fat Tuesday.

I've read that forty percent of Italians think they are overweight but only twenty-six percent actually are. Italians do not shy away from using the word 'fat'. "You are too fat for this store," a shop assistant once said in a friendly, gentle tone to an ex-pat friend of mine while she looked for something in her size. It's mind boggling how they can eat pastries for breakfast, pasta every day and have such tempting bakeries and not be as big as houses.

With shelves loaded with Carnivale supplies, the supermarket looks like a jollier version of an Irish store coming up to Halloween. Kids costumes, confetti, Venetian-style masks and packets of Carnivale cicerchiata; or 'frappe' as my friend in Rome called it, when she introduced me to the sweet wafer-thin and crunchy strips of fried dough.

Italy has a whole range of treats exclusive to Carnevale. Each region has its own variety of dough balls filled with custard, Chantilly, chocolate or lemon cream or made with liqueurs and honey and sprinkled with sugar.

Mam is delighted with the amount of Carnivale sugar-sprinkled cakes and deep-fried dough offerings to choose from at the bakery counter.

They are displayed alongside sweet varieties of focaccia and fritters and dough-based cakes, such as Torta Magica (magic cake); so called as it turns into three layers while being cooked. And soft and fluffy Berlingozzo di Carnevale, named after the Tuscan dialect term 'berlinganaccio', which in the Middle Ages meant having a good time around the table.

"Oh, that looks interesting," Mam says, pointing at a beautiful golden-coloured cake. The baker overhears and responds in English.

"This is Migliaccio, it is from Napoli and is made slowly in a very particular way with ricotta, semolina, essence of wild flowers and cinnamon. This is a very particular one as it includes capellini."

"Isn't capellini spaghetti?" I ask the jolly man who, by the attention he is giving my mother and the previous customers, obviously has great respect for all nonnas and loves talking with them.

"Yes, the very thin spaghetti gives it a special texture."

"Spaghetti in your cakes? Are you all mad? I wouldn't like that at all," Mam says, pulling a face.

He chuckles. "Where are you from?"

"Ireland," says Mam proudly.

"Ah well then for Carnivale you need sfinci or graffe both their doughs are made from boiled potatoes."

"That's more like it. Cake made from spuds, I'll have them."

"I don't have sfinci but I can give you some graffe. The potatoes make them incredibly soft." He lifts the fried donuts covered with icing sugar with his prongs for Mam's nodding approval.

"You also must have fritole and close your eyes and imagine you are at the Carnival in Venice when you eat it. They are flavoured with rum, pine nuts and lemon zest. The fritoleri used to make them on the streets of Venice in huge pans of oil."

He lifts another sugar-dusted, calorie-filled donut from the display and adds it to Mam's bag of sugar treasures.

Styles of cakes and dough balls are not the only differences in regions of Italy during Carnivale. There are also a whole heap of different traditions that have gone on for centuries. In the small town of Corniglia, residents have a tradition of throwing buckets of water out of their windows to celebrate the start of the carnival season.

Italians like throwing things out windows. Some towns have a tradition at midnight on New Year's Eve of throwing crockery, clothes and sometimes furniture and even old TVs out of their windows. It symbolises letting go of what is useless and getting rid of anything bad accumulated during the year to make room for a fresh start.

When we get home, Ronan is up. "The health service place in Ireland emailed to say you are not entitled to the S1 as my dependent as you are not in receipt of a medical card in Ireland."

"Unbelievable," I say. "So because I was a taxpayer in Ireland and not in need of a medical card, I am not entitled to the medical card a tax payer in Italy is entitled to?"

I know longer care. The urgency is gone; I have been exercising and looking after my diet since my visit to the osteopath and feel fitter and better than I have since my twenties.

"There is something else in the news you should read," says Ronan, handing me his iPad with an online news clipping open from ANSA–the English-Italian newspaper.

The news report is something I have been fearing to hear; the government has more or less pulled the plug on Green home improvement bonuses.

They have already approved a decree ending the so-called 'invoice-discount' ('sconto in fatture') scheme under which people could use credits from the State to pay for renovations. That's us.

The government said the scheme needed to end as it was too costly for the public coffers, inflated the prices of building work and was susceptible to fraud. The decree also stops public authorities buying credits linked to the scheme. That's our bank.

It's not just us affected, 115k home renovation sites throughout Italy, more than 32k companies and 170k workers are affected according to a building firm association. Some 115k Italian building sites are at risk of closure because of the "explosive" situation.

'Essere in alto mare,' is a common Italian phrase used when someone has procrastinated and discovers they are behind on a project. It literally means 'to be in deep water', with a long way to go before getting finished. It's how I feel about Mick Kelly and approaching him about the refund we have been waiting on.

I message him.

"Yes, the bank is no longer buying credit." He responds and then follows with 'Mi fa cagare!' Which is a blunt way of saying 'It's awful' but directly translated is; "It makes me shit."

But I don't care. I don't have breast cancer and my back pain has eased. And I'm going to Peru to meet the spirit world and getting a tattoo. But first I am going back to Ireland to hang out with my brother and find my Mam a nice place to live.

38

"I can't remember it being this cold last year," Mam says, tutting at the snow falling again the following day.

"It was colder last year," I remind her. "We didn't have the front door repaired, so it was arctic in the hallway, do you remember? We had clothes freeze into odd shapes on the clothesline a few mornings. So this winter is milder in my opinion. I think we could do with more rain though."

Having lived in rainy Ireland all my life, wishing for more rain is not something I ever thought I would hear myself say, but the lake is still low compared to other years.

It has been cold, but the house is definitely less drafty than the previous year because of the super job Alex's cousin had done on the front door. With the pellet stove on and the heating working, I would nearly go as far as to say the house was feeling... cozy. However, there is still something disjointed about the house's layout, but with time I know it will fall into place.

We go for an aperitivo with my yoga group friends. It's the first time we've got together in the new year after most of the group have spent Christmas back in the UK with their families. With every round of drinks ordered we are presented with a platter of foccacia, olives and bruschetta.

Ruth is talking about how an Italian guy who lives up the road from them removed a lot of scrub trees from a piece of land he has bought and the forest police arrived and argued with him for hours.

He was previously fined for removing trees on property he owns on the far side of the lake. Three guilty pleas of cutting down trees without permission gets you prison here. Whereas owning two guns and a rocket launcher is not such a severe issue, apparently. Ronan hasn't told our friends his crime story, he's too embarrassed about it.

Instead, he's telling stories about heights; The time he encouraged a group of friends in Germany to go para gliding and watched while a truck pulled a giant elastic and propelled them into the air. Just before it came to his turn, he hopped out causing havoc.

And the time, also in Germany, when he climbed to the top of a ten-metre diving board and then chickened out and had to get everyone on the board to back down the tall ladder. Causing havoc again. Mr Bean comes to everyone's mind.

Like Mam's stories, I've heard Ronan's stories dozens of times, like he has heard all mine.

Sitting in the same position has made my back hurt again. I want to go back to the house, but don't at the same time. My mind wanders to Jim and what the new year holds for him.

More chemo? Will he go into remission, will all his hard work of keeping to a strict diet pay off?

If I'm planning to go to Peru and do more travelling, I need to follow Jim's example and start looking after my health better. So, with the pain intensifying, I send Doctor Fab a text from the bar, 'Can I get an x-ray on my back?'

It's 9.30pm on a weekend, I don't expect him to respond but within minutes my phone buzzes. "On Monday come see me between 8am and 2pm at this address."

I presume the address is the clinic where we have always gone to see him. I arrive on Monday a little before 2pm but the door is locked. There are no lights on inside but I can see boxes in the hallway as if the place is being cleared out.

"I think we are at the wrong place," I say to Ronan who just automatically comes along as driver whenever I'm doing anything medical. I check the address in my Google Maps and it gives me directions to a destination two minutes away. We follow the road around to what looks like a block of flats. "You have arrived at your destination," my phone announces.

The empty Covid tampon testing tent outside looks dystopian. I am completely out of touch with what is happening with Covid as I haven't listened to a news report in months.

With my hand cupped between my face and the glass door to block the sheen, I can see it is a clinic alright, but that door is locked too. The sign stuck on the inside says 'Opening hours are from 2.30pm until 8pm. Monday to Saturday.' My head tightens as my stress level tops up.

"I'll just find him another day," I say, getting back into the car.

"No, call him. This is important Rosie."

Reluctantly I do what Ronan says. It's why he probably comes with me–to ensure I follow through.

"He's not answering," I say, about to hang up and then, "Pronto" Doctor Fab says. I still find it funny that Italians answer the phone with the word for 'Ready', instead of 'Hello'.

"Hi Fabrizio, I think I am at the right place?"

"Are you outside?" and he repeats the address.

"I think so, there are no numbers but there's a tampon tent." Again another thing that still tingles my funny bone–Italians calling Covid tests 'tampons'.

"I come and let you in."

It's nearly 2pm and, sure enough, he appears at the door and unlocks it. I follow him past a waiting area and we enter a labyrinth of highly coloured hallways with big and small colourful footprints on the ground leading in different directions. The place is completely empty. He leads me to a consultancy room with giraffes, elephants and lion stickers on the door and walls. There's a baby weighing scales and a smaller than usual examination bed.

Has he been sitting here since 8am waiting to write me a prescription? There is no explanation offered as to why we are here but I am guessing that while he waits to get his own clinic, he has to take whatever medical space he can get for his growing patient list. And today it is an out of hours pediatric clinic.

"Your back pain has been going on a long time. I think it might be sciatica. Have you pain going down your legs?"

"No."

"Did the anti-inflammatory work?"

"No."

"If you were older, and you had a trauma to the area I would say perhaps it is a cracked vertebra."

"But I'm not older."

"Yes, you are too young for this. What are your Vitamin D levels?"

"I don't know." Is that something the common person should know? If I stopped and had a chat with an Italian in a bar, and said "How's your kids? How's your Vitamin D levels?" Would they be able to answer? "The kids are doing great, but my D levels are dipping a bit at the moment so let's drink this outside."

It's unlikely this will ever happen as I don't think I will ever get beyond my clunky basics of Italian to ever have a fluid conversation about Vitamin D levels.

"Have you had them checked?" he asks.

"No."

"Hmmm. I will send you for the x-ray."

He writes out a prescription for the x-ray on white notepaper. If I had the Tessera Sanitaria, he would write it on the paper with the red box areas, he tells me. Red prescriptions mean you don't pay for them. On the white prescriptions, you do.

"I will also write you a prescription for Vitamin D just in case. You need to get this one not any generic one. This will cost €4.20 and last you three months," he says as he writes a second prescription on his headed notepaper.

"You take twenty-five drops on breadcrumbs after lunch on a Sunday," he says with a straight face. I am glad masks are still mandatory in health facilities as I don't want him to see I am laughing. It's not because his magic potion-like prescription includes breadcrumbs, but because he is prescribing that I must only take it on a Sunday.

I take my prescriptions and then get completely lost in the labyrinth of hallways following the reversed colourful feet on the floor, trying to find the exit of yet another completely empty Italian medical facility.

Back in the car, I am trying to decipher what he has written in a classic doctor's scrawl.

"I wonder if understanding doctor's handwriting is a module in university courses for pharmacists? I'm trying to figure out if he has actually specified on the prescription that I have to only take it on Sundays."

Ronan is still laughing at the specifics of the prescription. "Maybe it needs to be blessed bread to make the spell work, that's why it needs to be only taken a Sunday. Anyway, I'm glad you have the prescription for your back x-ray, we'll go straight to the clinic and get the appointment made, otherwise you will procrastinate about it for months."

Ronan knows me too well.

39

A t the clinic I hand my prescription through the booking window. I know the drill. The guy inputs the information of the x-ray request and finds my details from my previous visit for the MRI.

With a constant stream of numbers being called in the background, I can't hear what the receptionist mutters at me behind his mask. I lean my ear closer to the glass and say "Scusi?"

"Ah in English... eh, this will cost €51, okay?"

He must have recognised me from last time, either that or my ear looks like it can only understand English.

"Ok. What date?" I ask and he prints out the page.

"Okay, it will be 74 five."

As he hands me the page, I say 'okay' again, and wonder how fast inflation is going up in Italy for the cost to go up by €23 in two minutes. The x-ray is set for three days' time at 7.45 in the morning. So it wasn't inflation, it still cost €51 but the appointment time is 7.45. That makes more sense!

When the day arrives, I've got everything on the list that I need to take to the appointment in a folder, plus extras such as my MRI scan and results, the osteopath pictures, my doctor's details, and my ID. Everything they could possibly want.

I arrive on time, take a number and wait until it is assigned to a window where I hand in the booking sheet the guy gave me when I made the appointment along with my bank card.

She hands me back an A4 receipt of payment, a form to complete to collect the results the following day between 11 and 1pm, and the sheet with the details of the x-ray required and tells me to follow the green line and wait near the coffee machine.

There is only one other person in the waiting room so I'm guessing I will be in and out before 8.30am.

Just as I am thinking how much I love the efficiency of this clinic, the girl from the pay desk arrives looking for me. "Sorry, I need the prescription from your doctor."

"Hmm the one I gave to the guy to make this appointment?"

"Yes."

I search through my folder. All the papers are there from the day when I handed the clerk the prescription from my doctor and he copied all the details onto the official sheet, the receipt of payment and all the other bits.

"Damn, it's the one thing I haven't put in my folder," I say, searching a second time through every other bloody thing I brought with me. "But when I made the booking, the administrator copied all the details. All the information from it is on this form, do you still need the original?"

"Yes. I need to photocopy the original."

"I don't have it with me. Can I send it to you after the x-ray when I get back home?

"No, I need it before you have the x-ray."

She takes me back out to the admin area. I'm texting Ronan. He is not at home and even if he was, I wouldn't know where to tell him to look for the little piece of paper. I can't remember where I would have put it other than the folder I have with me. Maybe it's in the car? Ronan searches the car. But it's not there, he's not far from the clinic so he's heading back.

"How far away is your house?" she asks.

"Twenty minutes."

She discusses it with the guy who copied all the details of my prescription the day before... 'why didn't he take a photocopy or scan of it then?' I want to ask, but I don't have the words. Or the patience. I'm miff-deified. It's a new feeling I've added to my range of emotions since moving to Italy and dealing with their bureaucracy.

"Okay if you go home and come back with it, we can fit you in one hour from now."

So I run out to the car park and jump into our waiting car.

"We have an hour to get home, find it and get back. I can't believe it, everything they need is in this folder. I didn't think they would need the prescription again, I feel so stupid."

"It's not you being stupid, it's the system. You've already given the 'order' to them and they have all the details, what do they need the original for a second time?"

He's already driving and has turned onto the motorway... He has turned onto the motorway...why?

"Why have you turned onto the motorway? We're heading for Siena... why?"

"You didn't tell me the directions," huffs Ronan as if I'm to blame.

"Ronan, we are twenty minutes from where we live. How do you get this so wrong every bloody time we are in a hurry? Why can't you just think for yourself for once? Why do I have to take charge and direct every movement of our lives, even simple bloody directions? I'm so fucking sick of it." My short fuse had been ignited again and the everlasting gunpowder inside me exploding. Ronan doesn't say anything.

I look out the window; the lake is so still, giving the surrounding scenery time to reflect but not letting it get inside, keeping the upside-down version on the surface. It's like oil on water. I take in a deep, shaky breath and bite my nail. I don't bite my nails.

"Forget it, don't rush," I say more calmly, hoping he didn't detect the slight quiver in my voice. "There isn't a turn back on this road for another ten minutes so by the time we double back then get home and back to the clinic, I'll be late for the appointment. Let's just forget it." I've had enough of living to deadlines and chaos. I just want to forget I ever discovered the additional stresses that lay dormant in my body waiting for my big five zero year before all appearing at the same time.

"Italians are always late. I'll get you back there. You are going to have this x-ray today."

How could he be so bloody calm when I've said such a horrible thing to him?

Back at the house, sure enough, there is the prescription neatly folded and tucked in behind the tea caddy on the shelf. I take my time and get back into the car. I don't care if they can't fit me in.

But they do. The waiting room is full, the girl spots me and waves me to the top of the queue. She takes the piece of paper, copies it, hands it back to me and leads me back to the x-ray waiting room.

The radiographer is in her late twenties. She has the longest thickest false eyelashes I have ever encountered, and I have encountered quite a few false lashes in my years of wedding planning. It's a standing x-ray in a modern small room, it's comfortable but alien. The silence brings thoughts; so many medical checks in such a short amount of time when my life is in tatters... Why am I feeling so angry and disconnected from the love I used to feel for my mother and Ronan? The x-ray only takes five minutes, but it's long enough, fractured alone time for me to dislike the person I have become all the more.

The following day, Ronan is going to a rugby match in Rome between Ireland and Italy with Shelly and Sherwin. I would like to be going but I can't leave Mam for twelve hours alone. And anyway, I need to collect the results of my x-ray. I'm glad Ronan has gone for the day, it means I can collect them by myself and take time to translate the diagnosis back home.

At first none of the diagnosis makes sense. But then I break down each sentence, and google each component. 'Scoliosis on the left side with rotation in the spine.' That doesn't sound good. But the next line is even more of a surprise... 'Osteoarthritis in the spine.'

The Italian word 'Diffuso' is used. I'm guessing it means 'diffused' - sprinkled and just starting. I look up 'Diffuso' and it hits me hard. Diffuso means 'widespread'.

All I want to do is curl up in bed and have a good cry but I can't. Mam is downstairs waiting on her dinner. I need time to digest this, to research it and learn what is happening or has happened to my body.

After dinner, I consider telling Mam to see when her scoliosis started or if she has arthritis in her spine and her hips and what I should do. "I got my x-ray results," I say, broaching the subject.

"That was quick. It wouldn't be that quick in Ireland. My legs feel like they are going to break off when I walk or stand. I'll need to get them looked at when I get back. We'll need to put a full day aside just to sit all day waiting on an x-ray. They should never have closed down the local hospitals in Ireland. Having emergency rooms, maternity and small appointments and everything under one roof is just stupid. The Italian system of having smaller regional hospitals where they deal with everyday, less serious stuff is better."

"How about I try to get you an x-ray here before we go back? Getting the x-ray done here privately will probably cost less than going to the public hospital in Ireland to get it done."

"Could you?"

I am already texting Doctor Fab. I want to meet him anyway to discuss my results. Better to discuss it with him than my mother.

"I can see your mother tonight at 8pm at the clinic and to discuss your results."

"It's my hips, but it's my knee that really bothers me," she says to him at the appointment.

She hasn't mentioned this to me before.

"Ok, I'll send you for an x-ray. If you had come sooner, I could have given you a cortisone injection and then some weeks later given you an injection of a substance that replaces the cartilage and you would have no pain for six months."

"I'll suggest that to her doctor when we get back."

He asks about Izzy. "Is she still working on the movie with that actor?"

"Yes, she is.".

"I love that actor."

"Me too."

I hand him the CD with my x-ray pictures on it but it's not showing up on the computer of the borrowed surgery we're in.

"I can't get it to work but I can read here what is written; you have scoliosis and your spine is twisted, rotated," he says with a smile. Why are he and the osteopath both so delighted with me having scoliosis?

"You also have osteoarthritis. But it is the scoliosis causing the pain, it should have been corrected when you were young."

From online research I have done, I know there is adult scoliosis and childhood scoliosis. I got checked as a child by the school nurse, everyone did, at the same time we got our polio drops and sugar lump. I didn't have it then.

I had no intention of my mother being in the room while I discussed my results with the doctor, it just happened. There was nowhere else to put her at that moment.

"What about a good corset?" chips in Mam.

"Corsets are great for backs. When I–"

"Mam, stop! I am not wearing a bloody corset. Let the doctor talk."

"A corset could help perhaps, but it would need to be made for you."

There is nothing else he has to say, other than, can Izzy perhaps get an autograph from the actor.

With a water baby attached to my liver, scoliosis and now osteoarthritis in my spine, I need to press on about getting into the national health system of Italy.

I'll think about it after I get the next major hurdle in our life out of the way next week; Ronan's court case.

40

L ast names are funny in Italy. With three hundred and fifty thousand varieties, Italy has the largest number of surnames in the world. Only one percent of the population have the ten most common names.

As the population increased during the fourteenth century, surnames became a necessity. They were often assigned based on nicknames, physical characteristics or occupations. Many people didn't know what name they were being assigned by the local comune because they were illiterate. So, while they assigned one person the surname of Bellagamba (beautiful legs), another was assigned Troia (whore). Some orphaned babies were assigned harsh names such as Malfatto (badly made) and Pancione (big belly).

Some other names were decided by what the person was known for.

'Fumagalli' is a common surname in Lombardy which translates to 'smoke the chickens' meaning chicken thief, as blowing smoke into a chicken coup was a method to stun the fowl so they didn't make noise when being stolen.

Chicken thievery is also the origin of the Italian saying, 'Conosco i miei polli', meaning "I know my own chickens". It is used when you can predict how someone you know well will behave or react to a situation.

Another two great sayings are 'Ho peli sul mio stomaco' which literally means, "I have hairs on my stomach", meaning you're not taking something seriously.

'Ti scureggia il cervello' means, literally, "your brain is farting". It's a Roman expression meaning you are talking crap, and is only to be used with friends, unless you really want to insult someone.

Perhaps they were short of imagination at times and used the Native American way of naming the person after the first thing they saw as there are a lot of surnames based on animals, insects and objects; 'Piccione' (Pigeon), 'Legume' (Bean–the name of the original owner of The Sighing House) and 'Finocchio' (Fennel). However, Finocchio is now a common slang word for being gay. So it may not suit everyone who has the name.

There is also Mezzasalma, which means "half-cadaver"; I can't imagine how that came about. Another interesting name is Pelagatti. "Pelare" means 'to skin', "gatti" is 'cats'.

Ronan's solicitor's name is Rana which means frog in Italian.

On the day of the court case, we go to meet Signore Rana in his office in the centre of Perugia. We've arrive with time to spare, so stop for a cappuccino.

"I was watching Italian court trials on YouTube last night to prepare myself," says Ronan, fidgeting with his saucer and spoon–very uncharacteristic of him. "I had to stop–the wigs and cloaks and dark and moody rooms with all the people watching..."

"I'm sure it won't be that bad. It's not like you are going to the criminal court with a jury."

"Italy doesn't do juries. Nobody is tried by a jury, it's by a panel of judges. They don't do bail here either."

"Gosh, you have really done your research."

"Yeah, this has been playing on my mind for months. I've been trying to turn myself off from liking Italy in case I have to leave or not see much of it for a while, other than through the bars of a cell."

"Stop. You are letting your imagination get carried away and just being dramatic," I say firmly, "Do what I have been doing, live in the moment and avoid the 'what ifs'."

Even though we were facing a criminal court situation in a foreign country where we do not know the language, I can't help but feel relaxed in the palazzo sipping my cappuccino while Ronan offloads his research on Italian prisons. Apparently I was right, prison food isn't too bad.

At his office with a fantastic view over the hills below the town, Signore Rana sits us down. "It is difficult to know what will happen. The law changes every month in Italy, we constantly have to stay updated." He pats the cover of a thick paperback 'The Penal Laws of Perugia 2023' on his desk.

Like a lot of countries with 'old' laws, it is good that laws in Italy get updated. For instance, in Italy, killing your daughter, sister or more commonly your wife who had brought dishonour to the family could justifiably be excused as a fair way of bringing honor back to your family. Infidelity was the number one cause for this law's justification, and it was only abolished in 1981.

"They may postpone it," says Rana. "This is the best result I will try to achieve. If the case is pushed to beyond next March it will be beyond the statute of limitations. Can you speak Italian yet?"

"No," responds Ronan.

"Good!"

"Really?" I feel like saying, "Please don't encourage him to give up on at least trying to speak the language of the country we live in."

"So they will ask if you can speak Italian and you will say 'no'. And so they will need a translator to come to court and they will adjourn the date. However, they may disbelieve it and say, 'you live here five years, why can't you speak Italian?' Do you not go to the supermarket, the butcher, the bar?"

I get the feeling Rana actually finds it unbelievable Ronan can't speak Italian after all this time and wants to be sure they won't catch him out.

"Yes, but at the supermarket you just say 'thank you'. You don't have discussions. Will they really ask that?" Ronan asks.

"It depends on the judge and public prosecutor, they might say 'okay, there will be a translator here in twenty minutes.' If so, and they proceed to pursue with the criminal trial to condemn you–"

Criminal trial, condemning–he's using a lot of scary words beginning with 'C'.

"Then we will move to the second best option which is an offer to pay a fine to close the case. A trial in Italy must start and finish. It is not like the US or UK where a case can be thrown out of court or a prosecutor can say, 'I do not have time to do these small cases' and cancel it."

"How much would the fine be?" asks Ronan.

"Four or five hundred euro perhaps."

"That would be okay, Rosie, wouldn't it? To fast track the end of this?"

Rana interrupts, "It is not up to us, we have to see what the public prosecutor wants to do."

Prosecutor... Another scary word.

He continues, "It's about hopping back and forth."

"That's funny." I chuckle a little, he looks at me perplexed. "Because your name is Rana... frog?"

"Ah, yes!" he grins.

We walk through the old town streets towards the stone walls of the courthouse where the weather-worn mythical creatures guard the entrance, "Fuck this is the criminal court I've seen on reports I was watching last night." Ronan grips my hand and I try not to look nervous.

"We are not going to this one, we go to the tribunal court. It is down the hill," says Rana, giving us some relief.

The tribunal court building is much less intimidating with its ocher-plastered facade. The security staff speak to us in English. One handsome guy with a wide smile even says "Welcome," as he takes my bag for scanning, like we are arriving for a stay at a five-star hotel.

Down a flight of stairs into the bowels of the building and we walk through corridors leading to a room that looks way less intimidating than the ones Ronan has seen on YouTube.

We sit on the line of seats secured to the far wall. At the top of the room there are six people sitting behind a desk on a raised platform. The guy who is the judge is central, he's in his forties. Four large modern desks with enough space for two to sit facing the front plinth, gives the room more of a classroom appearance than a court of law. There's a woman at the end of our row of seats scribbling notes. I hope she is not a journalist–I don't want to be scandalised in the local paper again.

Everyone around the room is cheery towards each other. I'm not sure if some are civilians on trial or lawyers.

The first case is about unpaid alimony. The second, about a work injury, and then Ronan's case is called.

The two younger women to the left of the judge are reading the notes of the case and they are smiling at Ronan either to make him feel more comfortable or chuckling at him for being so stupid at buying a gun over the internet to keep rats and cinghiale away.

As Rana predicted, the judge asks in Italian if Ronan can speak Italian.

"No, he doesn't understand a word," responds Rana.

"Well then, we will need to postpone the case." The judge checks his diary and postpones it to eighteen months from now at 8.30am and we are dismissed.

"So in eighteen months' time I will return to court without the need of Ronan being present for the formality of finishing the case," says Rana, walking out through the hallways. "And then they will return your gun and firework launcher."

"Return them? Are you serious?" I ask, having to stop for a moment to comprehend what he just said.

"Yes, of course. He has not been charged with any wrongdoing and they are your property."

Ronan is looking chuffed with himself, whereas I feel like exploding.

"You are not getting those guns back." I can't believe he was even considering it after all the unnecessary anxiety this whole situation has caused, just because he won't read instructions.

Living with Ronan for the last thirty years has been exciting, in the same way living with a blindfolded person with a box of matches in an old barn with puddles of petrol dotted across the floor and hay bales in the corner would be exciting. I've been great at throwing sand over the small puddles and a few times the hay has gone up, but the roof is still standing. However, I am tired of the firefighting and with my emotions very raw in the last year, this gun issue has my patience with Ronan paper thin.

We thank Mr Frog profusely for his help. I no longer feel the need to go to Doctor Chicken for some anxiety medicine over my husband being a potential criminal. Instead, we will just return to our house previously owned by Mr Bean.

41

Things were happening fast; Jim and his wife visited three nursing homes and were sending videos and photos of their favourites. Jim's count, of whatever it is they count when people have cancer, was up again but considering it was five thousand when he was first diagnosed and it has edged up to fifty-three from twenty-six, it still wasn't bad, bad.

One of the preferred nursing homes said they would have a place available for Mam in April. It would probably be the summer before another place came up again. But before she could take the offer, she needed to be accepted into the government funding scheme–this would involve assessments and forms and meetings and more assessments spanning over a month. And she needed to visit the nursing homes herself to make sure moving into assisted living was really what she wanted to do.

I book one-way flights back to Ireland for Mam and me. I don't know how long I will be gone for, all I know is I'm not leaving Ireland until Mam is settled and happy.

I am going to make the most of the impending trip and have quality time with family and friends I haven't spent proper time with since before Covid lockdowns. Luca will be nearby, and I'll spend lots of lovely time with Jim, his wife and kids.

My other two brothers will visit Mam while I am there and Izzy is going to be working in Ireland for the month. Everyone alive who I am closely blood related to is going to be in Ireland during March. Ireland would be my island full of love for the month.

It all happened on the same day. The day before we were to leave for Ireland, just as the stress bubble dissolved about the court case something else swooped in to take its place.

It was Izzy who told me Luca had broken up with his girlfriend. To take time out, he was going to go over to London to take care of Izzy's cats while she worked in Ireland for a month. But that wasn't it. Luca, being forgetful over dates just like his Dad, had booked his flight to London for the sixth of March; my birthday. But that wasn't it, I wasn't bothered.

I was, after all, going to be celebrating my fifty-first birthday in style; with Mam's appointment arranged with the district nurse at nine in the morning, followed by a doctor's appointment for Mam to get her knee checked and two viewings of nursing homes in the afternoon.

Izzy was working at the other end of Ireland so even though we were going to be in the same country, looking at her tight schedule, it was unlikely I was going to see her for the month she was there, let alone on my birthday. But that wasn't the cause of my stress bubble either.

I reminded myself of my word for the year; Love. Even though I would not see my husband or kids on my birthday, it didn't matter, they still loved me. My saving grace was going to be dinner at Jim's for our joint birthday celebration. He already had the menu planned weeks before I had even left for Ireland.

With an ongoing need to remind myself of my word for the year and as a way of inner apology to my mother for all the anger I had felt since Dad died, which she must have sensed, I buy a Mimosa tree to plant in the garden before we leave. I chose a Mimosa as the flowers of the tree are exchanged between women in Italy on La Festa della Donna on the eighth of March (which is also Jim and his wife's birthday) as a sign of respect and support of each other. Teresa Mattei, one of Italy's first women in Italian politics started the tradition in 1946. Her activism first got noticed when she was a young girl who got suspended from school for criticising the anti-Semitic laws adopted at the time by fascist Italy.

Just as I am taking the tree out of the back of the car, a truck pulls up with the delivery of the paving we ordered last year.

"That will keep me busy while you are away," Ronan says as the truck's crane arm lifts the four straining pallets and precariously swings them into our driveway. My jaw clenches. I wanted to be here when the terrace was being laid, not just to help but because as usual, I didn't trust Ronan to do it right–the way I wanted it done. But I can't say that, instead I say, "Let's work out a plan of how it should be done."

Ronan is not stupid, he can see right through what I'm saying.

I stride to the back of the house and with chalk in hand I start mapping out the starting point and diagonals.

He's watching but I know he's not absorbing what I am saying, I can feel the annoyance at him creep up my back. These are instructions after all, and Ronan doesn't follow bloody instructions. My jaw gets tighter. Perhaps I just won't come back from Ireland? It's an option I hadn't thought of, I could just stay travelling... go to Peru from there... then I wouldn't have to face the future and I wouldn't have to scream at Ronan for making a mess of the terrace and spend the same amount of time and money again getting it redone professionally.

"What will we do with these?" Ronan says, pointing to the grey plastic mini-manhole covers Danny Boy implanted into the ground so that we could do future work. Some are for the down pipes of the new gutters that will be installed when the old small roof is replaced, and some have tubing for future outdoor lighting cables. Although I don't know where the tubing for the wiring runs to. That is a puzzle for another day. Today we just need to figure out which manholes we want to keep and which we are okay about covering over with the paving.

Ronan lifts one of the covers. "What the hell is that?" he says, staring into the sunken plastic receiver box under the cover. I look closely at the five-inch-deep stagnant rainwater that is wriggling with so much life that teeny waves are forming on the water's surface. "That's mosquito larvae, I recognise it from our garden pond we had growing up," I say, double checking the larvae pool in the neat modern facilities we have built for them.

"There's more here," says Ronan lifting another cover and another.

"That explains why we were infested with mosquitoes all summer when no one else had them as bad. We've basically been running mosquito maternity hospitals with kindergartens attached."

"What do you say to me cleaning them out and covering them over with paving? If we decide to install enough lights for a U2 concert on the patio, we'll remember where they are."

"Agreed." For once in a long time we are agreeing about something without me losing my patience. But I am sick at the thought of him trying to start this project without me finding the starting points, checking the gap lines–if they are not straight, they will drive me crazy for years. I don't want it to be an 'it will do for now' project like Ronan has treated many renovation projects he has done by himself in previous houses. The house is coming together so well, I want the garden to be the same. I want this to be permanent–something I'll look at and love. Can't I have one of those houses rather than an 'it will do' survival project?

"Just wait until I get back," I say. I don't trust him, and he knows it.

Mam and I plant the Mimosa tree together while I tell her about its symbolism of respect and support between women. We had developed a new sense of respect and support for each other during her stay this time. Like the time she first moved to Italy, we were now entering another new adventure together–finding her a new place to live.

I had no idea what the alternative could be if she changed her mind and decided assisted living was not for her. Me moving back to Ireland to live with her permanently would not make her happy nor me happy. We would drive each other nuts in her tiny cottage.

My inner voice constantly nagged me with the 'you shoulds'; you should be your parent's carer, you should do your duty as a good child and sacrifice your own wants and needs for your elderly parent's needs, you should be a 'good' daughter; a martyr like all the other generations of daughters before you, like your mother was for her mother. She did her duty, you should do yours, did she not bring you up to believe this?

The last thing Mam wants to do is to be a burden, I know that. My other two brothers had jobs and families and life stuff going on. They lived 'away'. They knew Jim had cancer, he had told them his full diagnosis last summer.

None of us had mentioned the word 'incurable' and what it meant to us about our brother. My brothers didn't mention it and it was not something I felt I could talk about over the phone. I needed to be near them to utter the word, to have time with each other to talk about our brother and our Mam. Perhaps they would hug me, even though they weren't huggy men. It's not an Irish male GenX thing to do with your siblings.

Since Ronan had come into our family with his bone-crushing bear hugs he'd give to everyone as freely as snuff at a wake, it had become the norm for Jim and I to hug each other hello and goodbye. The Italians don't have this problem they shower everyone they meet with embraces and kisses not just family members.

It was also from hearing Ronan say 'Love you' at the end of every call to his brothers and sister that made me begin doing it nearly thirty years ago with all my family. While we knew we all loved each other, it was not a thing you said in the Seventies. Except for Mam, she'd sing love songs with her gorgeous sweet voice and showered us with love with the best birthday parties and Christmases even if money was tight in our little house. I don't think it was just my siblings; I think the words 'I Love You' went unvoiced in most Irish families during the generations born pre-Nineties. Breaking the 'love you' silence was cringy at first and I still remember sniggers and exclamations of 'what did you say?' in the early test days, but with persistence my family soon got into the swing of it and it became as normal as hello and goodbye on our calls.

I had eased information to Mam about Jim over the months. About how his treatment would be 'ongoing' and how he really needed to look after himself. There was no need to mention incurable as he was doing great and he could go on for years like this and, who knows, they might have found a cure by then.

She just needed to be aware he may not always have the time or energy to pop around to fix something or run errands for her like he used to. She understood. Instead, she switched to her positive old self and talked enthusiastically about looking forward to her new life in assisted living. None of this was the cause of my new sense of rising stress.

The day started with a message from the guy running the trip to Peru "I'm sorry we are going to have to cancel the trip because of the rising political civil unrest in Peru." Typical... the year I book to go, Machu Picchu closes to tourists for the first time. But that wasn't the cause of the stress either.

The stress was from the call from Jim. He looked seriously fed up, lying in bed. "My temperature is bouncing up and down, they can't control it so they are admitting me to hospital... I've got bloody Covid."

42

"When I get out of here, I'm going to have lobster."

"Jim, you know they are cooked alive? Not very Saint Francis of you."

I've been back in Ireland three days and Jim has sent me photos of the hospital food each day, usually with a Star Trek description. 'Star Trek Cheese' he calls the pale, globular mould-shaped excuse for scrambled egg.

"There's food Jim but not as we know it," is the caption to a dish that neither of us can make out what it is supposed to be. For an evening snack they gave him a bag of crisps and fizzy lemonade.

"Seriously? How can they give anyone who is sick such unhealthy food, never mind someone like you, who is on a strict diet to keep your liver calm? I hope you didn't eat it?"

"Of course I ate it, I was starving."

It's such a relief he is on the road to recovery but we are worried how the hospital food will affect all the dietary work he has done to keep his liver under control.

Ronan sends me a photo of Truman cycling by, blue sky behind him in Italy while it's pelting rain in Ireland, with the caption 'Just in case you missed him'. He also sends me a picture of a tomato plant Shelly gave him. He has named it Tiny Tommy and planted it in a random spot in the garden.

With the Peru trip cancelled and everything so up in the air at the moment I need something solid to aim towards, so I can say 'on this date I am doing X so I will be in Y.' Something to look forward to.

And besides, it would be nice to book something today since 'Oggi compio gli anni' - 'Today I have accomplished the years'. It's how you say, 'It's my birthday', in Italian. So after I have breakfast with Luca and drive him to his early morning airport bus to catch his flight to London and keep a brave face as I say a gut-wrenching goodbye to my kid yet again, I look up retreats.

Are there any with screaming rooms I can sit in all day? No such luck... Maybe something more calming would be good. I find a fabulous retreat centre in the north of Italy.

It will be a perfect start to my travels. However, all the retreats they offer are booked up for the year. Some of the instructors have links to their details, so I tumble down the rabbit hole of links leading to links and end up on a webpage offering a retreat in May in Umbria, so I email for more details and forget about it. I need to get Mam to her assessment with the district nurse.

Mam treats the assessment for long-term care like a combination of an audition for Mastermind and a job interview for working at the care home, rather than becoming a resident.

"What's one hundred minus seven?"

Mam doesn't just answer, she rhymes off the minus times table backwards so quick even the nurse can't keep up. That's okay I tell myself, she isn't being assessed to go into a care home for dementia.

"Who does your shopping for you?" asks the nurse reading from her clipboard of questions.

"Oh, I do. I drive to the shops and get what I need," says Mam confidently.

"Can you stand up and walk to the window for me?"

Mam launches herself out of the chair without her usual loud groans, curse words, squeaks, and several failed attempts, and practically does an Irish jig across the room.

"I'm wrecked after that, but I think I got everything right," Mam says when we are outside.

We spend the day going from one appointment to another. By the evening we are both exhausted and with Jim in hospital and our birthday dinner not happening, I take the easy option and stop for a takeaway on the way home.

Our spirits are up though as we had found a nursing home Mam and I both really like; lots of activities, outings, live music once a week. Of course, it is the one with a bar. They will have a place available in three weeks—a big relief.

"Is that a car pulling into the drive?" says Mam just as I sit down for the evening having cleared up our plates. I hear stifled laughter outside just as the doorbell chimes.

It's Jim's wife and kids surprising me with a cake and candles and Izzy taking part in their rendition of 'Happy Birthday' by video chat from the asshole of nowhere in Ireland. So with the solidarity and love of the closest women in my life, I celebrate being grateful for getting to the age of fifty-one.

The following day, my other brother arrives to stay with Mam after her five months in Italy. It presents an opportunity for me to catch up with old school friends in Dublin.

"No one told us hitting midlife would be so bloody hard!" says my old school pal, Friend Number One. "I mean, as if we haven't been through enough and then we are hit with peri menopause, menopause, medical stuff, kids turning into humans with their own brains, divorce, work burnout, parents getting old and sometimes dying–very inconsiderate of them."

"No wonder we all feel like running away," I add.

"I'd be happy with just a holiday by myself," says Friend Number Two. "Just to go and remember who I am again. Do you ever feel you've forgotten who you are?"

"That's Alzheimer's, not menopause," I say.

"Don't fancy travelling by myself," says Friend Number One. "I don't mind travelling by myself but I'd like to go somewhere I know there would be other women my age. Sitting in a hotel alone looking at couples and young ones in their bikinis doesn't really appeal to me. Frankly, I'd find it depressing."

"I'd love to travel without a return date. I'd like to go some-where and live like the locals, not just for a week, more like a month or two," says Friend Number Three.

"You could! You work from home since Covid, so you could become a digital nomad," says Friend Number Two.

290 | ROSIE MELEADY

"I have thought of it," says Friend Number Three. "I looked at AirBnB but working all day by myself looks lonely too. Do old fashioned boarding houses still exist anywhere? You know, where women could safely go and get to know the other residents but still have their independence?"

"There are co-living places for digital nomads," I say, having researched writers' retreats during my recent escape planning. But then I realised I was living the retreat experience in my 'villa' in Italy by the lake with all the quiet time I needed. And it worked for me. The house and time to myself were just what I needed to focus on the books I always wanted to write. It's what lots of writers crave and need–a beautiful place they can go with time to themselves to work.

"I saw those co-living spaces, but it sounded like everyone is in their twenties or thirties," says Friend Number Three. "Some of them sound like party houses. I would need somewhere I can stay working quietly during the day. Meet people for dinner or a drink and go to bed by ten–absolute bliss."

We all skipped on to a different topic but the conversation planted a seed of an idea in my head.

43

After having a fun weekend away with my friends, within an hour of being back in Mam's house I'm angry, frustrated and upset to the point of crying. A letter is waiting–they have not passed Mam for full-time care. They have not said 'no' exactly, but they want her to go for further assessment.

I'm on the phone to the person in-charge immediately.

"The fact that she can drive and get her own shopping affected the decision," she explains.

"But she doesn't drive or shop by herself! She is waiting on a cataract operation for goodness sake, she would be dangerous behind the wheel of a car. Surely you have had people in assessments before holding onto their pride and bluffing? She was a 1950s housewife, of course she is going to tell you she cooks and cleans like the perfect example of her species."

"Yes, we get it all the time. It is why I argued her case and got the board to agree to further assessment."

"How long will it take?"

"Well, if you add up the time frames between everything, it will be finished about mid-June."

"Mid-JUNE? That's three months away!... What will happen if she doesn't pass the second time?"

"You can appeal it."

"And how long will that take?"

"About six months. But let's see how the further assessments go, shall we?"

I go to see my doctor in Ireland. She's lovely and has known me since I was pregnant with Luca.

It all pours out of me, what's happening with Jim and Mam, my dad passing, my kids gone from the house, my cyst and my back... my friggin' back. My anger at Ronan, and how I am feeling bloody angry about everything, just everything. She listens and that in itself helps ease the stress and sadness.

She checks my spine, it's only in the lumbar area and she tells me the area of back pain is muscle spasms caused by the scoliosis.

"Back strengthening and core muscles as you are doing, will ease the pain and stop it getting worse and things have changed with arthritis, most women in their fifties have some arthritis and it's manageable. We know a lot more now; how things in our diet can be inflammatory and aggravate it. You are doing all the right things."

She takes bloods and gives me a full MOT.

Jim calls. "I'm Covid clear and I can leave today, can you pick me up? I'm just going for a scan, they said they might as well do it now that I'm here rather than waiting until after next week's final chemo session, so I'll be ready to go straight after."

"I'm on my way!"

Jim, still in his dressing gown, nearly runs out to the car. He looks rough, his skin yellow but his eyes white. He's smiling and laughing, delighted to be out of hospital. "Oh my God, get me home and let's have some decent delicious food."

Getting Jim back home, seeing him prep food again with his wife and kids in his own kitchen and having had a good chat with my doctor, has me feeling much more positive. My anger has eased since hearing my back pain will go and I am not destined to become bent over like a question mark.

I'm too busy to miss Ronan or Italy. And being busy here, means I don't have to think about me and Ronan nor do I have to face up to the looming admittance; without the 50/50 bonus money we were expecting back, we should sell the house.

But I don't want to admit it. Being here helps me to procrastinate about it so I don't mind staying for a while until Mam's situation is sorted, even if it does take until June.

Maybe afterwards I could go visit my friend in Spain, go spend time in London with the kids before going to Costa Rica, Belize and maybe by then Peru will be open to visitors again. It will extend my procrastination for another while. Yes, that is what I'll do. Unless, of course, Jim gets the go-ahead from his consultant for him to travel. Then I would of course go back to Italy and possibly take him with me.

Three days later, Jim and Ingrid go to see his consultant to discuss the results of last week's scan and the next steps. Hopefully, a break from the chemo to let him get his strength back to normal and then he we can arrange his next trip to Italy. To Pompeii and the house. The idea of him coming back with me has grown, the weather would be just right, not too hot for walking around Pompeii, maybe Ingrid could ask at the appointment how soon he could travel–

–Speak of an angel, there she is calling me. She has a lot of words to say and she says them slowly, so she only has to say them once. Because she can only say them once.

"I'm calling you before Jim gets to the car. They said... they said they can do no more for him. No more chemo. They say Covid attacked his already damaged liver. They are referring him to palliative care."

"But palliative care is..."

"... End of life care." She finishes my sentence.

And with that, all the light from my world is sucked away.

———

"We're not giving up," Ingrid says with determination.

I don't know how long I stood staring out the window at the heating oil tank in Mam's garden. But long enough for my fighting rage to kick in. Out with my laptop and I pen the longest, angriest, saddest email to the person in charge of Mam's assessment. I tell her of the new unspeakable situation that has come to be... Our mother needed to be settled in her beautiful nursing home asap, with a support network around her urgently... before the future happened... so Jim could relax knowing she was looked after and I could be a support to Jim and his wife. Enough was enough, we needed this now.

Fair play to the women of the healthcare service, they came up trumps. A district nurse was out the next day.

"I actually haven't driven since before my husband died fifteen months ago. I've been too nervous." Mam has left her ego at the door this time. "I've been living with my daughter in Italy most of those months, and when I was here alone, my son Jim brought me to the supermarket and helped me, you see I can't stay on my feet too long. I haven't been to the supermarket or anywhere outside by myself in the last year and a half. I don't cook for myself as I can't stand for long and I don't see the point of just cooking for myself anyway to be honest."

Within a few days, the rest of the assessments are complete. They hold an emergency meeting and Mam gets her placement. She can move in the next day.

Mam's room at the care home is beautiful, ensuite with a balcony for flowers and plants. She has the carers in knots of laughing and chatting before I've even finished setting up her easel in her painting corner. I hear her trademark 'Ha Ha' and roars of laughter as she recounts the story of getting the heating fixed. She has an audience and I find myself laughing again at her stories, the stress band around my head is easing; It must have been cutting off the blood supply to my funny bone.

I feel moving a parent into assisted living is like dropping your child off at boarding school for the first time. You hope they'll settle in quick, make friends and enjoy the food and activities. I'm teary eyed but relieved leaving Mam the first evening, seeing her chatting to new friends, choosing what she'll have for dinner from the menu and laughing again.

Back at Mam and Dad's house, I am without Mam by my side for the first time in five months. It's the first time I have been here alone since Dad died. He was a small man, but he had a big presence, he filled this house. It's quiet.

I think too much and the sobbing starts, so much so I vomit. Sob. Vomit. Sob again because I have vomited because I sobbed so much. It's not good for me to be here alone so I get myself together and go to stay at Jim's. It's where I want to be, close to him as he's not doing well since being released from hospital.

I've been busy with Mam all day so it is the first time I have been in touch with Ingrid in the last 24 hours. He had a bad night. The doctor was called, he said Jim won't be getting out of bed again.

44

The medical profession handed him back to us, and we rally. We rally like the beautiful coven we are, who love this man with all our hearts as a brother, father, husband and son.

Turkey tail mushrooms, vitamin Bs and C, electrolytes, mangos, nectarines, kiwis, kale, spinach, greens of every variety in forty shades.

Tinctures, tonics, soaks and rubs, compresses, poultices, cannabis and weed. Teas and coffee, soups and broths—no sugar, carbs or grains of any kind. With the help of paracetamol to ease the pain in his feet caused by the chemo, we rally until his skin turns to tones less yellow. His energy returns enough for him to get up and spend time in his garden, go out for coffee, take part in life again and enjoy his family.

His eyes remain clear, his skin tone changes to normal.

We continue to rally around Jim as he gets stronger again. There are lilts of laughter in the house, lightness in a heavy situation. It comes from the courage of his wife and kids. Facing things head on. I step back and watch them swarm around him; I see pure love in their interactions. He is soothed and comfortable with them near. Their time is precious with him, I had him for all of my childhood. My place is not to be here, it's time for me to go back to Italy.

I book my flight for the following week.

Mam is flying around the corridors of the nursing home with her walker, getting her steps in, making friends and flower arrangements. There's a hula party planned for next week so she needs something yellow to wear brought to her. She's doing okay.

Back on his feet and in good form, Jim visits her and is delighted by how great the place is for her. She is being looked after, she will be looked after for the rest of her days. We both take a deep breath. We did it.

I wake to the rain beating down on the skylight window in the attic room of Jim's house. My head and chest are tight. My strong stone shell is crystallising into something much more fragile. I feel like I am turning into glass. Ronan is sending me photos of Juno in the garden with blue sky in the background, celebrating her first birthday playing with Paddy in the joys of the warm Italian spring air.

The flight I booked for tomorrow is the later more expensive option, as the earlier flight would mean needing to stay in Dublin for the night before. I am not in the mindset to be in my own company for any length of time with nothing to distract me, like cleaning or organising. I need to hold back the creeping fragility until I get back to Italy.

The feeling of needing to escape is overwhelming me again, I feel trapped by a limited timeframe before my back and body fail me, before my heart is drowned in grief, before my head explodes trying to manage the emotions my mother is going to have to face again with losing a child while still grieving for Dad.

I write to my Greek friend Ria and ask her to help me plan a trip without end around Greece. I will be travelling by myself in the autumn, I say. I need to have somewhere to run away to from the red-hot monster pacing the room panting with impatience. Maybe I won't go home... wherever home is... it's not here in Ireland and I'm not sure if it is Italy. How could Italy be home? I have no roots there, no family. Home was where my parents and brothers and sister were.

After Eileen went, we still held it together, but since Dad passed it is as if 'home' and everything in it has been rapidly sinking into the quicksand I always feared. I'd wade across quicksand without a second thought, if it meant getting that feeling of home back again.

Dad's grief blob just sits in the corner reading his paper as usual. He hasn't bothered me in months, he gave up trying to make his way across the room to me when the thrashing new monster arrived. The blob promises he'll just pay the odd gentle visit when this monster goes; but he's not going away.

The 'Incurable' monster is morphing into something much worse, something heavy and black that will stick to my body like a thick coating of tree sap.

I need a plan. And I need to think about what I want. I always have a plan. Without a doubt we need to sell The Sighing House. So I'll get started.

I fill in an Italian online evaluation which gives an estimated house price in five minutes. I can't remember the square meterage so I put in three hundred and I am not sure what some of the Italian words mean so I guess. It comes in at €453k to €650k. I am guessing I have entered incorrect information. I've also ticked a box saying three estate agents can approach me about a valuation. Why did I tick the box? Now my info has spread throughout our region before Ronan and I have even discussed this properly.

An hour later, while getting dressed, I get a call from an Italian number. I assume it is Shelly, but I am greeted with 'Pronto' followed by a deluge of Italian words. I focus, he is from an estate agency and is enquiring when I am thinking of selling my house and when can he come to do a valuation. He sounds pushy and too desperate. I say 'May' in Italian. He says he will call at the beginning of May. It has all become real.

"I think I might get a corn snake," says Jim. "I always wanted a pet snake."

His wife and children are at work. We are in the house on our own, so I grab the opportunity to hang out with him.

I burst out laughing. "Do you not think Ingrid has enough to think about at the moment other than having a snake in the house?"

Only hours before, this man was groaning in discomfort from the lasting side effects of the chemo treatment. I love his positivity and optimism. I need to be the same.

"What? I always wanted a pet snake."

Ingrid doesn't like snakes and what the hell is she going to do with the snake when he's gone? But he's not thinking of the future. Jim will live in the moment until he dies.

He's painting a watercolour of an exotic parrot alongside the blue tit he's just seen in the garden. He won't get to see parrots in the wild. Even if he was well and lived until he was ninety, he probably never would travel as he had no sense of direction. But he'd come back to Italy in a heartbeat, to the house he helped us find.

"We are going to put The Sighing House up for sale. Izzy wants to buy her own place in London and so I want to give her back her investment and I am not a BnB owner type of person. We don't need nine bedrooms."

He says nothing, just paints.

"I'm going to go and buy Mam a bird feeder for outside her window," I say, changing the subject.

"They have nice ones in the garden centre. I'll come with you."

I'm surprised he's up for it as his energy undulates. His belly looks seven months pregnant with an expected liver, but he's up and ready to go within thirty minutes.

We go to the garden centre and buy forget-me-nots for Mam's window boxes, a bird feeder for outside her nursing home window and we have a coffee.

"So what about the house, you are going to sell it?" he says, pulling on his home-rolled cigarette.

"There are things I'll finish first. But we saved a beautiful building from dying. Revived it in time for its hundredth birthday. It's too big for just the two of us." I actually don't feel this I am just repeating what everyone keeps telling me.

"Or you could do something with it. Something cool. So it is less empty."

"Like what?"

"I don't know, you'll think of something. Get people into it. Stop it sighing," he smiles.

He's right. The Sighing House needs company, to be admired and respected for all the history it holds and the stories it has inside it. Like our mother, it needs an audience. It also needs a new name, so it is not sighing anymore.

As the cloud of marijuana-scented smoke sits above our heads and we drink our coffee, he tells me how to build a path in our garden in Italy without digging. I savour the moment. The coffee. We have never gone out for coffee together before and I know... I know we will never again.

Back at his house, we watch vintage Top of the Pops from the Seventies. We laugh at the memories of our sister Eileen with her tape recorder beside the TV while we had to stay silent as she recorded the Top 10 every week. David Bowie, one of Jim's favourite artists, is performing 'Heroes'. Jim sings along.

Though nothing will keep us together,

We could steal time just for one day,

We can be heroes for ever and ever,

What d'you say?

I, I wish you could swim,

Like the dolphins, like dolphins can swim,

Though nothing, nothing will keep us together,

We can beat them, for ever and ever.

Oh we can be Heroes, just for one day,

We're nothing, and nothing will help us,

Maybe we're lying, then you better not stay,

But we could be safer, just for one day,

Just for one day...

...We'd just had our one day.

Jim is uncomfortable, his feet and legs have severe pins and needles and although he wants to sit with me on my last evening here, like every evening since he got out of hospital, he needs to go to bed early to get some sleep before the irritation becomes unbearable.

I am leaving tomorrow so I kiss and hug him goodbye.

"I'll be up to say goodbye tomorrow," he says.

I knew he would, but I just wanted to have an excuse to give him an extra hug.

The following morning while having a cup of tea with Jim, I read on social media it is Rome's birthday. I read it aloud;

"Romulus and Remus founded the city in 753 BC. At noon, every April twenty-first, the sun enters the oculus of The Pantheon creating a beam of light centred perfectly on the entrance doorway and at that moment the Emperor would cross the threshold of the temple, into the light... Oh bloody hell, I forgot I brought you a present," I say, jogging out to the hall and muffling my hand around in my inside coat pocket. How had I forgotten to give it to him?

I return to the kitchen table and place the little iron statuette of the wolf and her cubs in front of Jim. "Romulus and Seamus. I brought it back from Italy for you, for luck."

"No, you take it," he says, pushing it back towards me on the table. "You know I have huge admiration for you? You've always gone after what you want and not let anything hold you back. Always so strong. Dad said that about you–you were stronger than the three of us boys put together. You are the alpha wolf of the pack, determined to live life to the full. Don't lose that Rosie, keep it going... bring the wolf back to Italy, it's where she belongs."

Hearing something Dad said about me makes me need to change the subject before I well up.

"If I'm the alpha wolf, who are you?"

"I'm the Emperor of Rome!" His lips grin as they draw pain relief from his cannabis cigarette.

Time is ticking by. My car is here. I kiss and hug Jim. We both say 'love you' glassy eyed and I say I will be back in June.

He stands at the door smiling, a powerful smile with not a single ounce of regret or sadness, and throws kisses with force from both hands and all his heart as the car reverses slowly down the drive. The love I have for him responds with my widest smile and my hands to my heart.

We nod a last nod as the car turns away. We both know I will be back in Ireland before June. We both know this moment will be the last time we see each other.

45

From the plane I can see pools of lights, silver white and orange gold. They look as though they've been dropped in random heaps in the blackness, like Christmas decorations being unpacked. Two parallels of lights weave their way, zigzagging solo in spots of blackness as a lone car makes its way up an invisible hill. Maybe to his secret truffle hunting place.

Hello Italy, I am here again. I need you to wrap me in your softness, whisper your tender singing words in the darkness that lays ahead, hold me gently in your hand. Perhaps someday I will get into your heart but for now your hand will do.

Staring out the window, I think back to the conversation I had with the manager of Mam's nursing home before I left. "I can't do it, I can't be the one who tells her when it happens."

"It is what we are trained to do. She has friends here and our support. I will look after telling her and we will give her the support she needs." She had her hand on my arm, and like my doctor in Ireland she's my age, giving me the support I craved, saying a combination of words my body needed to hear to untighten, for my pounding headache to lift and for my heart to stop beating so hard, fighting the pull to break.

Back at The Sighing House, the stars shine brighter, the evening is still. I can hear the sound of toads by the lake, the wisteria is out. The owl that sounds like a truck reversing is about five houses away. I am so glad she moved on from considering nesting in our attic.

I sit staring at the long table in the garden.

If Dad was still alive and if Jim had not got sick, they would probably both be here this week. Dad living in the downstairs apartment with Mam. Jim over for Dad's eighty-ninth birthday in six days' time. Any excuse to come to Italy, any excuse to have a beautiful party under the stars in the warmth of the Italian evening like we did for Mam and Dad's sixtieth wedding anniversary at La Dogana six years ago. It was such a precious night.

The central seats for the two people I enjoyed sharing the house progress with most, and who I could not imagine laughter happening without at the long family table; Dad and Jim. The vision is now empty of warmth, laughter, love. The house is pointless. Its purpose gone.

He was supposed to be with me when we are in our eighties, sitting on the deck we built together in his garden beside the pond of koi, making things out of clay and wood. Painting. Planning recipes, enjoying our kids' families. We discussed it, how it was supposed to be, all our lives. It was the ultimate end goal. And now this monster has gone and spoiled it. What sort of fucking universe or loving God creates these monsters? All I can see ahead are years of emptiness. Without him.

Ronan joins me in the garden, bringing me back from my thoughts. He, being sixteen years older than me, is more than likely to go before me. More grief I'll have to deal with.

It's best to get it over with. Get all the sadness and grief over with at the same time. It's time to tell him my big life decision, and it's not about travel.

"I want a separation."

Ronan looks at me bewildered. "Are you serious?"

"We might as well. We live separately in the house anyway, we don't eat together because of your spaghetti bolognese addiction and we stay in separate rooms."

"Only when we are asleep, just because we snore."

"Because you snore."

"You snore too."

"Bloody hell, is this some sort of competition?" I say. "I don't want to fear living on my own, I don't want to be a burden on our kids, I want to be independent of everyone. I'm going away."

"What? Where?"

"We need to sell the house."

"What?"

"Well we are not getting the bonus refund back so we can't give Izzy back a lump sum from it and the house needs to pay for itself. We'll sell the house, buy you a small apartment wherever you want. Give Izzy back her money and I will go travelling. It's what I always wanted to do."

"I'd like to travel too."

"No, you wouldn't, not like me. I am not talking about a week in a hotel in Greece. I'm going to get my back strong and go backpacking. While I still can. If I still can. If I can't I'll just bring a small suitcase. Whatever. But it will be solo, to places you don't want to go. Camping in rain forests and things like that for the next ten years." I'm nearly breathless saying it all without pauses.

"What about the dogs?"

"You can have custody of them." I mumble, "They are just going to die someday too."

"What?"

"Nothing. I don't want to live this version of my life anymore. I don't want to live like this, feeling this way. I don't want to hurt you, I just want to go. We have heard all of each other's stories, we know everything about each other, so much so we predict what the other is going to say. We are so bloody boring and I'm tired of firefighting all the stupid things you do because you don't bother reading instructions."

"This is about me not reading instructions?"

"NO! I just want a separation, okay?"

"Okay... Okay... But maybe we should wait and discuss this in a couple of months? You have a lot on your plate at the moment. And the way the last year has gone, since your dad died, the pressure of the wedding business, your mother here, Luca moving out and Jim... we haven't really had time to be... us."

But I stay practical. "We don't have a choice. We don't want to run a BnB and the house is too big for just us, so we need to sell it. You were right suggesting it months ago, I should have listened. I never listen to you, I am always the one controlling, being angry, telling you what to do, I must be horrible to live with. Selling the house is the best thing to do, the right thing to do, right?"

"Right," he says low and slowly, as my mind and mouth run on.

"And by the time we give Izzy back her money, there will be enough left for one small place. Too small for both of us, so you can have it. I'll become a nomad and visit you now and then."

As always, I am not giving him a choice. I've thought it through. But I, for the first time, am choosing how I want to live without having to take anyone else into consideration. I am my own person.

By June when I leave, I won't have to care for anyone. I won't have to plummet into grief and sadness again or take Ronan into account as we are separating. Dividing. Breaking the bond. I'll just go away, far away and keep everything and everyone at a distance. Life will be easier. No more heartbreak.

I need this agreed and sorted quickly because I know what's ahead and it will happen soon... I know the date.

After a restless night, I go out into the garden and whack ivy and dig and pull weeds. I know the date. But I don't want to voice it.

Jim's wife calls me. "He had a bad day, so he took a sedative. The palliative nurse care team arrived early this morning and they are keeping him sedated."

She's like me. She knows the date too. The date it will happen. But neither of us voice it.

For the next two days I spend twelve hours a day whacking ivy, pulling weeds, digging a bed–around Tiny Tommy, Ronan's tomato plant that is no longer tiny, it's huge–for planting something... anything... I don't care. The action of digging keeps me in the moment, passes the time without thinking as the date gets closer. And closer.

'Hug him for me, kiss him, tell him I love him.' I text sobbing before I go to bed on the eve of the day.

And then it was here. Our Dad's birthday.

And I get the call. The Beautiful Soul we knew as Jim, Seamus, Jimmy, James, Jamsie, Jim Bob, peacefully crossed the threshold of his temple into the light in the early hours of the morning.

46

As soon as they heard the news, my tribe of women stepped in to support their broken friend. "Don't worry about the dogs I'll be over with Chloe and stay until you get back, take as long as you need," Karen said immediately, already rearranging her work schedule.

Lucia arrived on her motorbike. "I am here, what do you need me to do?" She is armed with hugs and practicality and helped my shaking hands to book the flights for the next day.

After a week we're back in Italy from Ireland. The dogs are excited to see us.

Karen has left flowers and incense. There's a card from Shelly beside a queue of pots with jasmine, lavender and rosemary ready for planting in the flowerbed, where Ronan is standing admiring his tomato plant that has grown out of control while we were away. I'm walking from room to room dazed, feeling lost in my own house. The dream is over.

I can feel the walls sending me the love they've absorbed from the laughter, the excitement, the amazement Jim, Ronan and I shared running around the house during the first visit. This house holds our memories.

Everything I did in this house is tinted with Dad and Jim's enthusiasm and advice and ideas to be added; the shutters Jim advised me on restoring to the tile grouting dad talked me through. My energy input into the renovation was fuelled by how much they would enjoy the finished result.

I stand in the stairwell, not knowing if I need to go up or down.

My heart races then slows. I have no purpose. The house feels low, its energy has changed, it too is without purpose. It needs love bouncing off the walls. Laughter. Togetherness. Luca and Mam are gone and they are not coming back, but their laughter and voices are in the walls, Izzy's too. It's like the house has absorbed the spirit of my family.

It's just me and Ronan now. Our kids have left the nest, our duty is done, and we have fulfilled all the dreams we had dreamed when we first got together thirty years ago. We are just a couple in a house who are separating.

I have already made five cups of tea today. Two I don't know where I've left. I make another cup of tea and notice when I lift it, the surface of the liquid is moving like there's an earthquake. But there is no 'earth-cake' happening; it is my hand trembling. I need to get out, to go somewhere, I can't be here. I can't be alone. Upstairs, with my tea still steaming and my whole body trembling, I can't write, I can't... my phone buzzes. 'Calendar Reminder for today: Retreat.'

I completely forgot I had booked it. I can't even remember what type of retreat it is. Yoga? Meditation? Pottery? No, it was something calming not a craft. Sitting on my bed, I try to find the email about it. Eventually I do. Introduction is at 7pm, check in time; after 11am.

Fuck it, I'll go. It will give me a focus away from the monster, who has not yet caught up with me since I left Ireland. He has crystallised into a much more terrifying beast, and will return to move in permanently with his heavy grief baggage, like the Ghost of Christmas Past's heavy chains.

If I go away, I can hide from the grief monsters. If I go to a place where no one knows of their existence, then grief won't find me for a few days.

I empty my unpacked suitcase from Ireland onto the bed, grab a few things from the pile and repack it. "Ronan," I call out. "I am going. I'm taking the car."

He's at the bedroom door. "Where are you going?"

"I'm going to a retreat I booked. I need to go. Now."

"Where is it?"

"I don't know, somewhere in Umbria. I remember checking before and it was about an hour and a half drive away."

"I'll drive you. Just give me a minute to get my jacket."

In the car, I'm trying to find an email or message from the retreat coordinator. My hands are trembling less now that I'm in the car, away from being alone in the house without a purpose. I have something to do; I don't have to think about anything or anyone I can focus on the retreat. I can be distracted by people who have no idea of what happened last week, last month, last year. For the last fifteen months.

"Which direction?" asks Ronan.

"Towards Perugia. I think it is in Spello."

I scroll through the messages again and eventually find the address. "Oh, it's not Spello, it's in Spoleto."

"You haven't told me anything about this retreat, what type of retreat is it?"

I'm reading the message properly for the first time... a qigong and Breathing retreat.

"Qigong," I state.

"What's qigong?"

I'm ahead of him, I have just googled it as I don't know what it is either.

"It's ehh. It's like tai chi... I think. It was before tai chi. Tai chi came from qigong. It's part of traditional Chinese medicine. It involves using exercises to optimise energy within the body, mind, and spirit, with the goal of improving and maintaining health and well-being. Included in the practice are exercises made up of postures, breath work, and intention setting."

"Are you reading that from the internet?"

"Yes."

"Because you don't know what it is either?"

"Yes."

"It's interesting though. I remember when we first met, you

were thinking of doing a course in Chinese medicine and tai chi."

Flash back to the Eighties and my 'Guide to Evening Courses' book, where I'd spend hours circling things I wanted to learn. The full-page ad on Chinese medicine had a big star, it faced the yoga instructor page which also had a big star.

Yoga was not popular then, but I loved anything eastern and ancient. The only two locations in Dublin where you could learn Chinese medicine and yoga teaching were beside each other on Dawson Street and my sixteen-year-old brain had worked out a detailed weekly schedule of how I could do both courses if I gave up school.

To do the two would cost £635 per year and I would be qualified in three years–by the time I was twenty–and then I could travel with my new qualifications... My parents listened, I went on about it for months, but it was a lot of money we didn't have and part-time jobs were not available in cash strapped Ireland then, so I stayed in school and my 'Guide to Evening Courses' sat on the shelf beside my 'Work Your Way Around the World' book.

It was the only 'what if' I had about my life. And one I had forgotten.

I have read more of the email and we take a pit stop at a shopping mall so I can buy a required yoga mat and soft shoes.

We travel into the green heart of Italy. Trevi melts into the rock it is perched on. The sun has broken through, illuminating the cream facades and steeples flowing down the rock face of the mountain they are built into. It looks like a carving. I forget my broken heart for a moment as the lush greens and beauty of the region I live in makes me double take my breath. I have not travelled this road before. Or perhaps I have but have never seen it through tear-glazed eyes, making it look all the more like an Impressionist's painting.

I have had no time to develop any expectations of this retreat.

Ronan drives me so that he can have the car while I am away. Also, I am still chicken about driving anywhere I am not familiar with by myself on Italian motorways.

An hour into the journey, we see grey black clouds ahead of us. Turning left, we follow the road away from the motorway. The directions are straightforward, leading us to ever smaller roads until we find ourselves climbing up hair-pin bends through a forest.

We follow the GPS as the clouds gather and darken to the point where cars have their headlights on. Up, up, up we go. We see a cyclist coming down and wonder how he had got up that far without dying. Steep hair-pin bend after steep, hair-raising bend are darkened by the enclosing forest. The last stretch of road on the GPS looks like someone with a blue marker has been given electric shocks while trying to draw a hexagon.

It crosses my mind that perhaps there isn't a retreat. Maybe it's just a ploy by some lunatic to entice women to an abandoned hotel and he's going to murder and bury me in the forest. With a flash of lightning, followed by a clap of ominous thunder, rain beats down.

"I hate to bring it up, but when you get back you really need to focus on getting your Tessera Sanitaria sorted," says Ronan, probably worried I'm having a breakdown.

"I don't care about it anymore. If I get sick and they decide to leave me to die, so be it." I mean every word as the rain pelts against the windscreen like a hoard of very strong forest nymphs shooting water balloons at us.

"I'll walk you in," says Ronan as we pull up at the hotel the GPS has led us to. There are about eight cats gathered on the porch sheltering from the rain, sitting on a cobwebbed collection of parked vintage motorbikes.

"No need," I say. The way I'm feeling being buried in the forest would be a welcomed escape.

"Are you sure? It looks dark."

"I can look after myself..." Do I have to remind him we are separating and he is free of his husbandly protector role? "It's just a quaint old hotel, perched on top of a mountain. Probably doesn't get many people staying here. I'll be fine. Best you get back down the mountain before that bigger darker cloud reaches here."

I may be leaving him, but I still care.

My hotel room smells of cleaned old stuff reminding me of my Great Aunt Kitty's old house, the one Mam and I used to visit before Aunt Kitty moved into the so-called nursing home. It's only 2pm but I need the lights on. Pulling back the thick net curtains doesn't help lift the darkness of the room which is angled towards the rest of the building, with its small window facing north.

Thunder is rumbling and the rain running down the roof is overflowing the gutter. A crack of lightning, the lights go off and I'm in semi-darkness. I can't get a phone signal never mind Wi-Fi and the room is too dark to read, so the only thing I can do is meditate and nap.

When I wake, the rain has stopped. It's still dark and threatening and it's hours before the intro session. It's too tempting to stay in bed, be alone and let grief take over. I need to literally push myself. I roll out onto the floor. My foot still tangled in the sheet, I crawl to the bathroom, climb into standing position with the help of the sink, throw some water on my face and creep down the quiet dark narrow passageway between bedroom doors.

Outside the hotel, I follow a path lined with trees, work around the puddles left from the storm and around the scattered picnic tables.

Ahead there are brick pillars on either side of an ancient stone wall enclosing a wood beyond. A hiking trail signpost reads: Il Bosco Sacro di Monteluco. The Sacred Wood of Monteluco.

To the right there is a small cloister with a bell tower silhouetted against the brightening sky. The sound of chanting entices me towards it. A string of monks in brown robes file from a doorway and cross the small courtyard and disappear though another doorway under the arches. I walk tentatively into the courtyard and follow the piped chanting to a church dedicated to some saint.

Of course, as this is Italy, the saint's body is on display in a glass case in the church. Around his neck, he's wearing a Saint Francis's wooden cross. Just like James did a week ago at his wake. It was a special occasion after all. I realise since he died, I have flicked back to my childhood name for my brother. Jim, Jimmy, Seamus was always James and Jamsie to me as a child. That was his christened name. The name our parents called him.

I go back to the brick pillars and into the woods, the sacred woods, followed by a cat with one eye. Another cat sits up a tree, perched in a comfy dip where two branches split from each other, watching me lazily.

The trees are tall, with ancient and gnarled moss-covered trunks. "That way is north," I find myself saying, "because it is the side the most moss is growing on." It is something James taught me as a kid.

Not too far along the path stands a stone with an inscription in Latin. The information notice board explains it is a replica of an original stone dating back to the third century BC now kept in the Civic Museum in Spoleto. The translation states; If anyone knowingly takes anything from the forest or cuts down a tree in the sacred woods dedicated to Jove, "they must pay atonement to the god Jupiter. An ox and 300 donkeys will be the fine."

I spot another cat further on, watching me from the stone wall. I'm beginning to think someone misunderstood and paid their atonement with three hundred cats.

Deeper into the lush Sacred Wood of Monteluco, climbing some crooked embedded stone steps, I stand surrounded by rock on the edge of the wood, looking over a panoramic vista of forests, valleys and the spectacular Ponte delle Torri aqueduct connecting the hill to the city of Spoleto below. I am completely alone.

"I could have a good cry here if I wanted," I tell myself.

But I don't feel the need. I am at peace. And in that moment I know, so is James, Jamsie, Jim, Jimmy, Jim Bob, Seamus.

47

A fter the intro session, it's time for dinner. There are several women on the retreat of similar age to me and we naturally gravitate towards each other at the dining table.

Chicken fillets seasoned with lemon are barbecuing on grills laid out on the huge hearth over glowing embers stolen from the roaring wood fire that warms the unusually cool May mountain air.

I immediately walk over to take a picture of it. But stop. I was taking it to send to James.

This happens again during dinner. I want to send him a photo of the black cabbage cooked in juniper berry juice giving it a near luminous aqua blue tint and the shredded wild chicory scooped onto my plate. It reminds me of last meal I made for him; purple cabbage with apple and shrimps–the closest I could get to lobster.

I could send the photos to other friends or family and they will glance at it, give it a heart or a thumbs up. Whereas James would have examined the picture, looked at it repeatedly, lingered on it and then have called immediately. By discussing enthusiastically every detail, he'd be there in the moment, living it with me through my words. His infectious enthusiasm would increase both our senses and our appreciation of every detail.

The same with the house. He experienced it in its raw dilapidated form, saw its potential and loved every second of its transformation; the renovation of the roof, the frustration and joys of each room being brought back to life.

He had always been available to help with a practical solution during the house renovation and to make me feel better during the most difficult times of my life. And here I am, facing one of the worst times of my life and he isn't here. It's the worst, because it is because he isn't here.

It doesn't take long before the group of women I find myself amongst at dinner are chatting like old friends.

"It was completely homophobic, but I thought it was the truth," says Gloria the seventy-eight-year-old sitting beside me talking about her previous existence as a leader in a cult Christian mission. She is now a psychic and astrologer. "And then my husband, came out as gay and they expelled us. Our two sons grew up and they are gay too. God teaches us lessons in the most loving way."

"Pretend you can't see any cats, I'm freaking Anna out saying I can't see any," says Jenn–a Dutch space engineer who helped build the satellite on its way to explore the moons of Jupiter in 2028. She has rushed to a seat beside us before her pilot friend Anna strolls over and sits down opposite us.

The place is riddled with cats, beautiful cats, all very different in breed and colour. The wheezy oldest one curled up in a chair is eighteen and the hotel owner introduced him to me as Jupiter.

"Jupiter keeps cropping up in my life today; the woods, your work Jenn and the name of the c-," I nearly let the cat out of the bag about the cats, just as Anna joins us. "–cat-astrophic hurricane happening..." I say adding to the word cat and covering my tracks.

"Oh no, where?" says Anna. Jenn is biting her lip trying not to laugh.

"Nowhere important."

Anna looks at me oddly, "But it is catastrophic?"

I ignore her. "What is important is for Gloria to tell me what it means for Jupiter to be popping up in my life. She has studied astrology for twenty years you know?" I say changing the subject.

"Jupiter is the guru planet," Gloria says, happy to share her knowledge. "You said your dog's name is Juno? Jupiter was married to Juno, there's another connection for you. Jupiter is called the Jeeva or soul of a person in astrology and relates to soul searching."

She takes a pack of well-thumbed oracle cards out of her pocket, fans them out and tells me to pick two.

"They are contradictory," she says, looking at my choice. "They are saying stay where you are but you need to go in a different erection than what you are thinking. Something involving women." English is not her first language. There is laughter amongst the group about how I need a different erection and it continues when Jenn lets it slip that there actually are cats all over the place as Jupiter walks slowly in with his tail in the air.

"Oh my God," says Anna. "I was going to book to see a shrink when I got back, I can't believe you kept that up since we arrived!"

I can't remember the last time I laughed until I cried, but it happens several times that evening and the following evening too. Being around like-minded women is healing me; Anna has an elderly mother and teenagers, Jenn is the breadwinner of the family and has an artistic husband, Gloria has... well Gloria has been through every type of grief and survived. It can be done.

It turns out Gloria can speak ten languages. Six fluently.

"The language of Ireland is the most beautiful," she says as we have lunch outside at the picnic tables one of the days. "I spent a year in the west of Ireland when I was younger learning the language. I have forgotten a lot of it but I really loved the structure and depth of meaning in the phrases."

I am embarrassed to admit to her even after all this time, she probably still has a better command of the Irish language than I have.

"The Irish had the essence of mindfulness through their language millennia before it became trendy. Emotions are temporary not absorbed," observes Gloria.

I understand what she means; instead of saying 'I am sad', Gaelic translates into 'Sadness is on me'. Instead of saying 'You made me smile', we say 'You put a smile on me'. The language instills in us that feelings will pass.

"Like oil on water," I say. "You let emotions touch you but you don't absorb them into you." As I say it, I feel something shift inside me.

"I love the writings of the Irish philosopher John O'Donohue, do you know him? He wrote a wonderful book called Anam Cara?" asks Gloria.

"I do! I just put our ragged copy of it on our bookshelf recently. My husband's brother had called his house Anam Cara, the book was his."

"It's a great name for a house. And a great book, why did he part with it?"

I see a distant shape coming closer waving at me. The grief monster of Ronan's brother Niall. "It was something my husband inherited, when his brother passed away eight years ago."

Niall's monster skips off into the distance again.

"I'm sorry for your loss," says Anna. I feel like saying you don't know the half of it. But I stop myself and let Niall have his moment of being remembered.

"What does it mean, Anam Cara?" asks Jenn, breaking my thoughts.

Gloria and I take a simultaneous deep breath; how do you describe one of the most beautiful phrases in the world? I can hear the piped chanting from the friary a short distance away while a heavy mist has risen from the floor of the surrounding woods, the coolness of the damp earth rising to enjoy new summer heat.

"The Celtic Irish believed each body has a light and energy radiating from it," I start.

"Like an aura?" asks Anna.

"Yes, or you might call it a soul but it's more about an energy. And Anam Cara is when two souls bond and intermingle," I say.

"Soul mates?" says Jenn, scooping up a second helping of spelt salad.

"Not really," says Gloria. "It is above a sexual or romantic connection of souls. Anam is the word you could translate into 'soul' and 'cara' means friend so it is more 'soul friend'. But for a person to make this genuine bond with another, they first need to see beauty and light in themselves."

A surge of love for my own Celtic heritage rises in my chest, it's something I haven't felt in a very long time. My anger for everything had included Ireland for its health service, weather, cost of living, lack of public transport from the airport, you name it. But I love being Irish and I used to love everything good about it, especially its Celtic mysticism and language and here it was resurrecting itself in a sacred wood up a mountain in Italy.

"It's the connection between people on a spiritual level, on a deep level. And souls can only make this everlasting powerful bond when the owners of the souls involved are open and honest about themselves. Then their soul flows and mingles and connects with other souls; you become each other's Anam Cara."

"Like us all here at this table?" Anna grins.

"Yes, I suppose so!" I'm smiling.

"By the way," I say, mopping up the sauce on my plate with a scarpetta. "Anam means name, so when someone in Irish asks you what your name is, they are asking you what your soul is called. Like it is some sort of spirit animal attached to you." I've never made the association between the two before now.

Of course, this moves the conversation on to what each of our spirit animals would be. I feel safe enough to talk about how I identified the hedgehog as my dad's spirit animal. But I still have not mentioned James. It's too raw and anyway James had such an affinity with so many bloody animals it is going to take time for me to figure out what is his.

"Here, I found the writer guy O'Donohue you were talking about," says Jenn, looking at her phone.

"His description of Anam Cara is; In Anam Cara love, you are understood as you are without mask or pretension. The superficial and functional lies and half-truths of social acquaintance fall away, you can be as you really are. Love allows understanding to dawn, and understanding is precious. Where you are understood, you are at home."

That's how I would love people to feel in my home...

"Jenn, how the hell are you getting Wi-Fi here? I can't even get phone reception," I say, miffed. While everyone in the group has an internet connection, I am the only one who can't get phone reception never mind Wi-Fi during the entire retreat. I did manage to send Ronan a message from the rock in the woods on the first day to say; all was okay, I hadn't been buried in the woods, but I could not get phone reception and I'd call him from the train station when I was on my way back after the retreat.

"I'm going to order his book," Anna says, tapping while saying off-hand, "Anam Cara, it is a very nice name for a house. Do you have a name on your house in Italy?"

"It was The Sighing House. But it's time for it to finish sighing, I think it's time for it to change to Anam Cara."

"A nice way to keep Niall's spirit alive." Gloria winks.

48

The monastery bell dongs at seven in the morning.

"The friars are such light weights," Jenn laughs to me. Our retreat group had already meditated and started our pre-breakfast qigong practice.

I did not know what I was getting into when I arrived at the retreat. Every day, I just take each breathing exercise, moment and movement as it comes and let it work its magic through my body as heaviness lifts and my energy shifts.

The class after breakfast is outside in a field shaded by the sacred forest. We are instructed to, "Find a focus point. Use it to empty your mind for thirty minutes."

I chose a daisy. But my mind does not empty, instead it floods with a memory of sitting on grass in the convent field behind our childhood home. Eileen is there showing me how to make a daisy chain, and Jim is showing me the secret hideout amongst the bushes with the white berries we can squish but can't eat. Love and Kindness. My eyes burn. But I blink the sensation away and feel the year of anger shifting and an enormous sense of gratitude flooding my body for the love and kindness I had in my life from them. And for the love of Ronan.

He's been there for me through the last eighteen months, bending like a bamboo to my mood swings and my needs.

In the afternoon, as we move through another qigong technique, I feel my body being flooded with the same sense of love and kindness.

I acknowledge the grief monsters who have weighed me down like a heavy, wet overcoat. They are here to stay, but I need to make them my allies, more fluffy and less fierce while they stick by my side for the rest of my life. I need to train them to sit with me quietly so they don't take over conversations, situations, or me when I am alone.

Them and their bags of overwhelming sadness had turned me into a monster. But it's one I can get rid of, push out the back door and gladly say goodbye to. I am in control of this one. I can do this.

Before dinner, I wander alone in a different direction through the sacred wood where the trees create strange forms but I'm safe.

I walk to the friary again and go into the cloister. The historic sleeping cells in the friary are open to be viewed by visitors through the four-foot-high doorways–making it necessary for the monk entering to bow his head and stay humble. Spots on the walls have shed their rough plaster, revealing a structure of woven saplings between beams.

I pick up a piece of literature in English on the donation box table.

"During the Middle Ages, not too far from Monteluco in the town of Assisi, the son of a wealthy merchant experienced a spiritual conversion and became a revered mystic, known throughout the world as Saint Francis of Assisi. It is here in the Sacred Woods of Monteluco where Saint Francis started his Franciscan Brotherhood, now the largest religious order in the world."

He was here!

I wish I could tell James, he would have loved it here... but the wording changes in my head. He is loving it here, with me.

After some more powerful breath work and energy-building movements, we have dinner outside next to the woods.

I have not shared my recent year, I'm not ready to yet. I'm enjoying having a break from grief, training the monsters to sit with me and not to take me over. Even when Gloria mentions death—"it is like stupidity, as the person it has happened to isn't affected, only the people around them"—my monsters give me breathing space.

It turns out that all of us at the table backpacked in our twenties, and I'm not the only one who wants to feel that freedom again.

"Life is much better after fifty, we have time to ourselves and realise life is too short not to fulfil dreams. It is what brought me to Italy from Argentina; what woman doesn't dream of living in Italy for a period of her life?" says Gloria. "But I enjoy making connections with people, proper soulful connections. It is difficult to find places where I can meet like-minded women who are travelling by themselves—like a retreat house, where we can talk and support each other like we are doing now, no?

That is why I came on this retreat. I knew it would be mostly older women, we like to nourish our souls."

Everyone is nodding and humming agreement.

"Women at our stage in life need to be around other women. It's the way it is in the tribal communities I have visited around the world. We have lost it in the western world. Women need each other's support and to share our wisdom and joy," says Gloria.

It was while sitting outside, sharing dinner in the warmth of the summer night with these wonderful women, that I noticed the grief monsters were not beside me or on top of me. They were sound asleep under a tree.

The healing sisterly connection of Anam Cara and the Italian sacred wood were working their magic.

49

S aying goodbye to the group was full of hugs and promises to meet again. Gloria was driving in the direction of the train station, so she gave me a lift.

She was the one I had shared most with during the retreat but I still didn't let my guard down about James. I couldn't talk about him, not yet as it would mean talking about him in the past tense and I didn't want him to be there–in my past.

On the way to the station, I talk to her about the idea that had kept me awake for hours the night before. It excited me so much I scribbled about twenty pages of notes before I could sleep again.

"It's a great idea but what will your husband think about it?" smiles Gloria.

"Conosco i miei polli" I answer. Gloria laughs, she speaks fluent Italian so is familiar with the meaning of 'I know my chickens'.

Arriving at the station the air feels damp, nearly chilly, so I take my denim jacket from my case. I haven't worn it since Ireland. I slide my phone into its pocket and hear a clunk of resistance. Fumbling into the pocket I can feel what it is without taking it out. The wolf and her cubs figurine.

As Gloria gives me a last hug and a goodbye, she says, "And don't worry, he's okay. He'll give you a fun sign on the way home to show you he'll always be close and around to listen when you need him."

I want to say "who?", but I know who. How did Gloria know who? I hadn't mentioned him, I was so careful all week not to let my guard down. Not to open the Pandora's Box of emotion.

I lift my suitcase up the final step to the platform. There is a woman walking further ahead of me in vintage 1920s attire. I notice her white stockings first with the seam up the back of her leg from her cream-heeled laced leather shoes to her knee-length dress. Her short hair, perfectly curled, peeps out from under her blue, felt cloche hat. She is pulling a dark red leather vintage replica suitcase and matching doctor's bag.

By the time I get up the last step to the platform she has found the perfect place to stand; under a vintage-style sign with her back against the red brick wall. It's then I notice she is about the same age as me, taller but similar build. There's a long string of clear beads around her neck over her short sleeve, blue dress with a white outline art nouveau pattern and white collar.

Messages that have been hanging around in cyberspace begin to ping on my phone as it reconnects to a network.

There's one from Izzy: "Dad told me you have been talking about selling the house to give me back money. I've thought about it and don't want you to. It was a gift not an investment.

I'm getting some work, don't worry. Everything will work out. Love you. xxx"

It's nice of her to say, but I don't want to be the one to delay her dreams, I'm still going to pay her back the contribution she made to the purchase of the house. The house will pay her back. It will be the house that buys itself.

Rain is threatening again, so the few of us on the platform group under the shelter with the vintage sign. An older woman beside me, possibly Australian, smiles at the vintage dressed lady, "you must be going somewhere nice?"

"I am going home to The Netherlands. Does anyone know what station I change for the train to Perugia?"

"I am going to it, so you can follow me," I say.

"Thank you. I get terribly nervous travelling on my own."

She sits opposite me; she has a sweet round face, her thin lips emphasised with red matte lipstick.

We chat. "When I got divorced ten years ago, I decided I was going to live the way I wanted to and vintage is my passion and now my way of life."

She since married her childhood sweetheart who she was travelling home to, having spent a couple of days with two friends going to fashion museums in Europe. She had met these women online through their mutual passion for vintage clothes.

"It's difficult to find clothes to fit, as the women back then were a lot more petite. Even their feet. I get my clothes online, or vintage shops or sometimes people call me and say their grandma has died and they have some clothes I might like. The dress I am wearing is one hundred years old."

The same age as my house.

I admire someone who can wear something so delicate and beautiful and live without the fear of spilling anything down the front of it–something I would have managed to achieve before I even ate something.

She hates travelling by herself as she has debilitating chronic migraines twenty-four days out of thirty in the month. She has tried everything, every medication and diet. But she was determined to take this trip and not let her chronic illness get the better of her. I suggest no grains, as it works for my sister-in-law. She will try it.

The conversation comes around to my story of buying the house by accident. I mention my brother was with us when we found the house and cautiously tell her he died recently–it's like I'm testing how it feels to say it. She sympathises. The look in her eyes is genuine, filled with kindness.

I don't go into the detail of James 'borrowing' the wolf figurine with Romulus and Seamus and then gifting it back to me on what was to be our last Christmas together, but I do think of it safely stashed in my pocket close to my heart, and like when someone is listening to a sad song they need to get over, she sees me dip and says something completely different to lift me out from under the wave.

"You bought a house by accident, well six years ago I bought a wolf as a pet by accident."

"Wow, a wolf? What's it like having a wolf in your house?"

She sees I am genuinely interested.

"It's very different from having a dog, although my chihuahua now howls and thinks he's a wolf too."

We're both laughing a little, relieved the mood has lightened again.

"He can carry a duck's egg in his mouth back home without breaking it but can crush a golf ball with his back teeth in one bite—the wolf, not the chihuahua. He's very instinctive. James senses one of my migraines before they come on and cuddles into my neck. He also kept nudging my back before I discovered I had kidney stones, I—"

"I'm sorry, James is your husband?"

"No! My wolf. My wolf's name is James."

And there it was. The little fun sign he promised, to say he will always be close.

————

"So, how was your Shih Tzu retreat?" asks Ronan, lifting my bag into the boot of the car.

"Shih Tzu? That's a type of dog. Do you think I was on a dog grooming retreat?"

"What was it again?"

"Qigong... Shiatsu is a type of massage... is that what you are confusing it with?"

"Ah that's what it was. Easy mistake. How was it anyway? You look different... a lot more relaxed than when you left, if you don't mind me saying." He's being cautious with words, picking them carefully. He knows I'd have been over thinking during the last five days and planning which direction I want to go, possibly changing my mind about where I want to live or what I want to do like the flip of a coin. That's how his life has always been with me; 'I kept life interesting', he'd always say.

"I have an idea I want to talk to you about..." I am unable to hold back my enthusiasm.

"I guessed you would, go on, tell me. What is it?"

"Well first, I want to say sorry for being so angry and such a pain to live with during the last year or so–"

"There's no need to apologise, I wasn't always the bag of laughs to live with during our relationship either. Hadn't really considered how tough it must have been on you, so I have been thinking and I understand if you want–"

"Let's not go there. I want to tell you my idea," I say while pulling out the notebook I had spent the night before nearly filling as he turns onto the motorway.

"I don't want us to sell the house. I love it, but it needs to make an income and we don't want to do BnB... and you know how I need a purpose?" I don't wait for him to answer this. "Well, I have come up with a different idea..."

Although he's driving, I can see his face relax. He doesn't want to sell the house either.

"First of all, I have a new name for the house... Anam Cara."

"Like Niall's?"

"Yeah, it will be a way to keep his memory alive and the meaning is what I want the house to be."

"But it's not Italian?"

"I know. But we are not Italian, we are Irish living in Italy. We are now part of the house's history so it makes more sense for us to give it an Irish name rather than an Italian name. The same way we gave Paddy an Irish name even though he's an Italian dog. And the Celts were all over that area with Hannibal so Gaelic words reverberated across the hills around the lake at some point in the past."

"Okay, never mind that. What do you mean by what you want the house to be... I'm nervous."

"Where people can be themselves and connect with like-minded souls."

"Go on," he says cautiously.

"Being around women has got me through the last month. Women my age thrive around other women. There are so many of us who have been through stuff and decide life is too short, and like me want to travel solo, like we did in our backpacking days. There are so many who want to experience living in Italy, not just stay for a couple of nights in a hotel doing all the tourist stuff." I pause.

"Keep going." He's still cautious.

"Well, the house has eight bedrooms, I'd like to open it for writers' retreats and a place where women can stay—a base for them to live amongst other like-minded women in the heart of Italy for a week or a month or two months. Not like a party house, a quiet house, a retreat house; somewhere they can work remotely, or work on a writing project or solo travel in Italy but experience it in a house with other women rather than a hotel."

He isn't objecting, so I continue.

"It will bring in an income so the house can fund itself, we can finish the bits that need to be done and we can pay Izzy back gradually... I don't want to sell the house."

"You want to start a business in Italy? Even with all the bureaucracy and taxes it would involve?"

"Lots of people run BnBs in Italy. It's different but the same basis. We'll figure it out. But it isn't so much about the money, it's more about the communal space, about the women, about me having a purpose. And that's what we can gift the house for its one hundredth birthday; a new purpose. A beautiful one."

I realise I am talking a mile a minute as usual about a massive freaky idea and expecting Ronan to fall in with it. "Even if it's just for a year and we then decide it's not for us, at least we tried. What do you think?"

"Well..." He leaves a long pause. "I'm glad I got the terrace finished while you were away. It will be perfect for you to do your qigong on and have dinner with your women." He grins.

"You got it finished?"

"Check your phone. I sent you photos, you should have reception now you are off the top of the mountain."

"Well done!..." I say looking at the beautiful, impressive courtyard he has laid. I kiss him on the cheek spontaneously. "But what do you really think of the idea?"

"As ever with your ideas Rosie, it sounds crazy but I know you will make it work and we'll figure it out. We always do, don't we?" He takes my hand and kisses it. "I'm just happy to see you back to your old self again."

It's like all the anger has magically melted away and been replaced by my word for the year. The two grief monsters are still with me, but they are sitting in the backseat chatting to each other, distracted by the scenery of where we live.

"Other than working on the courtyard... How was your week?" I ask, knowing I had left him in a whirlwind of emotion.

"Well, not as exciting as yours... I picked up a shell in the garden today and saw there was a snail inside. It was roasting, so I ran him under the cold tap and then left him in the shade beside a puddle of water. Ten minutes later I checked in on him and he was having a drink."

Why did I ever think of leaving this man? Saving the creature that will probably have eaten his prized Tiny Tommy tomato plant before we get home. Home to Anam Cara.

———

If you enjoyed this book please leave a kind review on Amazon or Goodreads. They mean a lot to me!

As this is a living memoir series, I don't know what is going to happen next.

While Book 5 is about gut wrenching grief (wasn't expecting that), Book 6 is a lot more fun! You can get Rosie Lets Herself Go; A Rosie Life In Italy 6 here.

Sign up for my newsletter on www.rosiemeleady.com for updates about my books, the house, and opportunities to stay at Anam Cara .

In The Air Around Us

Come sit beside me under the shade of the trees,
Come wrap your arm around me in the shape of
      the breeze.
Share your adventures amongst the galaxies and
      stars.
Tell me excitedly of the jungles you have swung
      through,
The ocean depths and mountain highs you have
      gone to.
Whisper how love is all of you gone wholehearted,
Your new adventure is just getting started.
Holding my hand, within the touch of soft moss,
You are here, there is no loss.
But I miss you... Terribly.

xxx - Rose

ACKNOWLEDGMENTS

Many thanks to:

Marco Marella for his fabulous cover illustrations

Suzy Pope, Lucy Hayward, Rosemary Beard for their editing skills.

Jordan Barnes and Elizabeth Reed for motivating me up to write every morning from 6,000 and 10,000 miles away.

And of course Ronan for putting up with me throughout this book.

ABOUT THE AUTHOR

Dubliner Rosie Meleady was a magazine publisher and editor for twenty years. She won the International Women in Publishing Award 1996 at the ripe old age of 24. She couldn't attend the award ceremony in London as she decided it would also be a good day to give birth.

She lives happily ever after in Italy running writers retreats, while renovating the villa and writing long into the night.

Follow Rosie on her blog: www.rosiemeleady.com

ALSO BY ROSIE MELEADY

A Rosie Life in Italy 1: Why Are We Here?

A Rosie Life in Italy 2: What Have We Done?

A Rosie Life in Italy 3: Should I Stay or Should I Go?

A Rosie Life in Italy 4: Potatoes, Pizza and Poteen

Cozy Mystery Series

A Nun-Holy Murder

A Brush With Death

Women's Fiction and Rom-Coms

Tilly Fox's Fabulous Midlife Crisis

Made in United States
North Haven, CT
05 March 2025

66465054R00209